VOLUME 1

FROM POVERTY TO WELL-BEING AND HUMAN FLOURISHING

Integrated Conceptualisation and Measurement of Economic Poverty

Julio Boltvinik

With a foreword by
Meghnad Desai

P

First published in Great Britain in 2025 by

Policy Press, an imprint of
Bristol University Press
University of Bristol
1-9 Old Park Hill
Bristol
BS2 8BB
UK
t: +44 (0)117 374 6645
e: bup-info@bristol.ac.uk

Details of international sales and distribution partners are available at
policy.bristoluniversitypress.co.uk

© Bristol University Press 2025

British Library Cataloguing in Publication Data
A catalogue record for this book is available from the British Library

ISBN 978-1-4473-6846-5 hardcover
ISBN 978-1-4473-6847-2 paperback
ISBN 978-1-4473-6848-9 ePub
ISBN 978-1-4473-6849-6 ePdf

The right of Julio Boltvinik to be identified as author of this work has been asserted by him in accordance with the Copyright, Designs and Patents Act 1988.

All rights reserved: no part of this publication may be reproduced, stored in a retrieval system, or transmitted in any form or by any means, electronic, mechanical, photocopying, recording, or otherwise without the prior permission of Bristol University Press.

Every reasonable effort has been made to obtain permission to reproduce copyrighted material. If, however, anyone knows of an oversight, please contact the publisher.

The statements and opinions contained within this publication are solely those of the author and not of the University of Bristol or Bristol University Press. The University of Bristol and Bristol University Press disclaim responsibility for any injury to persons or property resulting from any material published in this publication.

Bristol University Press and Policy Press work to counter discrimination on
grounds of gender, race, disability, age and sexuality.

Cover design: Robin Hawes
Front cover image: Robin Hawes/ León Boltvinik

To my beloved Araceli

Contents

List of figures and tables	viii
List of abbreviations	x
Acknowledgements	xvii
Foreword by Meghnad Desai	xx

Introduction 1

PART I Conceptualising poverty

1 **Households' reproduction logic, their well-being sources, and concepts of needs and poverty** 13
    1.1 Households' reproduction schemes and articulation with enterprises and government 13
    1.2 Well-being sources (WBS) and resources 26
    1.3 Central definitions: needs and poverty 33

2 **Critique of the Political Economy of Poverty (CPEP), Part 1: on different answers to the question of the constitutive elements of the good/full life** 42
    2.1 Sen's and Rawls's critiques of utilitarianism: Sen's critique of opulence and primary goods approaches 42
    2.2 Internal and external critique of Neoclassical Consumer Theory 44
    2.3 Sen's and Nussbaum's capabilities approaches: a critique 51
    2.4 Synthesis of my New Paradigm of Human Poverty and Flourishing 55

3 **Critique of the Political Economy of Poverty, Part 2: conceptual maps and definitions** 59
    3.1 Critique of the dominant definitions of poverty in the PEP: comparison with the definitions of poverty in my New Paradigm 59
    3.2 The narrow conceptual map of the PEP compared with the broader one of my New Approach to Poverty and Human Flourishing (NAPHF) or New Paradigm (NP) 69

4 **Principles and good practices of poverty conceptualisation** 81
    4.1 Introduction 81
    4.2 Principles and good practices: a complete panorama 82

PART II Measuring poverty

5 Principles and good practices of poverty measurement — 97
 5.1 Poverty measurement — 97

6 A typology of poverty measurement methods: a critique of direct and indirect poverty measurement methods — 109
 6.1 A systematic typology: comparison with Gordon et al.'s and Ringen's views of poverty measurement methods — 109
 6.2 On non-normative Poverty Measurement Methods — 112
 6.3 Description and critique of normative (and semi-normative) direct and indirect methods — 116

7 Combined methods of poverty measurement — 129
 7.1 Description and critique of combined methods included in the typology — 129
 7.2 Prevailing disagreement on the poverty criterion among combined methods — 133

8 The Integrated Poverty Measurement Method (IPMM) — 141
 8.1 The genesis of the IPMM — 141
 8.2 General description of the IPMM — 143
 8.3 Detailed description of IPMM poverty indicators, Part 1: UBN — 146
  8.3.1 Housing quality and space ($QSDwA_j$) — 146
  8.3.2 Durable goods — 154
  8.3.3 Sanitary services — 156
  8.3.4 Communication services (CS) — 159
  8.3.5 Energy adequacy (EnAJ) — 160
  8.3.6 Educational achievement indicator (EAI) — 162
  8.3.7 Health Services (HS) and Social Security (SS) — 167
  8.3.8 UBN composite indicator — 174
 8.4 Detailed description of IPMM poverty indicators, Part 2: income and time — 174
  8.4.1 Income (Y) — 174

9 Aggregate poverty measures (APM) — 188
 9.1 Description and critique — 188
 9.2 Critique of aggregate measures sensitive to distribution among the poor — 202

Contents

    9.3 A new aggregate measure of poverty sensitive to social inequality   208

    9.4 A final note   211

Epilogue   213

References   219

Index   229

List of figures and tables

Figures

8.1	Components of IPMM and integration procedure	144
9.1	Well-being as a function of access to resources	206
9.2	Probability (π) of not having a health breakdown as a function of BMI	208

Tables

1.1	Production and circulation schemes by type of household (HH)	15
1.2	Circulation and production schemes in private capitalist enterprises and in the state	20
1.3	Equivalences between well-being sources (WBS) and the concepts included in the reproduction schemes	27
1.4	Resources considered by several authors	32
3.1	Dominant definitions of poverty: critique and comparison with the two definitions of economic poverty in my NP	62
3.2	The economic process of needs satisfaction: a totalising view	72
4.1	Principles and good practices of poverty conceptualisation and measurement	83
5.1	Procedure for generalised dichotomisation (replicable full cardinalisation)	103
6.1	Typology of poverty measurement methods	113
6.2	Ringen's typology of approaches to the measurement of well-being	115
7.1	Poverty criteria in combined methods	134
8.1	Contingency matrix: poor by PL and by UBN, Peru, 1985	142
8.2	IPMM basic procedure	145
8.3	Strata used in IPMM	145
8.4	Stratification of population (%) by the value of $HQSD_j$ in their corresponding Dw	154
8.5	Updated prices of durable goods, August 2020	155
8.6	School attendance standard/threshold	165
8.7	Annual $VIMSS_i$ per person, voluntary IMSS HS insurance, 2020	169
8.8	Scores for $HSAA_{ij}$ and HSS_{ij}	171
8.9	UBN components and weights	174
8.10	UBN integrated strata of individuals	175
8.11	Adjustment factors of Y captured by ENIGH to NA, 2020	176
8.12	Structure of HH Y sources from ENIGH	177

8.13	Some statistical descriptors of the distributions of YaA$_j$' and YaD$_j$	179
8.14	Income individual's strata by values of YaD$_{ij}$'	179
8.15	Norms for: IRT, (EDWT + DWT + comm), ET + comm, by AG. HrsW	185
8.16	A big contrast: IPMM's and Coneval's diagnosis of poverty in Mexico, 2020	187
9.1	H, q, I, and q$_E$ results for the IPMM by poor strata in Mexico, 2020	193
9.2	Energy survival requirements (r) and % of total requirements for two estimates of survival (1.27 and 1.4 BMR), various occupations	208
9.3	Values of HI, P$_S$, P$^2{}_{FGT}$, G$_{PR}$, P$_R$, P$_{SB}$ by poor IPMM strata, Mexico, 2020	211

List of abbreviations

$VHS	cost of voluntary affiliation to health services (IMSS)
$VSS	cost of voluntary affiliation to social security (IMSS)
α	parameter of aversion to extreme poverty
ΔM	surplus value generated
$\dot{\omega}CD1$	depreciation of the purchased consumer durables
A	achievement
A_{MI}	amortisation and interest
A_μ	mean achievement indicator
$A_\mu P$	average achievement index of the poor
A^{ee}	egalitarian equivalent achievement
AF	adjustment factor
AG	age group
A_G	geometric mean of H (incidence of poverty)
AHS	achievement of housing space
A_i	achievement indicator of individual I
A_J	achievement indicator of household J
AMPI	Acute Multidimensional Poverty Index
APM	aggregate poverty measures
APOA	alimentary pension for older adults
B	bedrooms
BA	basic assets
BMI	body mass index
BMR	basal metabolic rate
BNAD	Basic Needs Approach to Development
BSA-PL	budget standards approach to PL
C^2	squared coefficient of variation
CA	capabilities approach
CBEP	economic poverty of circumstantial being
CD	consumer durables
CF	cooking fuel
CFA_J	cooking fuel achievement
CHH	combined household
CIESAS	Centro de Investigaciones y Estudios Superiores en Antropología Social
CM_C	commodities for consumption
CM_E	vector of production commodities including equipment and facilities
CM_{In}	vector of production commodities including inputs
CM_{LF}	vector of production commodities including labour force
CM_P	commodities for production

List of abbreviations

CM_{RC}	ready-for-consumption commodities
CM_S	commodities for sale
CN6NeB	cost of the normative six-N basket
CNFB	cost of the normative food basket
CNGB	cost of the normative generalised basket
CNnFB	cost of the normative non-food basket
CNONeB	cost of the normative other needs basket
CPEP	Critique of the Political Economy of Poverty
CPL	capacities PL
CROP	Comparative Research on Poverty
CS	communication services
CSA_J	communication services achievement indicator
CT	Compulsory Time
CWFWT	carrying water and firewood
CY	current income
DGA_J	durable goods achievement indicator
DGV_J	durable goods value
DM_J	deprivation mass
DMP	domestic mode of production
DMWB	diminishing marginal well-being
DP	domestic production
DPSC	domestic production for self-consumption
DRAE	Diccionario de la Real Academia Española
Dr	drainage
Dw	dwelling
DWHCT	time of domestic work dedicated to household chores
DWT	domestic work time
E	Engel coefficient
E	equipment
E	years of schooling completed
E★	normative years of schooling
E★A	normative years of schooling according to age
EA	equivalent adult
EA_J	education achievement indicator
EB	equivalent bedrooms
EB★	normative equivalent bedrooms
EDWT	extra-domestic working time
E_{IJ}	observed years of schooling
El	electricity
El_J	electricity access indicator
$ElLB_JA$	electricity access and quality achievement indicator
$ElLB_JD$	electricity access and quality deprivation indicator
ELSPN	enforced lack of socially perceived necessities

EnA_J	energy adequacy
ENCUBOS	Survey of Objective and Subjective Well-Being
EnD_J	energy deprivation indicator
ENIGH	Mexican National Survey of Household Income and Expenditure
EP	extreme poverty
EPL	extreme poverty line
EW	excess work
EWT	excess working time
FG&S	free goods and services
FGT	Foster, Greer and Thorbecke
F_J	floor achievement
FPL	food PL
FRT	family replenishment time
FSNA	failed searches for a new approach
FT	free time
G	Gini coefficient
GD	generalised dichotomisation
G&H	Garfinkel and Haveman
G&S	goods and services
Gij	deprivation indicator score or gap
GNB	Generalised Normative Basket
GP	good practices
GPPC	good practices of poverty conceptualisation
GPPM	good practices of poverty measurement
G_{PR}	relative gap
GVT	governmental transferences
H	poverty incidence
HEA_J	household educational achievement
HED_J	HH educational deprivation indicator
H_{eE}	equalitarian equivalent incidence
HFA	human flourishing axis
HH	household or households
HI	equivalent incidence
HN	human need or needs
HQA_J	composite indicator of housing quality adequacy
$HQSA_J$	integrated indicator of housing quality and space availability
$HQSD_J$	housing quality and space deprivation indicator
HS	health services
HSA_J	health services achievement indicator
I	aggregate poverty index or poverty intensity
IAA_J	internet access achievement indicator
IA_J	internet access/connection

List of abbreviations

IDM	Individual Deprivation Measure
IEA_{IJ}	individual educational achievement
I_J	intensity of household J poverty or poverty gap
IMSS	Mexican Institute of Social Security
In	inputs
INDEC	Institute of Statistics and Census from Argentina
INEGI	National Institute of Statistics and Geography
IP	intense poverty
IPL	International Poverty Line
IPMM	Integrated Poverty Measurement Method
IPMM-PL	poverty line defined in IPMM
IPSMM	Integrated Poverty and Stratification Measurement Method
IRODw	imputed rent of own dwelling
IRT	individual replenishment time
IV-IPMM	improved variant of IPMM
KE	kitchen for exclusive use
K_p	Champernowne inequality index among the poor
LA	literacy achievement variable
LB_JA	lightbulb achievement
LDMU	Law of Diminishing Marginal Utility
LF	labour force
M	initial capital/money
M_C	vector of consumer goods and services
MN	Martha Nussbaum
MP	moderate poverty
MR	multipurpose rooms
MS	medium stratum
MSS	minimum satisfaction stratum
MT	monetary transfers
MTR	modified total rooms
MUT	time-use module
N	need or needs
N_O	normative
N_{HH}	universe of households
N_I	universe of persons
NA	national accounts
NAPHF	New Approach to Poverty and Human Flourishing
NBA	non-basic asset or assets
NBES	normative basket of essential satisfiers
NCT	Neoclassical Consumer Theory
NFB	normative food basket
NGB	normative generalised basket
NHHY	total national household current income

NN	non-normative
NP	New Paradigm
NP_R	non-protected
NPPHF	New Paradigm of Poverty and Human Flourishing
OA	Opulence approach
ODEPLAN	Planning Office of Chile
OECD	Organization for Economic Cooperation and Development
OP_R	over-protected
OT	transferences from other sources
OV	original variant
OV-IPMM	Original Variant of the Integrated Poverty Measurement Method
OWB	objective well-being
Pp	principles
P_R	protected
P	Poverty
P_1	poverty index
PEP	Political Economy of Poverty
PHH	producer households
PIM	poverty intensity measurement
PL	poverty line
PMI	private medical insurance
PMM	poverty measuring methods
PPC	principles of poverty conceptualisation
PPL	patrimonial poverty line
PPM	principles of poverty measurement
P^R	relative poverty index
PYI	property income/rent
PRC	people requiring care
P_S	Sen Poverty Index
P_{SB}	Sen-Boltvinik Aggregate Poverty Measure
$P_U PHH$	pure producing households
$P_U SHH$	pure salaried households
PVR	private vital rent
Q	number of poor households
q	number of poor people
q_μ	mean size of poor households
q_{EJ}	number of equivalent poor persons
q_J	number of persons in a poor household
$QSDwA_J$	housing quality and space achievement indicator
RC	ready-to-consume
RHET	repairing the house and its equipment
R_J	roof score
RT_{PRC}	replenishment time for people requiring care

List of abbreviations

S	satisfier or satisfiers
SA	school attendance
SA★	normative value of school attendance
SaA_J	consolidated indicator of sanitary achievement
SBEP	economic poverty of structural being
SaD_J	indicator of sanitary deprivation
Sedesol	Ministry of Social Development in Mexico
SFB	standard food basket
SHH	salaried households
SHHDP	salaried households with domestic production
SLA	standard of living axis
SMHHT	shopping and managing the household
SMP	state mode of production
SN	semi-normative
SNWT	socially necessary working time
SPHH	combined households (salaried and producers)
SPI	Social Progress Index
SPI-LTD	Social Progress Index – Lifetime Deprivation
SS	social security
SSA_J	social security achievement indicator
ST	study time
SUV	social use values
T_X	taxes
T	time
T_0	available adult hours for household tasks
TC	Tropic of Cancer
TCMP	Technical Committee for the Measurement of Poverty
Tl	telephone (fixed and/or mobile)
TNP	sum of non-poverty
To	toilet
TP	time poverty
TTP	total poverty
Tr	total (kcal) requirements
TR	total rooms
TT	total time
UBN	unsatisfied basic needs
$UBNA_J$	consolidated
UBN	achievement indicator
UBN-IV	UBN improved variant
UEA	University of East Anglia
UP_R	under-protected
US	upper stratum
UV_P	productive use-values

UV_{RC}	ready-to-consume use values
U_Z	referential level of utility
VCWT	voluntary or community working time
VCSSR	voluntary affiliation to the compulsory social security regime (IMSS)
VHSSS	voluntary affiliation to IMSS in-kind medical services
VIP	very intense poverty
VSSOR	voluntary affiliation to the obligatory social security regime
VW	virtual worker
W	wages/salaries
W★	normative wall achievement
W/P	wealth/poverty
WA_J	wall achievement
WB	well-being
W-B	World Bank
WBS	well-being source or sources
WF	water frequency
WP	water provision
WS	water source
$WSSA_J$	water and sanitary services
X_F	free budget
X_N	necessary budget
X_T	total budget
Y	income
Ya	available income
YaD_J	available income deprivation indicator
YOBSN	income of own business
Z	norm assumed equal for all
Z	poverty threshold/norm assumed equal for all

Acknowledgements

This book has a long story that includes a large list of persons who helped me, gave me a tip, recommended a reference, corrected a mistake, criticised my work, or encouraged my efforts. The story started in 1980. The first person I want to mention in this chronology is philosopher Arturo Cantú, who convinced me to join the research team at COPLAMAR – an office adjoining the Mexican Presidency and in charge of improving poor rural areas in the country. In this institution I found my vocation: studying the terrible fate of the disinherited of the earth and fighting to alleviate their condition. Those three years (1980, 1981 and 1982) yielded very fruitful collective research that involved many young researchers; I was young, but most of them were even younger, and my job was to guide and coordinate their work. Some years later, luck struck again: Luis Thais, a visionary Peruvian official in charge of the United Nations Development Programme (UNDP) office in Bogota and of the UNDP's Latin American Regional Project to Overcome Poverty, persuaded me that it was time for me to move. I spent four years in Bogota from 1988 to 1991 and travelled all over Latin America interacting with many brilliant minds and engaged souls, and those years were a blessing, both cognitively and personally. Among the people I met in that period was Libardo Sarmiento, a Colombian philosopher and economist who opened a door I did not know existed: the work of my greatest mentor, György Márkus. There I discerned the IPMM (Integrated Poverty Measurement Method), the central component of the present book, which would not have been possible without previous works by Óscar Altimir, Luis Beccaria, Alberto Minujin, and Rubén Kaztman. But most of all I would like to express my gratitude to Antonio Suárez McAuliffe, a Mexican economist who made a devastating critique of the *disintegrated work* carried out both in COPLAMAR and, later (1986–87), in the UNDP's Regional Project. This critique spurred me on to search for an integrated poverty measurement method, the inspiration for which I found in Latin America's rich and innovative research on poverty. When I returned to Mexico, I was fortunate enough to join El Colegio de México, the best place to do the type of social research I carry out and to interact with very special graduate students, not only from Mexico but from many Latin American countries.

At El Colegio I also met my beloved wife, Araceli Damián – who was then conducting her PhD field research for University College London– to whom I dedicate this book. Together we have raised one son and one daughter – already adults, both artistically talented: he (León) for cinema and photography, and she (Ema) for poetry – and written many papers and books on the topics addressed in this book. Araceli and I share our experiences in universities in Britain, where we both pursued postgraduate studies and have been visiting professors. We both owe the British Academy for its rigour and, above all, its openness to constructive critique: both of us were astonished to see how fiercely members of the Academy criticised each other in a seminar and then went to a pub without any resentment. I want to thank all the British scholars who hosted me at their universities, but I would like to make a special mention, first, of D.G.R. Belshaw (1932–2022), my most admired professor at the University of East Anglia (UEA), where I studied for an MA in Rural Development in 1972–73, and who later hosted me as a visiting professor to UEA in 1996. Second, I would like to extend my warm thanks to David Gordon, currently Director of both the Bristol Poverty Institute and the Townsend Centre for International Poverty Research, who twice hosted Araceli and me as visiting professors at the School of Policy Studies at Bristol University.

In Mexico during 2008–2012, I had a second opportunity to get involved in collective research on poverty and social policy at the Mexico City Evaluation Council (Evalúa CDMX), where I was a member of the governing council – a part-time position compatible with my work as Professor at El Colegio de México. During those very fruitful years I carried out innovative research which, nevertheless, ended quite abruptly. The team was dissolved, and the full harvest of what we sowed is still pending. During those years (the second term that Mexico City was governed by the leftist party PRD), Pablo Yanes, Director of Evalúa CDMX, gave me his full support and adopted IPMM as the official poverty measurement method for Mexico City. Since 2012, Yanes – working at the Mexico City office of the UN Economic Commission for Latin America (ECLAC) – and Hugo Beteta – the office director – have continued to support my research and my efforts to try to make IPMM the official poverty measurement method of ECLAC. This battle was lost despite the sympathy of Alicia Bárcena, Executive Secretary of ECLAC at Santiago de Chile. This shows how powerful bureaucracies are and how difficult it is to change statistical practices, especially in international intergovernmental organisations.

Starting in 1997 and until its conclusion in 2019, I participated in various tasks in Comparative Research on Poverty (CROP), mobilising critical research for preventing and eradicating poverty. I was vice-president from 1997 to 2004 and member of its scientific committee during various periods in this century. During all that time, the Presidents of CROP, Else Oyen, Asunción St. Clair and Alberto Cimadamore, gave me enormous support. An instance of this was the organisation of an International Seminar in 2012 in Mexico City on Peasant Poverty and Persistence, based on which a book was published in the Zed-Crop books series on poverty. All of them were very sympathetic to IPMM and frequently sent me to lecture on poverty measurement methods internationally.

Acknowledgements

Since 1990–1991, Meghnad Desai (member of the UK House of Lords and previously Professor of Economics at LSE, when we co-wrote *Social Progress Index: A Proposal* together with Amartya Sen) became both a colleague and a friend. He and Araceli Damián have been the two most influential people in the development of IPMM throughout these years. Desai, an outstanding cosmopolitan intellectual and activist, acted as a bridge between British and Latin American poverty research traditions. I hope his foreword to this book is not too severe.

Cuernavaca, Mexico
March 2023

Foreword

Meghnad Desai

Poverty has been a factor in history almost since time immemorial. It is only since the Industrial Revolution in the late eighteenth century that the idea of mass material well-being has become possible. Political Economy began around that time in Britain, France and Italy. In England at the time, the relief of the poor was supervised by the Church in every parish. Those who could not work – the elderly, the disabled, women with children – were called paupers. They received relief from rates collected by the Church from the local better-off households. The category 'poor' was applied to daily workers, mainly working on the land, who received a wage which traditionally was enough to feed the worker, his wife and their children.

It was when inflation of wheat (corn) prices occurred in the decade following the French Revolution that rates were collected for the working poor as well. At this stage Thomas Malthus conceived the idea that population grew at a geometric rate but food output only at arithmetic rate, hence there was a danger of overpopulation. His real purpose was to say that the working poor should not receive payments in addition to their wage since they would only breed more children and the money (paid in rates by the rich) would be wasted. David Ricardo, the most influential economist of his time and for centuries later, confirmed Malthus's view.

Political Economy became hostile to any idea of relieving poverty as inimical to the laws of the market. It took a century of democratic struggle to broaden the franchise as well as the First World War to bring about a universal franchise. It was then that the idea of income redistribution from the rich to the poor was introduced in Political Economy by Arthur Cecil Pigou (I have discussed this in my *Poverty of Political Economy*, Harper and Collins, 2023).

It took another world war to establish the idea that relief of poverty was the task of the government. This was especially so because democracy had spread across the world. International agencies were set up and began to make comparisons between nations. We became conscious of advanced versus emerging economies. To measure progress, we had to know not only income, total and per capita, but also the percentage of poor in a country. But the old prejudice of Political Economy lingered. Poverty was measured by what the poor ate and whether that was sufficient in terms of calories. The World Bank, in an infinite hurry to reach a single measure for billions of people, said a dollar a day (suitably adjusted down using purchasing power parity) was sufficient to be called not poor. Governments loved this as they wanted to spend as little as they could get away with because they had more prestigious items to spend money on. It was enough to give Political Economy a worse reputation than it already had.

Julio Boltvinik is one of those rare economists who has dedicated his life to studying poverty not as a disease to be minimised as a challenge to Political Economy but to integrate the study of poverty with treating the poor as human beings with the same drives and springs of well-being as everyone else. The poor are not a separate caste or a class but just the same as us. He has explored the idea of human well-being in the works of György Márkus, which are wide ranging rather than minimalist. He has then imaginatively adapted Marx's scheme of reproduction to develop an implementable measure.

The result is one of the most complete treatments not only of understanding the notion of human well-being in its full philosophical and sociological aspects but also supplementing that with practical measurement details which do justice to the richness as much as the complexity of the task. Julio Boltvinik has practised what he preaches in a variety of contexts, but principally Mexico and South America. We also worked together in the UNDP in its Human Development Programme back in the 1990s.

I have learned a lot from knowing, reading and working with Julio Boltvinik. Here he presents for the English-reading public his life's work. You will learn as much as I did.

Introduction

In March 1980, slightly over 42 years before I found myself writing this Introduction – one of the last tasks in preparing this book – I started working as Director of Essential Needs in COPLAMAR, an agency attached to the President's Office in Mexico and responsible for improving the living conditions in the country's poor areas and among groups designated as *marginalised*. My role was to coordinate a research team of around 20 professionals working on the unsatisfaction of essential needs in Mexico. This team was the largest part of the agency's General Direction of Socioeconomic Studies. I started studying poverty from the standpoint of unsatisfied needs, which has been the central element in my conception of poverty since that time. COPLAMAR was shut down in December 1982 with the arrival of a new federal government; however, understanding and fighting poverty has been my vocation and main occupation ever since. Although from the beginning of this century I have broadened my look and started aiming at the more ambitious purpose of human flourishing (to which I added, in the second decade of this century, the fashionable topic of well-being (WB), including subjective WB, poverty remains among my core tasks. I am aware that achieving human flourishing and generalised WB is impossible, or is only possible for a reduced elite, if poverty is not overcome first.

I have worked with international organisations (particularly UNDP and CROP[1]); in Mexican left-wing political parties; in the Mexican Congress; in the Mexico City government; as a journalist in the critical national newspaper *La Jornada*, writing a weekly column called *Moral Economy* since 1995; and primarily in the academic world as a full-time researcher and Professor at El Colegio de México – a postgraduate and research institution devoted to the social sciences and the humanities in Mexico City – since 1992, and also as a visiting professor at the British Universities of East Anglia, Bristol, and Manchester. My work in all these institutions has largely focused on poverty, social policy, and human flourishing.

The intention to put this book together grew out of my awareness that my work on poverty and human flourishing was scarcely known among people who don't read Spanish, since around 95% of my published work is in Spanish and very few texts are in English. In particular, my work on the

---

[1] CROP: Comparative Research on Poverty was an independent organisation created by the International Social Science Research Council in 1992. Its offices were hosted by the University of Bergen in Norway. In 2019–2020, it transitioned into GRIP, Global Research Programme on Inequality.

conceptualisation and measurement of poverty is practically unknown in English-speaking countries, as my writings on these topics in English are scarce. My publications in Spanish on poverty-related issues (and on unsatisfied essential needs in Mexico) span from 1982 to the present. My books, thematic journal issues, articles and book chapters in Spanish on the conceptualisation and measurement of poverty are quite dispersed through time and space (quite a few were published in Latin American countries other than Mexico, particularly, but not limited to, during 1990–1992). When I started developing the project for this book, I realised that it was also needed in Spanish, as readers trying to follow my work might have a hard time putting the literally hundreds of scattered pieces together and making sense of their sequence and interrelations. This book will therefore also be published in Spanish.

At present I am slowly writing an intellectual biography in Spanish, focused exclusively on my central scholarly interests: poverty, human flourishing, and WB. This might eventually become a book. It will be different from the present book, for it will be genetically structured and have a chronological format so that the reader can follow the development of my thought. The present book's structure is almost entirely logical, except for Section 8.1, which recounts the story of how I came to generate the IPMM. As I stated in the book proposal to Policy Press, this method is the core contribution of the book. In the same proposal, I added the following:

> Almost all the rest of the book can be construed as providing the holistic approach – and the critique on which it is based – that supports or leads to the IPMM. This is true of the initial conceptual discussions and critiques (chapters 1–3) that constitute what I have called the Critique of the Political Economy of Poverty (CPEP). I use the term 'critique' to mean an appraisal that allows appropriating the positive features of the assessed ideas and rejecting their negative aspects. It was this process that, throughout many years, allowed me to appropriate and bring together many positive ideas taken from various authors and intertwine them with the concepts I was required to develop (e.g. the typologies of needs, satisfiers, and well-being sources) in order to enable the narrative I finally attained. This is particularly salient of the principles and good practices I formulated in Chapters 4 and 5, and that systematise and axiomatize those developments. The critique would have been incomplete had it not included the systematization and critique of other salient poverty measurement methods. This is comprised in Chapter 6. Classifying all these methods systematically and proceeding to their detailed critique was a necessary step.

The book is divided into two parts: I Conceptualising Poverty (four chapters), and II Measuring Poverty (five chapters). Chapter 1, Households Reproduction

Introduction

Logic, their well-being sources and concepts of needs and poverty', is a slightly modified version of chapter 12 of my unpublished PhD thesis (2005): *Ampliar la mirada: Un nuevo enfoque de la pobreza y el florecimiento humano*, Centro de Investigaciones y Estudios Superiores en Antropología Social (CIESAS)-Occidente, Guadalajara, Mexico. This title could be translated into English as *Broadening Our Look: A New Approach to Poverty and Human Flourishing*. In the present book I refer to my thesis either as *Ampliar la mirada* or as *Broadening Our Look*. By building a typology of households (HH), and by describing the production and circulation processes, as well as the articulations with enterprises and government for each HH type, Chapter 1 acquires a foundational character, which is made explicit when the concept and a typology of the HH's well-being sources (WBS) are established.

Together with Chapter 1, Chapters 6 and 7 (both on the typology of poverty measurement methods [PMM]) are also closely related to *Ampliar la mirada*. Construction of PMM typologies is something I started writing – and publishing – about well before starting my PhD thesis, and I have continued writing on the subject since completing the said thesis. My first published text properly including a PMM typology was 'Poverty Measurement Methods – An Overview' (1998). This paper is based on a course on PMM I taught at the United Nations Staff College in Turin, Italy, in 1997. Thus, Chapters 6 and 7 are not based on my PhD thesis, but rather on later writings (for example, Boltvinik and Damián, 2020, pp 15–29). These chapters classify all pertinent PMMs I have found according to the following criteria: normative (N), semi-normative (SN), non-normative (NN); direct and indirect; and one-dimensional and multidimensional, describing and appraising all of them critically. These chapters provide the reader with an informed map of the existing PMMs.

Lastly, Chapter 9 was originally Chapter 14 of my PhD thesis and was published, with very few modifications, as Boltvinik (2011). The English version included in this book follows both texts closely. Chapter 9 addresses aggregate poverty measures (APM), which refer to the process of synthesising the poverty conditions of a country or part of it in one figure. These measures can also be used to express the overall poverty conditions of groups selected by attributes other than the place of residence (for example, social class, ethnicity, or religion). This chapter provides a rather original view of APM derived from my experience and from the literature on the topic. In addition, it critiques APMs sensitive to inequality among the poor and proposes instead an APM sensitive to macrosocial inequality.

Chapters 2 and 3 of this book (which present the Critique of Political Economy of Poverty [CPEP]) closely follow Boltvinik (2007a), which was my article in a thematic issue (centred around the topics of *Ampliar la mirada*) that I coordinated for *Desacatos*, a Mexican journal on social anthropology. Before I discuss the significance of this work, I must clarify some issues.

First, the present book is intended as Volume I of a two-volume work. Volume II will focus on human flourishing and WB. My PhD thesis – which I started around 2002 and finished in 2005 – reflected a profound change in my view of human beings, a change that started back in 1989 but remained latent for a long period. While living in Bogota – where I was involved in UNDP's Regional Project to Overcome Poverty in Latin America – the young Colombian economist and philosopher Libardo Sarmiento, aware of my interest in questions on the human essence, recommended I read György Márkus's *Marxism and Anthropology*. This reading was eye-opening and radically changed my view of the human essence. Márkus's narrative – described in detail in Chapter 2 of *Broadening Our Look* – informed all of my thesis. Márkus's influence led me to develop what I now call the New Approach to Poverty and Human Flourishing (NAPHF), or my New Paradigm (NP).

Volume II, which I also intend to publish both in English and in Spanish, has a recent Spanish precedent. In 2020 I published *Pobreza y Florecimiento Humano. Una Perspectiva Radical*, centred on the NP and its foundations, particularly on Márkus's *Marxism and Anthropology* and a comparative analysis of several theories of human needs (HN). The second volume of this work will be an updated and amplified English version of my 2020 book.

This two-volume book will thus provide integrated views of what may be seen as the two stages of my intellectual development: the conceptualisation and measurement of poverty, and the NAPHF. The two volumes are deeply interrelated, but each will be independent and may be read on its own. To ensure this, Volume I includes a synthesis of my NP (Section 2.5), and Volume 2 will open with a synthesis of the CPEP (Chapters 2 and 3 of this volume).

Having finished my PhD thesis, I was invited to coordinate the aforementioned issue of *Desacatos*, which revolves around the topics discussed in the thesis. In the brochure commemorating the tenth anniversary of *Desacatos* (2010, p 17), I explained the significance of the issue I had coordinated:

> When I decided to break out of the narrow frameworks of conventional studies on poverty and broadened the look to see the human being as a whole, connecting poverty with human flourishing and distinguishing economic poverty from human poverty – tasks that I carried out in my doctoral thesis – I did not fully realise that *broadening the look – and the concomitant radicalisation – was necessarily linked to 'projecting the look to the future', to a future in which human flourishing would be a widespread reality, whose attainment would require a radical social transformation*. However, although I failed to realise all this, I nevertheless sensed it and, therefore, when planning this issue, I convened two 'normative futurologists' …

Introduction

György Márkus [a critical Marxist philosopher] and Ruth Levitas [an expert in Utopian studies].

By way of conclusion to a brief commentary on Márkus's and Levitas's contributions to the issue, I pointed out that these works confirmed the centrality I ascribe to the development of needs, which led me to conclude (2010, p 18) that

> the approach I developed in my doctoral thesis is not only useful to broaden the look but also to project it into the future. Human flourishing is *the good thing*, and therefore, *the good society* is the one that promotes and encourages the development and satisfaction of needs, and the development and application of capacities, the essence of human flourishing. By introducing capacities alongside needs, the active aspect of human beings complements the passive aspect of needs, thus conforming a complete human being.

The first part of the title of the issue, 'From Poverty to Human Flourishing: Critical Theory or Utopia?' reflects the broadening of the look from economic poverty and its eradication towards human poverty and its overcoming, that is, towards human flourishing. But it also reflects the immensity of the task facing present and future generations: overcoming economic poverty and achieving universal flourishing. Later, I realised that the second part of the title – 'Critical Theory *or* Utopia?' – should have been 'Critical Theory *and* Utopia'. This would have coincided with E.P. Thompson's statement that Marxism (kingdom of knowledge) and utopia (kingdom of desire) are complementary, and with Ernst Bloch's idea of complementarity between Marxism's hot (passion) and cold (analysis) currents (Boltvinik, 2010a).

In the 'Presentation' of *Desacatos* 23 I stated:

> Before and after having formally presented my doctoral thesis, I had the opportunity to present its main ideas in various forums. In them, due to time limitations, I minimised or even eliminated the critique on which the developments of my thesis are based. In doing so, I recurrently perceived among the audience a perplexity that reminded me of a verse from the poem *El nuevo narciso* [The New Narcissus] by the Mexican poet Enrique González Martínez: 'The water's mirror is like an answer without a question.' Since I did not include the said critique in my presentations, my proposal for a different approach to poverty (linked to human flourishing) seemed in fact an answer without a question. For this reason, I decided to focus, in this issue of *Desacatos*, on its critical bases. [Once the critique evinces the inadequacies of existing

answers *to the question about the constitutive elements* of the good life, the good society, the search, and the presentation of an alternative approach makes sense.] The approach developed is an answer to this question, but if presented without showing the inadequacy of current theories, the proposal seems meaningless. This critique I have called *external critique* because it is based on the new paradigm (NP) developed to identify the flaws of the previous paradigm; meanwhile, the critique I had been making before the thesis, mainly focused on poverty measurement methods [and their underlying conceptualisations], I have called *internal critique* because, despite having adopted a broader vision than those prevailing, I remained in the old paradigm in a double sense: methodologically, because I addressed the standard of living axis [SLA] directly instead of deriving it from the human flourishing axis [HFA], as posited by the NP [see Section 2.5]; and substantially, because it maintained that the satisfaction of needs is the answer to the question about the constitutive element of both axes, sharing the essence of the dominant vision … that I have called the 'conventional approach to needs'. … In the new approach [the NAPHF], this response has been replaced by the development of the human essential forces – needs and capacities – which replaces the passive vision of the human being with one that integrates its active and passive sides. (Boltvinik, 2007b, p 14)

Summing up, in *Ampliar la mirada* I had moved *from economic to human poverty and human flourishing*; in *Desacatos* I moved from *broadening the look to projecting the look to the future*, and from *internal to external critique*.

Although the present volume focuses on economic poverty (an amplified vision of economic poverty that includes free time), it combines internal (mainly Chapter 6) and external critique (Chapters 2 and 3). It also goes beyond my usual formulations of concepts and PMMs by *founding them solidly on two sets of principles and good practices, one for poverty conceptualisation and one for poverty measurement methods* (Chapters 4 and 5). These chapters have various precedents in Spanish: Boltvinik (2010a, 2010b), and Boltvinik and Damián (2020). The first two references only included principles; good practices were added in the last one, which was however a much shorter text phrased as a series of recommendations to ECLAC. The text of Chapters 4 and 5 constitutes the most complete version of my work on the conceptualisation and measurement of poverty ever published in any language. The principles of poverty measurement (PPM) and the good practices of poverty measurement (GPPM) are very important innovations in the subject, which up to now lacked solid foundations. Both sets of principles and good practices are divided into those referring to conceptualisation (Chapter 4) and those referring to measurement (Chapter 5).

Chapter 8, which revolves around the improved version of the IPMM (IV-IPMM), is the longest and most complex chapter of the book, and the one whose preparation required the most work and time. One reviewer of the book proposal recommended adding an empirical example of its application. Since 2019, Evalúa CDMX has re-adopted the IPMM at its official PMM, which had also been the case in 2008–2012. Since 2019 I ceased calculating poverty in Mexico myself and started using the results obtained by this organisation. I was aware that the Council had made some innovations, such as calculating poverty at the individual, rather than the HH level – as was previously done – and separating the health services from the social security (SS) indicators, which I had maintained as a single indicator. I agreed with this. Evalúa CDMX had also reinstated the adjustment of income data from the surveys to national accounts, which is a very important practice to avoid overestimating income poverty (and underestimating inequality); this happens, for instance, with the income data captured in the ENIGH (Spanish initials for the National Survey of Household Income and Expenditure, a bi-annual national survey whereby members of around 80,000 HH are interviewed), which underestimates HH's income. This adjustment practice, already adopted by COPLAMAR (1983), was impossible to maintain during the periods in which the National Institute of Statistics and Geography (INEGI) postponed, for many years, the publication of the national accounts by institutional sectors, which include the HH sector. Additionally, in 2002 the Mexican federal government adopted a one-dimensional (income only) official PMM which did not adjust income to national accounts, so that my calculations using the IPMM without adjusting income seemed more nearly comparable to the official estimates. Ever since 1979, ECLAC has maintained the practice of adjusting income data to national accounts.

When I started writing Chapter 8, taking the methodology published by Evalúa CDMX as the starting point, I found I slightly disagreed with some procedures adopted by the now autonomous institution (especially regarding some indicators with a low weight in the integrated indicator). This led me to immerse myself in the details of the procedures and to start a dialogue with the authorities at Evalúa CDMX. We agreed to carry out an extensive review of the procedures. Chapter 8 presents the methodology that Evalúa CDMX and I adopted (first months of 2023) and that became the new methodology in force. This methodology reflects many other important improvements (implemented in different years) in the income dimension of IPMM:

1. The adoption of poverty lines (PLs) that reflect both the differing (quantitative and qualitative) requirements of goods and services (G&S) among persons of different age and sex (equivalent adult (EA) units), and

the economies of scale in consumption among large HH. In Boltvinik (2010a) I included, for the first time, the formula that we (Evalúa CDMX and myself) have since used to calculate each household's PL according to the number of members and EAs rather than the usual PL per capita (which does not reflect the age–sex composition nor the HH's economies of scale). This shows the big leap that this new PL represents. *It differentiates each HH's PL according to the number of its members and EAs.*

2. A procedure – adopted by the IV-IPMM since its very outset – whereby the PL only includes the costs of the G&S bought (or self-produced) in most HHs and, correspondingly, the HH income (Y) that is compared with the specific HH PL is available income (Ya) in HH J : Ya_j, for acquiring the G&S included in the cost of the specific normative basket of each HH, its PL_j. This implies subtracting expenditures in G&S not included in the PL as they are verified by unsatisfied basic needs (UBN). This makes the amounts of money on both sides of the equation (Y and PL) comparable. Other methods, such as ECLAC's, to calculate what it calls indigence, compare the cost of raw food (a portion of PL) with a HH's current total income, which is not totally available for buying food.

3. The IV-IPMM calculates the PL based on the cost of a normative basket of essential satisfiers (NBES) – a fully normative procedure – that includes all kinds of G&S required by a HH to satisfy all its needs. This corresponds to what English-speaking scholars call the *family budget approach*, developed in the UK in 1901 by Seebohm Rowntree (1901/1902). This makes a big difference with all currently applied PMMs in the world, none of which use this procedure (see Chapter 6).

4. In Boltvinik (2010a) I introduced – not in the income dimension, but rather in the UBN indicator of domestic energy – the needs for heating and water heating (something that had been neglected in COPLAMAR (1982 and 1983) and in IPMM since 1992). In that exercise (one of the most detailed I have conducted), I included that HH need to have at least a heater and a water heater. However, this does not apply to every HH in the country, but only to those located in places with at least some cold months. This exercise is very important, since it was the first time that a differentiation based on weather conditions regarding HH satisfiers (S) requirements was introduced in the IPMM. This exercise has now been thoroughly revised and all its consequences taken into account. Heating the house is clearly required in locations where cold weather is present for part or all the year, while cooling the house is a pressing need in most of Mexico, especially at low altitudes. Heating water, whose temperature varies greatly during the day and is usually cold since it comes from high altitudes, is a universal need of HH in Mexico, a country located between 12° N and 33° N and crossed by

the Tropic of Cancer (TC). Every state north of the TC (most of the territory of all states bordering with USA, plus most of Durango and Sinaloa) is located in latitudes where cold weather is present during the winter months, even at sea level. Moreover, the Mexican territory is to a great extent a high-altitude plateau where low temperatures prevail. Omitting these needs has been a big mistake. The highest cost to consider in this regard is that of the electricity or gas used to operate the heating or cooling devices. Electricity tariffs in Mexico have a very complex structure with subsidies designed especially for very hot areas. However, despite these subsidies, electricity charges are higher both in cold and hot areas than in temperate areas, a situation that is reflected on the variation of the PL. This exercise revealed that electricity costs are highly differentiated geographically. Municipalities (counties) were classified according to their weather: cold municipalities and others. The costs for cooling were calculated based on the use of fans; air conditioning was discarded for being too expensive. Meanwhile, the costs for heating water were estimated based on the use of liquid gas.

Important changes were also introduced in health care and SS. In the original IV-IPMM, these two needs (N) were defined as items whose (un)satisfaction was to be identified by a mixed procedure. In Mexico, as in many peripheral countries, SS covers health care services and risk-related income maintenance for only a fraction of the Mexican population, mostly salaried workers and their dependants. However, self- and family-employed workers, as well as most employees of small establishments, are not registered in SS. Those registered at SS institutions are considered as having both N satisfied and as being protected, but the rest of the population cannot be considered as not having satisfied these N, as there are other available options ('market alternatives'). Since IPMM is not only a PMM but also a stratification method, it was necessary to identify market alternatives that could situate non-protected HH or individuals both at the normative level and above it. The details of this procedure are explained in Chapter 8.

Other UBN indicators were also modified. In the durable goods UBN indicator, the following goods were added to the normative set: computer, internet modem, fan, heater, and water heater. Regarding domestic energy, the number of lightbulbs, as a function of the number of rooms, was added as a *proxy* of the electric network's quality in the dwelling. This indicator was previously used in Boltvinik (2010a) but had not been applied since. The indicators related to the availability of piped water and the frequency of effective water flow – which had been combined by Evalúa CDMX as an arithmetic average – are now combined in a multiplicative format, which is the correct combination procedure for attributes that are wholly dependent on other attributes to fulfil their purpose.

In short, the reader of this book will find a holistic, solidly founded conceptualisation of poverty and poverty measurement methodology that is unique in the literature and that, in its current version, improves on all that had been previously published in Spanish, and which is part of a two-volume *oeuvre* that constitutes a breakthrough seminal work.

PART I

Conceptualising poverty

1

Households' reproduction logic, their well-being sources, and concepts of needs and poverty

In Section 1.1, I present a HH typology and a reproduction scheme (production and circulation) for each type of HH. The reproduction schemes intertwine the three main institutional sectors: households, enterprises, and government. Based on these schemes, Section 1.2 develops the concept of WBS and its role in the critique of partial poverty measurement methods and thus in the development of my own method. Defined WBS are compared with the resource lists of several authors. Section 1.3 introduces the concepts of needs (N) and poverty (P).

1.1 Households' reproduction schemes and articulation with enterprises and government

As a core part of social organisation, HH carry out the tasks of biological and social reproduction. Keeping current members alive in adequate conditions to perform their social roles, as well as breeding and raising new generations, are the essential social functions of HH. These functions complement those of enterprises (specialised units in the production and marketing of commodities) and the state apparatus, whose main functions can be defined as arbitrating among other social agents and providing public goods and collective services.[1]

Although many HH constitute not only *consumption* units but also *production units*, this fact deviates from the ideal model of capitalism, in which all production/marketing is carried out by enterprises, while HH are the sole sphere of consumption. In this model, enterprises establish only two types of relationships with HH: buying their labour force (LF) and selling commodities for consumption. Under conditions of near full employment, the urban reality in the central countries was approaching this ideal model

---

[1] In orthodox economics the term *public goods* is understood as G&S in which it is not possible to exclude anyone from their benefits (such as national defence and public safety). Thus, they cannot be charged, and only government (or non-profit organisations) can produce them, not being dependent on sales-derived income.

at the end of the 1970s. However, there has been since then a strong trend of enterprise decentralisation, by which many tasks previously performed by salaried personnel in medium-sized and large enterprises are now carried out by independent people or small businesses, regaining the importance of independent individual work and family businesses in urban areas, while in rural areas family businesses never ceased to be important. In peripheral countries, that ideal model has always been far from being achieved, and this has been accentuated by economic stagnation. A significant part of current world's poverty is associated with non-salaried forms of production.

Therefore, to be useful, a global scheme of society must consider *HH as both consumption and production units*. Even if HH are involved in commodity production, their basic social function is not altered, as production of commodities is, for them, *a means* for their biological–social reproduction.

The first part of Table 1.1 shows the reproduction schemes of a typology of HH which distinguishes five types of HH. Type 1 corresponds to the ideal model of domestic-natural HH, isolated from any commodity link; Type 2 to salaried HH without domestic production for self-consumption (DPSC); Type 3 to salaried HH with DPSC; while Types 4 and 5 are commodity-producing HH, without and with DPSC, respectively.

HH without commodity links are called domestic-natural or 'domestic mode of production' (DMP) (Boltvinik, 1986). These HH produce everything they consume using their LF, the land/nature to which they have access, and self-produced tools/inputs. Everything they produce is for their own consumption/use. The DMP is therefore based on productive use values (UV_p) (such as LF, plough, maize) to produce ready-to-consume use values (UV_{RC}) (such as a dish) suitable for group reproduction. *HH produce to live, to reproduce themselves. Production at the service of needs (N)*. In the DMP there is no social division of labour, no values, no commodities, only use-values. It can also be said, paraphrasing Piero Sraffa (1960) that it is *production of UV by means of UV* (see Table 1.1):

$$UV_p \rightarrow UV_{RC} \qquad (1.1)$$

The arrow indicates production of what is on the right by means of what is on the left.

In this type of HH, the group's reproduction requirements are the maintenance (and replenishment) of the LF as well as the other UV_p. Production must be sufficient to replenish individuals' energy, protect their health, and repair or replenish other UV_p. This scheme could be extended, with some modifications, to the community by identifying the mechanism of reciprocity between members of different HH.

Table 1.1: Production and circulation schemes by type of household (HH)

Type of HH	Production/circulation scheme	Remarks
Domestic natural	$UV_P \rightarrow UV_{RC}$ Using productive use values, UV_P (LF, soil, tools), to produce ready-to-consume use values (UV_{RC}). There is no commodity articulation. Domestic and extra-domestic production have not been differentiated.	There is only a production-consumption cycle, with no social division of labour and no circulation. Domestic mode of production (DMP). *Sense: need satisfaction. Production of UV by means of UV.*
Pure salaried	$CM_{LF} - M - CM_{RC}$ Sale of the LF commodity (CM_{LF}) to enterprises, the state or other HH, to obtain money (M) and buy commodities ready for consumption (CM_{RC}) to reproduce itself.	Only a petty commodity-type circulation cycle, with commodities ready for consumption ($CM_{LF}-M-CM_{RC}$). There is no production in HH, only in enterprises. *Sense: need satisfaction.*
Salaried with domestic production	$CM_{LF}-M-CM_C$ $(+UV_{DC}$ or $CM_{DC} + UV_{LF})$ $\rightarrow UV_{RC}$ With money (M) from the sale of LF (CM_{LF}), commodities for consumption (CM_C) are acquired. LF (UV_{LF}) is applied to these CM_C using pre-existing consumer durables (UV_{CD} or CM_{CD}), generating ready-to-consume use values (UV_{RC}).	Two cycles, one of petty commodity circulation and one of commodity-articulated domestic production. This is *production of ready-to-consume use values by means of UV and CM*. *Sense: need satisfaction.*
Pure producers	$(UV_{LF} + (UV_E$ or $CM_E) + UV_{IN}$ or $CM_{IN})$ $\rightarrow CM_S-M-CM_{RC}$ The production of commodities for sale (CM_S) is carried out with own LF (UV_{LF}), purchased/self-produced equipment (E) and inputs (IN). Money (M) from the sale (S) of CMs is used to buy ready-to-consume commodities (CM_{RC}).	Two petty commodity cycles, one of production, one of circulation. *Sense: need satisfaction. Production of commodities by means of use values and commodities.*
Producers with domestic production	$[UV_{LF} + E + In] \rightarrow [(UV_C) + CM_S]-M-CM_C$ $(+ UV_{CD}$ or $CM_{CD} + UV_{LF}) \rightarrow UV_{RC}$. The production of commodities for sale (CM_S) and, in this case, use values for own consumption (UV_C) is carried out with own LF (UV_{LF}) and purchased/self-produced equipment and inputs. The M of the sale of CM_S is used to buy commodities for consumption (CM_C), which (as well as UV_C) the UV_{LF} with support of CD and inputs (commodified or not) transforms into UV_{RC}.	Three cycles. Two of production (one for sale, petty commodity, and one for consumption, domestic with commodity articulation) and one of petty commodity circulation. Petty mode of production and circulation. *Sense: need satisfaction Production of commodities by means of SUV and CMs.*

In the reality of today's world, isolated HH or communities are a rare exception; almost all of them are articulated to the commodity economy of companies and to the 'tax economy' of governments. This means that almost all HH are part of the social division of labour. Considering only commodity-articulated HH, I identify two types: 1) *salaried HH* (SHH) that sell LF and buy consumer commodities (CM_C, consumer G&S) for their reproduction; and 2) *producer HHs* (PHH), which sell CM (consumer or production G&S produced by the HH or purchased) and buy CM_C for reproduction. Some HH are both salaried and producers (combined households: *SPHH*), which is more common in rural than urban areas.

SHH are usually conceived in the social sciences only as *consumption units*, but peasant and feminist studies and the writings of Gary Becker (for example, 1965) have shown that this vision is biased. SHH begin the cycle with LF and some consumer durables (CD), such as the dwelling, purchased in previous cycles (CD_0).[2] The portion of LF sold is a commodity (CM_{LF}), while the portion used in the HH retains its UV character (UV_{LF}). In what I call *pure salaried* HH ($P_U SHH$), which are a rare type, all monetary income depends on the sale of LF and all consumption depends on the purchase of UV_{RC}. These HH can sell their entire LF because they have no other use for it. For them, available time (after discounting requirements for sleep, cleaning and feeding) is divided only between extra-domestic working time (EDWT) and free time (FT). In SHH *with domestic production* (SHHDP), LF sale will be partial, since it will also be a UV in the HH (to transform purchased CM_C into UV_{RC}). CDs may or may not have a commodity origin. To avoid complicating the notation more, I will not make this distinction and will always write CD_0 and CD_1 to refer to goods from the previous cycle and those produced/purchased in the current one. The reproduction cycle of SHHDP is:

$$CM_{LF} - M - CM_C (+ CD_0 + CD_1 + UV_{LF}) \rightarrow UV_{RC} \qquad (1.2)$$

The dashes indicate exchange (sales/purchases). The cycle has two components, one of a commodity nature ($CM_{LF} - M - CM_C$), which consists of the sale (−) of part of the HH's LF (CM_{LF}) for an amount of money (M) with which it buys (−) the vector of consumption commodities, CM_C. The other component is the utilisation of the use-value LF (UV_{LF}), relying on CM_C and CD to produce ($\rightarrow$) the UV_{RC}. Even if we look at this domestic production process in isolation, we will see that domestic

---

[2] They can also start it with an inventory of non-durable consumer goods, but for the purposes of the schemes to be developed it is not necessary to consider this fact, so I assume these goods are fully consumed in each reproduction cycle.

production of UV differs from that identified in the DMP because here commodities are involved. For example, once part of the LF is sold, the wage is used to buy raw food and fuel (consumer commodities, CM_C) that another part of the LF cooks and serves, using pre-existing (CD_0) or acquired (purchased or produced in the period) consumer durables (CD_1), such as a stove, pots, plates, or cutlery, thus turning them into UV_{RC} at the HH. This domestic production component can be described as *production of UV by means of UV and CM*. I have added the assumption, again to simplify, that the entire vector of consumer G&S (M_C) is bought, although as in the peasant economy, it is usually a mixture of bought, produced, or received as transference.

At one extreme there is the $P_U SHH$, in which there is no consumer work or the presence of CDs from previous periods; this is the case of some inhabitants of cities like New York or London who live in a furnished flat, have all their meals outside the HH, and hire the washing/ironing and domestic cleaning services. This is a model, however, that has serious difficulty functioning in HH where children are being brought up, since in these cases the intervention of the HH LF is desirable and practically unavoidable, although the employment of domestic servants (or the bringing up of minors in specialised establishments) can reduce this requirement. In $P_U SHH$, the reproduction cycle is constituted only by the circulation component. By emphasising the commodity character of the first element of the LF sold, we can write the reproduction cycle of the $P_U SHH$:

$$CM-M-CM' = CM_{LF}-M-CM_{RC} \qquad (1.3)$$

This is similar to the form of the cycle that Marx called *petty commodity circulation* and which he contrasted with *capitalist commodity circulation*. In (1.3) the household achieves the transformation of a CM not suitable for human consumption (LF) into a vector of G&S that allows its reproduction. It is *selling to buy* as opposed to *buying to sell* in capitalist circulation. *CM−M−CM' only makes sense if there is a quality change between the initial and final CM, in contrast to capitalist circulation in which the sense is given by the change of quantity between M and M'*. Note that in (1.3) there is no production, only LF sale and purchase of ready-to-consume (RC) goods (for example, cooked food). If all HHs were $P_U SHHs$, the social division of labour would be maximised, and all production would take place within enterprises (or the government). However, this pure model would require the bringing up of minors to be carried out entirely in specialised establishments or exclusively by salaried domestic personnel. The introduction of domestic servants in both types of salaried HHs could be formalised, but I will not do so to avoid unnecessarily complicating the equations by introducing the purchase of CM_{LF} to be used in the production of UV_{RC} and the bringing up of minors. This also applies to PHHs.

Let us now look at the cycle of reproduction of households articulated commercially through the sale of goods or services, which I call *producer households* (PHHs). I start with a PHH without domestic production: *pure producing households* (P_UPHHs). Equipment (E) and inputs (In) used in production can be purchased or self-produced. To simplify, and leave the door open to both options, I will use neutral symbols (In, E). The P_UPHH reproduction scheme includes a production cycle and a circulation cycle:

$$(UV_{LF} + E + In) \rightarrow CM_S - M - CM_{RC} \qquad (1.4)$$

The last part of the cycle ($CM_S - M - CM_{RC}$) is similar to that of the P_USHH. However, in this case, the first term is not CM_{LF} but other goods intended for sale (S), so I have denoted it as CM_S. An example of this would be accounting services. This is the typical case of Marx's petty commodity circulation that consists of *producing/selling to buy satisfiers* (S). The production cycle (UV_{LF} + E + In) $\rightarrow CM_S$, *production of CM by means of UV (own LF) and (often) CM (equipment and inputs)*, is distinguished from capitalist commodity production by the absence of LF purchase.

This case, however, is not the most common among PHHs. Most of the HH that sell CM (especially in peripheral countries) also have domestic production (DP) processes: they are *producer households with domestic production*: PHHDP. If they produce consumer G&S, they might use part of it for their own consumption. This cycle can be written as:

$$(UV_{LF} + E + In) \rightarrow (UV_C + CM_C) + (CD_0 + CD_1 + UV_{LF}) \rightarrow UV_{RC}$$
$$\downarrow \qquad \qquad |$$
$$CM_S - \qquad M$$
$$(1.5)$$

A part of UV_{LF} is utilised in production for sale (CM_S) and another in production for consumption (UV_C). The two portions of the LF are supported by equipment (E) and inputs (In), which can be goods (purchased) or use values (self-produced), to obtain the production of the vector of goods destined for sale (CM_S) and the vector UV_C; the vector MC_C is purchased. The sale of vector CM_S obtains M, which in turn allows the HH to acquire the vector CM_C and consumer durables (CD_1). With these purchases and UV_C (again we assume that there are no self-produced CD), plus the CD from the previous periods (CD_0) and the portion of the domestic LF destined for one's own use, the ready-to-consume G&S (UV_{RC}) are produced.

Or in a simplified way:

$$(UV_{LF} + CM) \rightarrow (CM_S) - M - (CM) + (CD + UV_{LF}) \rightarrow UV_{RC} \qquad (1.5')$$

Where the first arrow symbolises production for the market and the second for consumption. The first dash symbolises the sale of the goods produced and the second the purchase of the goods intended for consumption. In Equation (1.5') we return practically to the scheme of petty commodity circulation of goods M−D−M, *except that here both production processes are made explicit*. In this case, three cycles have been made explicit: one of circulation and two of production (one production of commodities and the other production of UV for self-consumption).

In all the types of HH examined, the purpose of the cycle is, as in the DMP, need satisfaction. In all, however, we have found commodity articulation of a double character: the sale of some G&S (mostly not consumable by the HH) to finance the purchase of others that are S of N. What is sold is LF and/or CM_S.

Table 1.2 analyses circulation and production schemes in three types of private enterprises: producers of G&S, commercial and financial, as well as in two types of government institutions: producers of social use values (SUV) and producers of commodities (CM_S). Enterprises operate in a fully monetised scheme that starts with an amount of monetary resources, symbolised as M (initial capital). M allows the purchase of the vector of production commodities (CM_P), which includes equipment and facilities (CM_E), inputs (CM_{In}), and LF (CM_{LF}). The production process transforms this vector into another vector, which I call CM for sale (CM_S). Selling them closes the cycle and leaves the firm with an amount M' (M' = M + ΔM). Commercial companies sell the same vector of CM they buy, but in a different place and/or moment. In financial firms the ability of money to multiply itself becomes apparent (the cycle is M−M'). In the three types of enterprises, for the whole operation to make sense and be sustainable from the capitalist point of view, M' must be greater than M (that is, M' > M). This difference is called by Marx surplus value and in national accounts operating surplus. Thus, *money is transformed into capital*, which Marx defines in *Capital* (1867/1976/1990, volume I, chapter IV), as money that has the power of generating more money.

The circulation/production cycle of the enterprise producing G&S, or the capitalist cycle, is:

$$M - CM_P \rightarrow CM_S - M' \qquad (1.6)$$

The cycle can be read as 'to make money by buying and then selling (after transformation in the case of production companies, and without it in commercial enterprises)'. In the first type of companies there is a production

Table 1.2: Circulation and production schemes in private capitalist enterprises and in the state

Institutional sector		Production/circulation scheme		Remarks
Private Enterprises	Producers of G&S	$M-CM_P \rightarrow CM_S-M'$ $CM_P = CM_{LFT} + CM_E + CM_{IN}$	With the initial money (M), commodities for production (CM_P) are purchased, including LF (CM_{LF}), equipment (CM_E) and inputs (CM_{In}). They are transformed ($\rightarrow$) into 'goods for sale' (CM_S), and sold (−) for a larger amount of money (M = D + ΔD).	In the first type of companies there is a production cycle ($CM_P \rightarrow CM_S$) and a circulation cycle (M–CM–M'). In the second and third the production cycle disappears; in the third even CMs disappear. *Capitalist mode of production (production and circulation). Meaning: to make a profit.* All three cases start with M and end with increased M. First group: *production of CM by means of CM.* Second group: buy to sell at a profit. Third group: lend money to obtain interest.
	Commercial	$M-CM_S-M'$	There is no production process. CMs purchased are 'the same' as those sold. LF and other CMs are also acquired to support the commercial service.	
	Financial	$M-M'$	Money that is lent with interest.	
Government	Non-commodified	$M_T-CM_P \rightarrow SUV$ $CM_P = M_{LF} + M_E + M_{In}$	With money (M) derived from taxes (T), the state apparatus buys commodities (CM_P), including LF, and produces social use values (SUV) that it delivers to the population without *quid pro quo*.	A production cycle ($CM_P \rightarrow SUV$) and a circulation cycle (M_T-CM_P) that consists of *buying without selling. State mode of production in its non-commodity variety. Meaning: satisfaction of needs through social use-values. Production of SUV through CM.*

Table 1.2: Circulation and production schemes in private capitalist enterprises and in the state (continued)

Institutional sector	Production/circulation scheme		Remarks
	Commodified	$M-CM_p \rightarrow CM_s-[M + \Delta M-MT]$ $CM_p = CM_{FT} + CM_E + CM_{IN}$	The cycle is formally equal to that of the capitalist mode of production, except that the surplus value generated (ΔM) can be transferred to customers, suppliers or consumers (MT), so the sum of the terms in square brackets can be less, equal or greater than M, depending on whether $\Delta M - MT$ is positive, negative, or zero.	A $CM_p \rightarrow CM_s$ production cycle and a $M-CM_p-[D + \Delta M-MT]$ circulation cycle. *State mode of production, commodified variety.* Formally identical schemes to those of the capitalist mode of production, except that the sense is not (necessarily) the obtaining of profits, because the state apparatus has other sources of income (T). *Production of CM by means of CM.*

cycle (CMP→CM_s) and a circulation cycle (M−CM_p−M'). In the second, production disappears; in the third, even CMs disappear and only money remains (M−M').

As at the ends of the cycle there is only money that lacks quality (use value), the sense of the whole operation is quantitative: to increase M. It does not matter, therefore, through which CM this accumulation is carried out (food or guns). Only value matters, with UV being contingent. To use Sraffa's accurate expression, it is *the production of commodities by means of commodities.* It should be added: *and the circulation of these through money.*

It is necessary to introduce government, in a broad sense, including all levels of government, the legislative and judicial branches, and public enterprises. To understand government functioning, I have coined the concept of 'state mode of production' (SMP; Boltvinik, 1986), which comprises both activities that lead to the production of SUV (for example, the provision of free education and health services), the non-commodity variety, as well as activities that produce commodities (for example, producing gasoline or electricity), the commodity variety (Table 1.2).

The non-commodity variety of the SMP starts, like capitalist enterprises, only with M, in this case obtained through taxes and similar sources (T). With M it buys a set of CM_p, including LF, to produce a series of G&S which, in the non-commodity variety, are not sold as companies or PHHs do, but delivered to the population as SUV. The state can also use part of M to deliver monetary transfers (MT) to the population. This cycle is:

$$M_T - CM_p \rightarrow SUV \\ | \\ MT \qquad (1.7)$$

Depending on the design of social policy, the SUV may benefit all or part of the population. In any case, it will be necessary to reformulate the reproduction equations of HH, adding these SUV to the preceding equations, as well as the payment of taxes and reception of MT, which in the *SHHDP* will be:

$$CM_{LF} - [(M-T) + MT] - [(CM_C + CD_1) + (CD_0 + UV_{LF})] \rightarrow (UV_{RC} + SUV) \qquad (1.2A)$$

In (1.2A) I have added MT and subtracted T (including SS contributions), to the M obtained from the sale of LF; I have added SUV to UV_{RC}.

The *PHHDP* equation is:

$$(UV_{LF} + E + In) \rightarrow (CM_C + CD_1) + (CD_0 + UV_{LF}) \rightarrow UV_{RC} + SUV \\ \downarrow \qquad | \\ CM_s - [(M-T) + MT] \qquad (1.5A)$$

where T is subtracted and MT added to the M obtained from the sale of CM_s; received SUV are also added.

All schemes presented are single-period schemes, where the only things that can come from a previous period are the CDs, the E, and the In. In addition, the schemes lack other forms of assets, monetary savings and loans obtained that allow HHs to increase the amount of M available for the acquisition of CM_C and CD_1 but impose later payments of interest and amortisation. These elements explain the possibility of consumption expenditure differing from current income.

To add both possibilities in the schemes, we symbolise the saving/depletion of savings with S (positive or negative values) and the payment of interest and amortisations with A. Let's start with the *SHHDP*. Savings, in securities or in real estate, generate income (dividends, interest, rents) over multiple periods, expressed with R:

$$CM_{LF} - \{[(M+R) + (MT-T) - A]\} - [(CM_C + CD_1) + (CD_0 + UV_{LF})] \rightarrow UV_{RC} (+ SUV) + (S) \quad (1.2B)$$

Similar equations can be formulated for the other types of HH. Up to now I have not presented equations for combined households (CHH), which have both wage income and income from the sale of goods produced (or purchased) by the HH, and neither have I presented, except in HH with no commodity articulation, the production of goods for own consumption. In the most complex case (Equation 1.8) I include both absences. Production for self-consumption is denoted as UV_C. I also add FT as a new component of final consumption. When I read, watch TV, listen to music, or go to a show, I *spend time*. Possession of books or a TV set does not constitute consumption. Time dedicated by the individual is required. FT is not only necessary to consume CM but also to get involved in relationships and participate civically and politically.

$$(\alpha UV_{LF} + E + In) \rightarrow [UV_C + (CM_C + CD_1) + CD_0 + \gamma UV_{LF} + \delta FT] \rightarrow (UV_{RC}) + SUV + S$$
$$\downarrow \qquad\qquad\qquad | \qquad\qquad\qquad (1.8)$$
$$(\beta CM_{LF} + CM_S) - [M + R + (MT - T)] - A$$

Several issues can be appreciated in (8).

First of all, income (second row): CHH sell βCM_{LF} and CM_S which they produce, or market. In (1.8) I have also included income from property, R, and the net MT (received less granted), which may come from other HH or the state. To obtain available income in the period, it is necessary to subtract taxes paid (T) and amortisations and interest (A) on standing debts, a part of which may come from previous periods. For certain purposes it is appropriate to classify transfers in public and private. In addition (first row), a vector of self-produced consumer goods (UV_C), that constitutes *non-monetary* or *in-kind income,* has been included in (1.8). Total current income (monetary and non-monetary) is the sum of monetarily valued UV_C and monetary income [D + R + MT−T]. To obtain the usual concept of total current income, net T in kind (which does not include education, health services, or other public sector services, the SUV), payment in kind to employees and the imputed rent of services provided by the HH's own dwelling would be missing. All these should be added in the reproductive scheme to obtain total current income.

Second, *household consumption,* the components of which (excluding time used for final consumption), are formed by four types of G&S, in terms of their form of access and period of acquisition: the UV produced for own consumption (UV_C) using αUV_{LF} plus E and In; the CM_C and CD_1 acquired with M in the period; the pre-existing durable goods (CD_0); and G&S received from the state (SUV). The HH applies γUV_{LF} and δFT, relying on pre-existing CDs and those purchased in this period ($CD_0 + CD_1$), to transform the UV_C and CM_C vectors into the UV_{RC} vector. These UV_{RC} are the ones that Becker (1965) calls 'fundamental consumer goods (food cooked and served, clean and ironed clothes)'. The HH also consumes SUV and, finally, generates savings or dissavings. A TV set is a CD, but only television observed by one or more people is a UV_{RC}. Therefore, FT is included in the term between the two production arrows of the first line, which includes everything necessary to produce the UV_{RC}.

The situations described in the two preceding paragraphs can be illustrated by a peasant HH that grows maize and beans to eat and coffee to sell, and some of its members sell their LF. Their monetary income can also include rents (they can lease part of the plot), plus the MT received from the federal government or family remittances. T can be positive or zero.

Third, *saving and borrowing.* Part of the income may be committed by debts, whose payments A (amortisation and interest), must be subtracted to obtain *the available income for consumption expenditures in the period* $[D + R + T - I - A]$. If this income is less than consumer expenditure $[CM_C + CD_1]$, there will be depletion of savings (S will be negative). This clearly illustrates how assets such as savings (or debt capacity) can be used to finance consumption and their role as sources of WB.

Fourth, *distinction between consumption expenditure and actual consumption.* Consumption expenditure, CE $[CM_C + CD_1]$, is not equal to the consumption of the period, even abstracting at the moment from the other elements of Equation (1.8) (UV_C and SUV and added domestic work), since only a fraction (depreciation) of the CD purchased in the period will be consumed in it, what we could denote as the $\dot{\omega} CD_1$ product, where $\dot{\omega}$ is a positive fractional number that expresses the depreciation rate. In addition, a fraction $\dot{\omega}_0$ of the consumer goods accumulated in previous periods ($\dot{\omega}_0 CD_0$) will be consumed in the current period. Therefore, consumption (C) in a period, may be larger, smaller, or equal to CE, but in general it will be different:

$$C = CM_C + (\dot{\omega} CD_1 + \dot{\omega}_0 CD_0) \neq CE = CM_C + CD_1 \qquad (1.9)$$

Recalling that housing and domestic equipment is included in CD_0, and can be included in CD_1, it becomes clear that (1.9) can involve great differences between C and CE and that, therefore, today's standard of living is not fully determined by today's income (even without considering the SUV).

Households' reproduction logic, their well-being sources, and concepts

Fifth, the determining factors of the final vector of ready-to-consume consumption, whose total level expresses the standard of living of the HH/person (without considering interpersonal variations in needs) comprise two large components:

1. The amount, quality, and diversity of the UV_{RC} that depend, mainly, on *four elements*:
    a) The CD_0 or HH patrimony. The value of the 'services provided by these goods' could be called *imputed in-kind income*. This is carried out in national economic accounting only for the self-owned inhabited dwelling (and is called *imputed rent*). Despite the convenience, for certain purposes, of valuing this component in monetary terms and adding it to current income, other reasons advise keeping this item separate. On the one hand, because it is a component not affected directly by the conjunctural factors of the economy, contrary to what happens with the income from sales of CM_S or LF, in such a way that its behaviour is much more stable in the short run. On the other hand, being an income in kind, it cannot be used to acquire other goods. A dwelling cannot be used to eat.
    b) The purchases of the period, determined in the long run by *the level of current monetary income*, although in the short term they may differ from it. Therefore, the factors to be identified are those that determine the level of the different sources of monetary income.
    c) Consumption G&S in kind, produced, received (net) from other HHs and as part-payment for the sale of LF. The production capacity for one's own consumption depends on time allocated to it, the equipment, land, and real estate to which the HH has access, the technology and skills applied, and access to credit.
    d) Availability and application of LF in domestic tasks to produce the UV_{RC}. It could be said that by deciding on the relative allocation of time between LF time sold (extra-domestic work), domestic work, and FT, HHs decide (given their restrictions) a good part of the level and structure of their consumption. Not all members of a HH are available for domestic and/or extra-domestic work, although all are in principle available for FT. The time that members who, due to age, disability, illness, or study, are not available to work (domestically or extra-domestically) must be deducted (totally or partially). For those available, once the hours for sleep, self-cleaning, and food intake are discounted, there would be about 14 hours a day available on average. Therefore, hours devoted to $CM_{LF} + UV_{FT} + FT \approx 14$ for most individuals. This restriction forces the individual to decrease the time of one or two components if it wants to increase that of other(s). For a HH whose livelihoods depend on income derived from the sale of LF,

the allocation of time to it (given the income per hour their members are capable of earning) has a minimum determined by the monetary income necessary to meet needs. Once this allocation has been made, there is not enough time left for the other two uses. FT is more likely to be sacrificed when income is below, equal to or slightly above the minimum requirements (PL). When income is higher, it is possible to cut domestic work, increasing food consumption outside the HH and hiring some domestic services. In some cases, extra-domestic work could also be decreased, income decreased, and domestic working time and FT increased.
2. The level, amount and diversity of SUV for the average household in a country depends on social legislation and social policy. For a single-person household (HH/I) this level will depend, if the legislation establishes differentiated programmes by age, gender, stratum or social class, on its condition in this regard.

Sixth, knowledge and skills. In (1.8) four additional parameters have been introduced (denoted with lowercase Greek letters) that multiply the three terms of LF (portion sold, used to generate vectors UV_C or UV_{RC}) and FT. These parameters refer to the knowledge and skills that people put into play when they work and consume. The results of their activities will be enhanced the deeper and more relevant the knowledge/skills are. Regardless of their impact on income, the level and diversity of skills and knowledge deployed at work are associated with a higher likelihood of work satisfaction. In economic units with a technical division of labour, in general, people with greater knowledge occupy positions in which work done tends to be more rewarding (less boring and monotonous), such as management and design tasks. Partial work on the production line is left to those with lower levels of knowledge/skills. In domestic work there are fewer possibilities of technical division of labour. In consumption, there are consumer skills or capabilities that are required to be able to consume certain G&S. As Marx says, it takes a trained ear to appreciate good music. In other words, both from the point of view of the quality of human work (from total alienation to the self-active realisation of potentialities) and of the quality of consumption, the level of knowledge/skills is an enhancing factor. For these reasons, the parameters in this regard have been introduced into Equation (1.8).

1.2 Well-being sources (WBS) and resources

The pertinent WB to be measured for the study of standard of living is the one related to the satisfaction of needs that depend partially or totally on economic resources. In the reproduction schemes/equations outlined above, I expressed in a more detailed and formal way a thesis that I have been

Table 1.3: Equivalences between well-being sources (WBS) and the concepts included in the reproduction schemes

Well-being sources (WBS)	Concepts included in reproduction schemes
1. Current income/current disposable income	Current disposable income: $[M + R + (MT - T) - A]$.
2. Non-basic assets and borrowing capacity	A part of CD_0 and CD_1, financial savings and borrowing capacity. They can be used to finance consumption above current Y.
3. Basic assets	The other parts of CD_0 and CD_1: basic durable consumer goods, including own housing.
4. Access to free public sector G&S	Social use values, SUV.
5. Knowledge and skills	Parameters of UV_{FT}, CM_{LF} and FT which indicate the level of knowledge and skills mobilised in work activities (domestic and extra-domestic) and in 'consumption'.
6. Time available/FT	UV_{FT}, TL.

holding for many years (for example, Boltvinik, 1990a). This thesis holds that the WB of individuals/HHs depends on the following *direct WBS*: 1) current income; 2) family patrimony, understood as the set of assets and durable goods that provide basic services to a HH; 3) non-basic assets and HH borrowing capacity; 4) access to free G&S offered by the government; 5) FT or time available for rest, domestic work, education and recreation; and 6) people's knowledge and skills, understood *not as means for income earning, but as direct satisfiers of the HN for understanding*.

Table 1.3 sets out the 'equivalences' between these six WBS and the concepts used in reproduction schemes, particularly in Equation (1.8).

WBS 1–3 represent private economic resources, either in the form of flows or assets; WBS 4 represents the flow of public economic resources (the social wage). Together, these first four categories represent the economic resources *that can be expressed in monetary terms*. WBS 5 and 6 have their own units of measurement, which *cannot be reduced to the monetary yardstick*. In short, economic resources, knowledge/skills and FT are the three irreducible dimensions of WBS.

These six WBS can be characterised by their degree of *substitutability* and *specificity*. The dissaving of NBA or indebtedness can replace a low current income without affecting current satisfaction of any need, but it is an unsustainable practice in the long run. The sale/pawning of basic assets is not a plausible way to compensate for insufficient current income, even in the short term, because it affects the satisfaction of some need. If an individual reduces their bank savings (NBA), they can sustain current private consumption. But if you pawn your TV or refrigerator, the increase in liquidity implies the loss of the basic services provided by these assets. A higher current income can replace the lack of access to free services (for example, by paying for private education or health care); it can also replace the lack of a family patrimony (for example, by renting a furnished apartment). But a higher income cannot compensate for either the lack of FT or ignorance.

The fact that *there is no total substitutability* between WBS is related to their *specificity*. WBS are not generic and do not meet all needs. However, they have varying degrees of specificity. Monetary income and non-basic monetary assets allow the satisfaction of a wide range of needs (in principle, all that can be satisfied through the consumption of bought G&S); other WBS are more specific. Non-monetary current income and basic assets take the form of specific goods that provide specific services (for example, maize, a house, a table) that can only meet specific needs. Social policy generally provides G&S in kind (education, health care, food) related to a specific need.

One or more WBS may be required to meet each need: for a child to increase their knowledge, it is necessary to attend school, which entails dedicating FT. The government provides free school services, but the child will require school supplies, appropriate clothing, and transportation, which are usually purchased. Feeding family members requires (except in HH without domestic work) both income and domestic work (which involves use of FT).

An adequate measurement of poverty (and of the standard of living) requires taking into account simultaneously the six WBS and their interrelationships. Some examples will illustrate the consequences of not doing so. As a result of the increasing incorporation of women into paid work, monetary income increases in many HHs. National economic accounts will show an increase in both GDP and net HH income. The PL measurement method will record a decrease in income poverty. However, part of this GDP growth and poverty reduction will be spurious. Markets will have expanded (the realm of commodity values), but in terms of WB, of need satisfaction, the improvement can be much less or even null. Current income will have increased, but the FT of women who entered the labour market will have decreased. It might be necessary to hire a person or the services of a nursery and/or lengthen the working day of the woman. In addition, new transportation expenditure and meals prepared outside the home, among other things, will be required. Therefore, some *HH will have higher monetary income but also higher monetary expenditure requirements* for the same WB level. The final balance can be positive, neutral, or negative in a HH's WB. Likewise, between two HH of equal size, age structure and sex composition, and with equal current incomes, if their positions in other

WBS differ, they will have different standards of living. For example, if one is entitled to free medical services and education and the other is not, or if one has available time for DW and the other does not.

Social WB trends are the result of changes in the levels and distribution – between HH/individuals – of the WBS. The levels and distributions of each source are determined by specific factors. Average real yearly HH income is determined by the conditions governing the economy and by macroeconomic policy. Access to SUV, both in terms of level and distribution, depends almost entirely on legislation and social policy. FT depends, on one hand, on social customs regarding the length of the working day and on weekly and annual rest periods and, on the other hand, on HH income (HH with lower incomes will feel pressured to extend their working day) and individual preferences. Although determinant factors differ between sources, they are not totally independent of each other. FT and social policy, for example, can both be affected by what happens in the economy. The WB of the population is, in turn, a fundamental determinant of mortality rates, as evidenced by the empirical relationships between countries' living standards and life expectancy at birth.

Elements involved in the discussion of WBS are sometimes acknowledged by mainstream economic thought, by recognising the insufficiency of current income as an indicator of the control or disposition of resources, and by proposing *composite indicators of the economic status of households*. Aldi Hagenaars (1986, pp 9–10) describes successive additions of items to these composite indicators. Put together, access provision to resources would be equal to the sum of current income, the value of domestic production, the value of leisure, the annual flow derived from net capital assets and the value of non-cash transfers (public and private). Irwin Garfinkel and Robert Haveman (1977), relying on Gary Becker (1965), have developed the concept of *earning capacity*, 'designed to measure the ability of a HH unit to generate a stream of income if it were to use all its human and physical capital to capacity' (p 50). Although the departure point of these approaches and mine are similar (the holistic concept vision of the HH), three differences stand out: all the constituent elements are seen as *means* in the economic status approach, while I conceive time and knowledge, at least partially, as *ends in themselves*; a clear contrast is drawn between my position on the *irreducible character of time and knowledge* and the reduction to monetary terms of all elements in the economic status approach; my approach does not rely on assumptions on HH maximising behaviour, present in Becker and in Garfinkel and Haveman. While my approach is currently applied in the practice of poverty measurement, that of economic status is less applied.

In summary, I have identified six HH/individual WBS which can evolve in different, even contradictory, paths because they are subject to different determining factors.[3] Therefore, when studying the WBS trends of a given society, both the different WBS and their determinants must be taken into account.

The six WBS can also be construed as resources, although at the cost of losing some of the breadth of the concept, since knowledge and skills, as noted above, are not conceived as means to income, saleable commodities, or human capital, but as direct satisfiers of the need for understanding and for other HN, as substantive capacities whose development express human flourishing.

The main limitation of what I call partial methods of poverty measurement (as they only consider some of the WBS), among which are the income or PL and the UBN methods, is that they proceed *as if the satisfaction of needs depended only on some WBS*. PL proceeds as if the only WBS was current income, although in applications comparing current consumption with PL, NBA (and HH borrowing capacity) are also implicitly considered. The restricted variants of UBN used in Latin America utilise indicators of need satisfaction that basically depend on the ownership of consumer basic assets (mainly housing) or on the right of access to government services (water, elimination of excreta and basic education), so implicitly it does not take into account the other WBS.

That is, the PL method does not consider WBS 2–6 when comparing the PL with HH income, or 2 and 4–6 when comparing it with HH consumer expenditure. For its part, the restricted UBN method in its original variant does not consider WBS 1 and 2 (current income and NBA) and source 6, FT. That is, both methods have a partial view of poverty. Measuring poverty with them produces biased measures. In Boltvinik (1990) I concluded that the two methods are complementary rather than alternative because they take into account different WBS. This is how the IPMM was born (Boltvinik, 1992). The path for an adequate measurement must be sought developing methods that consider, implicitly or explicitly, all WBS.

---

[3] Beyond the logical possibility, this has happened in Mexico in recent decades. For an analysis of the radically different evolution of WBS in Mexico and, therefore, the incidence of human deprivation in different components, see Julio Boltvinik (2003b, pp 385–446). Among other things in this essay, I show that while the incidence of income poverty had a mixed evolution in the various sub-periods (it decreased between 1968 and 1981 and then increased uninterruptedly until 1996, and lastly decreased between that year and 2000), ending the millennium above the level of 1977 and 1981, the incidence of poverty in education, housing, housing services and access to health services decreased throughout the period, leaving their levels in the 2000 at less than half the 1970 level. These contrasting trends show that the WBSs of the different components are specific and may move in opposite directions.

Peter Townsend (1979), in the conclusions of his chapter 2 where he discusses different theories on poverty, notes that '*Other resource systems* than the wage system, and *other institutions than the labour market*, including the political and welfare institutions of the state, have to be brought into a general theory [of poverty] – even if they prove to be of lesser importance or to be indirect appendages of the labour market' (p 87). This author, in my opinion the most important researcher on poverty of the twentieth century, relates resources to his definition of poverty in this way:

> Poverty ... is the lack of the resources necessary to permit participation in the activities, customs and diets commonly approved by society. Different kinds of resources, and not just earnings or even cash incomes, have to be examined. The scope, mechanisms and principles of distribution of each system controlling the distribution and redistribution of resources have to be studied. ... Poverty is in part the outcome of these systems operating upon the population. Some, such as wage and social security systems, affect large proportions of the population and account, in aggregate, for a large proportion of the total resources which are distributed. Others play a relatively minor role. They have been developed in conjunction with the class structure and both help to reproduce but also to modify that structure. ... Therefore, the distribution of resources *between* resource systems can be as important as the distribution *within* any single system. (Townsend, 1979, pp 88–90)

The author presents a chart in which he associates various types of resources with the systems from which they derive. Apart from the wage system and the SS system, the chart includes the self-employment income system; the tax system; the property income system (rents, interest, dividends); social assistance; family; court-ordered maintenance payments; the industrial welfare system; and the central and local public welfare systems. Townsend failed to achieve an adequate taxonomy, since the initial quotation makes it apparent that systems and institutions became entangled. The idea of distribution systems is very suggestive and helps to understand the multi-determination of the standard of living and poverty.

As for resources, Townsend distinguishes five types, which I have reordered to be able to compare them with what I presented above: monetary income (which he divides into earned income or income from work, not earned or from property, and derived from SS); value of labour benefits in kind; private income in kind (includes *domestic production*, gifts and the value of services provided by the family or community); capital assets (family-occupied housing, others); and the value of public social services (including subsidies and services such as education and health).

Table 1.4: Resources considered by several authors

WBS (well-being sources) Boltvinik	Townsend	Bryant	Garfinkel and Haveman
1. Current income	Monetary income Labour benefits in kind Gifts in kind	Financial resources	Current income
2. Basic assets	Assets	Financial resources Physical goods	Net asset flow
3. Non-basic assets			
4. Access to free G&S	Utilities Family and community services		Transference in kind
5. Knowledge and skills		Skills and energy	
6. Time available		Time	Value of leisure
	Domestic production		Domestic production

Table 1.4 compares this resource typology by Townsend with the WBS, Bryant's (1990) typology, and with the elements that Haveman and Garfinkel (1977) include in the HH economic status approach. Aggregating monetary income with gifts and labour benefits in kind, these Townsend items are equated (approximately) with current income (monetary and non-monetary) that is included in both the WBS and the economic status of households. Bryant does not handle, in this part of his text (p 6) the explicit concept of income. Financial resources do not coincide, of course, with income, which is why I have repeated, in Table 1.4, the concept in assets. Regarding assets, there is an almost total agreement between the authors of the table, except that Garfinkel and Haveman (G&H) convert them into equivalent flows of income (Y). Something similar is proposed by Townsend (1979, chapter 5). Bryant does not explicitly handle free-of-charge or highly subsidised G&S received from the public sector. The equivalent item in G&H is that of transfers in kind, which include private transfers, which in Townsend are called gifts and which I have placed as part of current income. My concept of current income includes private monetary or in-kind transferences, although for purposes of aggregation it is necessary to arrive at a net concept, in which the item of each HH is 'transfers received less transfers granted', otherwise current income of all HH will not be equal to the sum of the individual HH income.[4] Townsend includes

---

[4] Alternatively, only received transfers could be included in HH Y and transfers granted could be seen as expenditures. This is, in fact the view I have adopted in Chapter 8, below, for income-poverty calculations.

an item that does not appear in any of the other authors: that of family and community services (not governmental, which he calls public services). These services resemble the concept of domestic production (last line of Townsend and G&H) but has a transference character (it is produced by one household for the benefit of another).

So far there is a broad agreement, in general, between the authors. The strongest differences are in the last items of the table, which are *less conventional resources*. Townsend does not consider knowledge and skills, nor FT, as resources. However, he includes domestic production, which is the result of HH members' activities, in which they use part of their FT and their skills/knowledge. G&H agree with Townsend in including domestic production, and they add the value of leisure. Bryant and I partly agree as he explicitly includes time, as well as skills, but adds *energy*, which is a very interesting concept, in the resources.

Much of the differences depend on two factors: the phase of the resource–use cycle in which each author is implicitly located; and whether the author wants to transform all resources into monetary terms to be able to add them up. When an author begins before the sale of LF, HH whose income depends 100% on this sale will only have their capacities, their time and, perhaps, some assets from previous periods as their patrimony. When an author (as in my case) includes current income among resources or WBS, they already assume that the sale of LF has taken place (or an equivalent element in non-salaried HH). The same goes for DPSC. One can depart, as I do, by taking as a given the elements from which DPSC takes place: the monetary income that allows buying the inputs, and the skills and the available time of the members of the HH that allows them to transform these into UV_{RC}.

1.3 Central definitions: needs and poverty

The concept of HN in philosophy

HN are defended, rejected or problematised by different groups of academics. In this book I address mainly the ideas of the defenders. For reviews of 'rejecters' and 'problematisers', see Doyal and Gough ([1991] 1994) (Introduction and chapters 1 and 2) and Springborg (1981) (especially the chapters dealing with Herbert Marcuse, Ivan Illich, and William Leiss). In Boltvinik (2005–2006) I synthesise Doyal and Gough's text and proceed to criticise Neoclassic Consumer Theory (NCT), which rejects needs explicitly but then lets them in by the back door. A detailed critique of NCT is presented in Section 2.3. HN are based on human nature, as Bernard Williams (1990) and Gasper (2004) argue. Márkus (1973/1985/1978/1988) systematises Marx's thought that locates HN within philosophical anthropology. According to this view, humans are distinguished from animals because their vital activity, work, is oriented towards N satisfaction through mediations (*tool-making animals*), a view confirmed by modern palaeoanthropology, as shown in Boltvinik (2020, pp 101–115). Marx conceives N (except original biological N), as produced in a sense like the one conveyed when speaking of produced goods. Marx's conception contrasts with the instrumentalist vision of production in neoclassical theory that conceives it as being at the service of the sovereign consumer and his pre-existing preferences, not N (Rothenberg, 1974). My detailed narration of Marx's conception of N, as construed by Márkus, can be seen in Boltvinik (2020, pp 71–115).

Wiggins ([1987] 2002) distinguishes N from wants/desires and rigorously defines N and distinguishes them from the needed object (or satisfier). The following paragraphs explain his ideas and incorporate other points of view.

To distinguish needs from wants/desires, this author points out that N are not strong or unconscious desires (or preferences).

> Unlike 'desire', or 'want' then, 'need' is not evidently an intentional verb. What I need does not depend on thought or the workings of my mind (or not only on these) but on the way the world is. Again, if one wants something because it is F, one believes or suspects that it is F. But if one needs something because it is F, it must really be F, whether or not one believes that it is. (Wiggins [1987] 2002, p 6)

Doyal and Gough ([1991] 1994, p 42) distinguish between *objective needs* conceived as purposes universally associated with the prevention of serious harm and *subjective desires* that are not.

The special force of the term N and the normative character of non-instrumental but categorical/absolute N stem from the non-controversial character of their purpose, to avoid human harm or to achieve human flourishing, according to Wiggins. Doyal and Gough ([1991] 1994, pp 2, 39) adopt the similar concept of avoiding serious harm ('significantly impeded pursuit of purpose') or achieving flourishing, and define N as universal, with which Fromm (1955/1990) and Max-Neef et al. (1986/1991) agree. Doyal and Gough assert: '*if all human beings have the same capacity to suffer serious harm or to flourish, they all have basic human objective human needs conceived as universalizable purposes*' ([1991] 1994, p 3). Fromm and Maslow identify the serious consequences of unmet needs as physical or mental illnesses: for example, Fromm (1955/1990, p 30–36) identifies narcissism (which in its extreme forms is equivalent to insanity) as the consequence of the unsatisfaction of the need for intimate relationships.

Wiggins defines the satisfier or object needed: 'A person needs x (absolutely) if and only if, whatever the morally and socially acceptable variation ... that it is possible to foresee that it occurs within the relevant time interval, will be damaged if it has no x' ([1987] 2002, p 14). And he defines needs as 'states of dependence (with respect to not suffering harm), which have as appropriate objects the things needed' (p 16). This distinction between satisfiers and needs is made by several authors, and Max-Neef et al. (1986/1991) also distinguish satisfiers from goods as different analytical spaces, in the sense developed by Sen (1983/1984). Orthodox economists, and paradoxically Amartya Sen, generally restrict satisfiers to G&S (objects), but Lederer (1980) identifies objects, relations and activities as satisfiers, while I, based on Márkus's description of Marx's conception of human nature and Max-Neef et al.'s matrix of N and S (1986), have identified six types of S: G&S; activities; relations; information, knowledge, and theories; capabilities; and institutions (see Section 3.2).

To continue with Wiggins' ideas, it is necessary to add that:

1. 'The political-administrative process, as we know it in Europe and North America, could hardly proceed (it could hardly conclude an argument) without constantly resorting to the idea of N.' 'Given the special force that comes with N we must try to grasp some special content that the word possesses by virtue of which it acquires that force.'
2. 'Although there is an instrumental sense of "need" where one can ask for a purpose to be specified ... there is another sense of N for which purpose is already fixed, and fixed by virtue of the meaning of the word: to avoid harm to human beings.' It is precisely the fact that this avoidance is not a controversial purpose that provides claims of N with their *prima facie* special practical and argumentative force ([1987] 2002, pp 4–9). Wiggins explains that this is valid only for absolute or categorical needs, not for instrumental needs.
3. 'The suggested elucidation in terms of harm ... expounds the idea, not innocent, of the metaphysics of personality, WB or flourishing, by reference to which we make judgments of harm' ([1987] 2002, p 11).

N is an example of what is called 'gross ethical concepts' when referring to which 'factual description and valuation can and should be *entangled*' (Putnam, 2002, p 27). To use this term 'with any degree of discernment, one has to be able to identify oneself imaginatively with an evaluative point of view'(2002, p 39). Needs, poverty and Sen's *capabilities* are entangled terms in which description depends on evaluation (2002). The entanglement thesis defeats many frequent criticisms directed at academics for incorporating values. One example is Fitzgerald's critique of Maslow. When Fitzgerald says, 'To speak of the N of self-actualisation is tautologically or unequivocally normative' (Fitzgerald, 1977, p 49) (that is, it is not synthetic or falsifiable). Fitzgerald adopts the tripartite classification of logical positivists of all judgements that constitute the expression of the fact/value dichotomy: 1) synthetic or falsifiable; 2) analytical (false or true only by the rules of logic, and therefore tautological; 3) without cognitive meaning (ethical, metaphysical, and aesthetic judgements). Therefore, he states that the discourse on the need for self-actualisation belongs to categories 2 or 3.

Poverty (generally defined as economic inability to meet needs) is a central field of application of the concept of N and is dominated by economists who defend the fact/value dichotomy and reject the concept of N. Since they conceive that rationality cannot be present in questions of values, they assume – and insist on it all the time – that the definition of the PL (highly loaded with values) is an arbitrary act by the researcher, thereby promoting a total vacuum in this subject and facilitating the task of those who wish to minimise the incidence of poverty through thresholds that deny most HN. They are impoverishing poverty studies in the same way that, as Putnam describes, they impoverished welfare economics (Putnam, 2002: chapter 3).

Definitions of poverty and needs in everyday life

The *Diccionario de la Real Academia Española* (DRAE) expresses the meaning of the adjective 'poor' as 'needy and lacking what is necessary to live, or that has it with much scarcity'. Likewise, it defines the noun 'poverty' as 'need, narrowness, lack of what is necessary for the sustenance of life'. Two issues are clear: the terms poverty and poor are associated with a state of need, with deprivation, and this lack is related to what is necessary for the sustenance of life. We can deduce that the term poverty in its daily use implies the comparison between the situation of a person, family or human group and the conception of the one who speaks or writes about what is necessary to live or sustain life. That is, *the concept of poverty bears the inevitable imprint of the comparison between an observed situation and a normative condition.* While this norm is implicit in everyday language, it must be explicit in philosophical and scientific language.

The same dictionary shows that the noun 'need' means, on the one hand, 'lack of the things required for the preservation of life'. Note here the deficiency meaning of the term and the limitation of the purpose (subsistence). On the other hand, it also means 'irresistible impulse that makes causes to work infallibly in a certain sense' and 'everything to which it is impossible to escape, fail or resist'. In expressing the meanings of the adjective 'necessary', it shows its opposite terms: necessary is opposed to contingent when it means that 'precisely, forcibly or inevitably it is to be or happen'; it is opposed to voluntary, spontaneous and free when it refers to what is 'done and executed by obligation of something else' or 'of the causes that act without freedom and by determination of their nature'; and it is opposed to superfluous when it refers to that which is 'indispensably necessary, or is required for an end' (note here that the end remains open).

It is clear that when we speak of N we refer to the lack of things that are necessary for the preservation of life, but also to situations from which it is impossible to escape and to the infallible action of causes. What is necessary to sustain life is not the superfluous, nor the contingent, nor that which we may voluntarily or spontaneously want or desire. On the contrary, it is something in which we cannot exercise our freedom, since it is something that is impossible for us to escape.

N contrasts with 'desire' precisely in the element of will contained in the latter term, whose meaning is expressed in the dictionary that we have been citing as 'energetic movement of the will towards the knowledge, possession or enjoyment of a thing'. You can desire what you need or desire what you don't need (the superfluous, the contingent). Wanting something is different from needing it.

The contrast between N and 'preference' can also be explored by analysing the meaning of the latter term, which the DRAE explains as follows: 'primacy, advantage or majority that one person or thing has over another, either in value, or in merit'; and also 'choice of one thing or person, among several; favourable inclination or predilection towards it'. While N refers to the indispensable character of a situation or an object, preference is the predilection, advantage, or choice between diverse objects that may be necessary or superfluous. In preference the subject compares different objects and chooses between them, and truly chooses only when he is free from N, since N obliges. Unlike desire, in preference there is no 'energetic movement of the will'.

There is thus a gradation between the 'irresistible impulse' of N, which has an involuntary character, the 'energetic movement of the will' in desire, and the primacy, choice or predilection that results from tastes or preferences that are also volitional acts but lacking the energy of desire. While I need to feed myself if I am to continue to live, I may wish to do it with a lasagne and be willing to cook it to achieve it. On the other hand, when choosing lasagne on the menu of a restaurant, I only express my preference among the various dishes contained therein, without one option or another involving an energetic movement of the will. The need to feed myself cannot be subtracted while I am alive. A desire, on the other hand, can be resisted without harming my physical or mental integrity, although it can lead to frustrations of varying degrees depending on the importance of the desired object. The preference for lasagne can be changed at the last minute to spaghetti without even causing frustration.

Let us now explore these same meanings in the English language. According to the *Concise Oxford Dictionary*, the adjective poor expresses one who lacks money or adequate means to live comfortably. The noun poverty means the state of being poor and the lack of the necessary goods (necessities or satisfiers) for life. As in Spanish, the word expresses the sense of lack of what is necessary. Let's look at the meanings of the noun 'necessity': an indispensable thing, an imperative necessity and, like the Spanish term 'necesidad', a 'state of things or circumstances that force a certain course', so it is the antonym of freedom, as in Spanish. This same meaning is contained in one of the meanings of the adjective 'necessary': 'determined, which exists or happens by natural laws ... not by free will'. An important conclusion is that the meanings (in Spanish) of 'need' are divided in two English words: need and necessity.

Let's contrast necessity or need with desire and preference, as we did in Spanish. 'Desire' is defined by the dictionary we have been citing as 'unsatisfied longing' or 'craving', while *Webster's New World Dictionary* defines it without the element of dissatisfaction as 'wish or long for'. In no case do we find the precise meaning of the definition of the DRAE that associates desire with 'energetic movement of the will'. 'Preference' is defined in the *Oxford Dictionary* as 'favouring one person over others', and 'prefer' is explained as to choose or 'like better'. Despite the diminished strength of the English definition of the term desire, the gradation of meanings from need to preference, passing through desire as an intermediate point, remains clear. The conclusions obtained in Spanish remain in English.

In English there is also the term 'want', which is a verb and a noun. *Webster's* defines three synonyms for *want*: desire, lack, and poverty. Want could only be translated into Spanish as wanting when it is synonymous with desiring, as in the phrase *I want a new car*. In this case it is close to preference. However, in other cases it is closer to N. It is synonymous with poverty in the phrase *to live in want*. It is synonymous with lack in the phrase *to suffer from want of adequate care*. In Spanish the verb 'querer' has a narrower range of meanings in our field. The noun *want* is difficult to translate into Spanish. My position is that it should be translated as 'apetencia' (related to appetite), since want in Spanish as a noun has a completely different meaning.

According to Gordon and Spicker (1999, p 9), in the *Standard Dictionary of Arabic*, written in 1311, poverty is defined as the 'inability of an individual to meet his own basic needs and those of his dependents'. Note how current this definition sounds. The authors add that another Arab source from 1037 defines eight different levels of poverty ranging from loss of savings until the individual/HH is reduced to ultimate poverty, passing through situations such as loss of some assets, being forced to eat millet bread (cheaper than the usual wheat bread), not having available food, no longer having belongings that can be sold to buy bread, or being humiliated and degraded because of poverty. According to the work *Economic Doctrines of Islam*, by I. Ul Haq (quoted in Gordon and Spicker, 1999, p 109), poverty from the Islamic perspective is the inadequacy of goods, means, or both that are necessary for the sustained WB of the human being. It implies a state in which the individual lacks the resources to meet N not only for sustained survival but also for healthy and productive survival. The Koran recognises the following types of poor: destitute poverty: *al fuqara, fakir*, people who lack material goods, possessions, or income to support themselves; needy poor, *al masakin, miskin*, who have some income or assets, but these are insufficient due to their low productivity or the large number of dependants; those who require temporary help, *al gharimun*, because they are overwhelmed by debt or have been affected by natural disasters; and the traveller, *Ibn al sabil* 'son of the road', who has no means for the expenses of the journey (Gordon and Spicker, 1999, p 109–10).

Orthodox economics is based on the idea of preference and rejects the concept of need.

On the nature of needs

According to Doyal and Gough, two conceptions of N must be distinguished. One conceives N as impulses with respect to which 'we have no choice but to conform'. The other conceptualises 'N as purposes that, for some reason or another, all people are believed to be trying or should try to achieve'. It is this *universality* that differentiates N from preferences and desires. They argue that the former conception 'is at least misleading because of its overly deterministic conception of human biology' ([1991] 1994, p 35), while they adopt the latter. N is often used to denote an impulse or some internal state that initiates an impulse. Here, N refers to a motivational force instigated by a state of imbalance or tension established in the organism due to a particular lack. This approach has inspired perhaps the most famous analysis of basic needs, that of Maslow. Doyal and Gough point out that in the rest of their book they will not use N in this sense. They argue that 'there are good reasons why we should completely divorce the discourse of N as universalisable purposes from that of motivations or impulses' ([1991] 1994, p 36). And they argue, citing Garret Thomson's book, *Needs* (1987), that 'having an urgency to act in a particular way should not be confused with an empirical or normative justification for doing so'. They use Thomson's example of the alcoholic who says that 'one can have an urge to consume a lot of alcohol, which one does not need' and argue, correctly, that in this case 'the impulse is not linked to the prevention of serious harm in a universalisable way'. It should be added that the satisfaction of addictions, in addition to not being universalisable, does not lead, in the long term, to avoiding serious harm. But they add, as a strong point of the conception of needs as impulses:

> However, the emphasis on drives and motivation alerts us to the biological background of HN: to the constraints on HN that our

genetic structure provides. If N are not identical to the impulses of the human organism, neither are they disconnected from 'human nature', or the physiological and psychological structure of *Homo sapiens*. (Doyal and Gough [1991] 1994, p 36)

My opinion on this is that *the key point lies in the word universalisable* and not necessarily in the dichotomy between impulses and purposes. Therefore, the notion of *universalisable impulses that prevent serious harm is a solid foundation for the concept of need*, combining both the central goal (prevention of serious harm) and impulses. This conception overcomes the dichotomy. On the other hand, it is important to clarify that Maslow's approach is not based (or at least not only) on impulses. Indeed, in the 'Prologue to the Theory of Motivation' (chapter 1 in his book *Motivation and Personality*, 1954/1987) he clearly saw what Doyal and Gough call the 'grammar of needs'. Under the heading 'Means and Ends', he says:

> We want money to be able to have a car because neighbours have it and we don't want to feel inferior to them, so we can retain our self-esteem and be loved and respected by others. Usually, when analysing a conscious desire, we find that behind it, there are other more fundamental purposes of the individual. ... It is characteristic of this deeper analysis that it will always lead, ultimately, to certain purposes or needs, beyond which we cannot go; that is, to certain satisfactions of N that seem to be ends in themselves and seem to require no further justification or demonstration. ... In other words, then, the study of motivation must be, 'in part', the study of ultimate human goals, desires, or needs. (Maslow, 1954/1987, p 5)

Doyal and Gough engage in a wide-ranging discussion of biology's influences on our N and, towards the end, say that 'the problem with much of what is now known as "socio-biology" is that it confuses restriction with determination and overestimates the extent to which innate, emotional, and cognitive grammar determines what we should and should not attempt' ([1991] 1994, p 38). They give as an example the supposed genetic predisposition of women to express strong maternal feelings towards their young children and say that there is no problem until this conflicts with their need to find employment and that in these cases 'it is the woman and not her genes' who has to choose what aspect of their nature to activate, so that 'our unique cognitive abilities as human beings still leave us with the problem of deciding what we need, regardless of what we feel we want' (Doyal and Gough [1991] 1994, p 38). From my point of view, Doyal and Gough make an obvious mistake here: it is one thing to choose what needs to be satisfied or what aspect of our potentialities to develop (maternal or other creative potentialities), a dilemma often inevitable, and quite another thing to decide what we need. If you compare the earlier ideas of Doyal and Gough with those of Wiggins (whom they quote), *it seems that they have not understood (or have not accepted without refuting it) that to need is not an intentional verb and that, therefore, we cannot decide to need or not to need.* On the other hand, they do not seem to clearly distinguish between instrumental needs (which obviously have less interest in a theory of needs) and categorical or absolute needs, as shown by the example of the woman working to pay the bills. They also conceive needs, as indicated above,

> as a particular category of purposes that are considered universalisable. N in this regard are commonly contrasted with 'desires' that are also described as purposes, but which derive from an individual's particular preference and cultural environment. Unlike N, wants are thought to vary from person to person. (Doyal and Gough [1991] 1994, p 39)

They go on to explain why universality is imputed to some purposes but not to others:

> The imputation is based on the belief that if N are not met by an appropriate [satisfier], serious harm of some specific and objective kind will occur. Therefore, not trying to meet N will be seen as something that goes against the objective interests of the individual involved and will be considered abnormal and unnatural. When purposes are described as 'wants' rather than N, it is precisely because they are not believed to be linked to human interests in this regard. (Doyal and Gough [1991] 1994, p 39)

2

Critique of the Political Economy of Poverty (CPEP), Part 1: on different answers to the question of the constitutive elements of the good/full life

The *external critique* of the Political Economy of Poverty (PEP) presented in successive sections in this and the following chapter comprises six aspects: Sen's and Rawls's critiques of utilitarianism, complemented by the former's critique of the opulence approach (OA) and other related approaches (Section 2.1); an internal and external critique of Neoclassical Consumer Theory (NCT) (Section 2.2), which complements the critique of utilitarianism; a very brief summary of the critiques of Sen's (and Nussbaum's) *capability* approaches developed in *Broadening Our Look* (Section 2.3); a summary presentation of the New Paradigm of Poverty and Human Flourishing (NPPHF) (Section 2.4); a critique of conventional definitions of poverty (Section 3.1); and a comparison of what I have called the *conceptual maps* of the PEP and of the NPPHF (Section 3.2). Unlike the *internal critique* I have been formulating for over 30 years, and which is presented in Part II of this book, the one discussed in these two chapters is not a critique of measurement methods and their public policy implications but rather an external critique that focuses on the conceptual foundations of the PEP. In Sections 3.1 and 3.2 the critique contrasts the criticised positions with the NPPHF, which makes its external character *evident*.

2.1 Sen's and Rawls's critiques of utilitarianism: Sen's critique of opulence and primary goods approaches

Amartya Sen defines utility theories as those that see value only in individual utility, defined in terms of a psychological metric such as pleasure or happiness.[1] *According to this interpretation, the moral importance of needs (N) is*

---

[1] The contents of this subsection are a summary of section 7.1 of *Broadening Our Look*. Sen's works on which I have relied for his critique of utilitarianism are Sen, 1980, 1987, and 1992. I have drawn on Rawls' critique of utilitarianism indirectly from Sen and G.A. Cohen (see below).

based solely on the notion of utility, says Sen, who distinguishes *utilitarianism* from *welfarism*. The former seeks to maximise total social utility by equalising everyone's marginal utilities, while the latter posits utility as the single value but does not seek to maximise total social utility.

According to Sen, if one accepts the *prior principle that the equality of the total utilities of all persons is valuable,* then utilitarianism should be condemned. Sen introduces here *human diversity*, a concept that is repeated time and time again in his work, and which in this case explains that equating the total utilities of each person yields different results than equating their marginal utilities. Sen also criticises *utilitarianism* using the *case implication perspective* between a disabled person who obtains a low level of utility from a given income level and a pleasure wizard; Sen sustains that utilitarianism would concentrate income in the latter, showing that it fails to perceive the abovementioned prior principle.

Sen's central critique of *welfarism* argues that the adaptation that paupers undergo to reconcile themselves with their situation means that they can derive great pleasure from small things; this means that, in the metrics of utility, *the resigned poor can be extremely efficient utility producers.*

This critique and the one by Rawls based on the concept of *expensive tastes* (see below) are symmetrical, and to emphasise this, calling Sen's critique *the cheap tastes critique* is quite useful. By combining both critiques, we can conclude that the measurement of utility (if it were at all possible) might place the poor in a better position (higher total utility) than the rich. Thus, the *egalitarian welfarist,* who attempts to equate the total utility of all persons, would demand *transfers from the poor to the rich.* Yet, paradoxically, the *utilitarian would transfer resources from the rich to the poor,* who are 'pleasure wizards', to increase total social utility. Sen does not entirely reject the welfarist approach; what he rejects is that WB can *be judged exclusively in terms of utility.*

G.A. Cohen (1993/2003) describes and analyses Rawls's critiques of utilitarianism based on the concepts of *offensive* and *expensive tastes*. The former holds that the pleasure derived from discriminating against others or subjecting them to restricted freedoms should not count in the calculation of justice. The latter rejects the idea that one should provide gourmets with a higher income, *since citizens are responsible for their preferences.* In my view, these critiques are irrefutable and show the severe limits of any approach (including Sen's capability approach) which, as G. Peter Penz (1986) states, assumes that individuals are the only authority to judge the appropriateness of their wants, without daring to formulate a universal principle or any value judgement.

Sen reintroduces personal diversity to criticise what he calls the 'opulence approach' (OA), which involves identifying *people's access to G&S or real income* as the constitutive element of the living standard: a person with a higher metabolic rate, Sen argues, may prove to be less wellnourished than a person with a lower income. He concludes that the living standard is not a question of opulence but rather of *the life one leads,* what *one can do*, and what *one can be*. Sen identifies the Basic Needs Approach to Development (BNAD) with the OA, arguing that basic N are typically formulated in terms of *possession of goods*, and criticises BNAD for failing to delve deeper into the foundational dimension of N, which he associates with the question of *why basic N are important.*

Variability in nutritional requirements (and in other N) among individuals has been acknowledged in the literature on poverty measurement. This makes it difficult to understand what phantom Sen is fighting. Once he has defeated utilitarianism – for his critique of cheap tastes is devastating – what he should refute to underpin his *capabilities approach* (CA) is not the OA but the one holding that *the constitutive element of the standards of living is the (objective) satisfaction of HN*. However, Sen fails to identify this approach.

Using similar arguments, Sen (particularly 1992) criticises Rawls's primary goods approach. According to Sen, the primary goods index proposed by Rawls (1971) to measure people's status fails to take human diversity into account and therefore does not acknowledge the *utility* disadvantage of disabled people. Rawls proposed postponing this problem rather than ignoring it – as Sen admits – although in his opinion, a theory of justice cannot postpone this issue, since *differences in N* are omnipresent.

In order to evaluate the importance of human diversity as stressed by Sen, in *Broadening Our Look* (chapter 7, footnote 24) I examine how serious persistent inequalities would be if all HH had the same resources per person. I conclude that these inequalities would be of tertiary importance.

2.2 Internal and external critique of Neoclassical Consumer Theory

For the orthodox economist, the 'objectivity' of N is *suspicious*. Preferences and demand are considered sufficient for the purposes of much of positive and normative economic theory, say Doyal and Gough (1991), following Penz.[2] Welfare Economics (a branch of NCT), Doyal and Gough continue, states two principles: the *subjective conception of interests* – individuals are the only authorities on what their actual interests or wants are – and *consumer sovereignty* – production is determined by individual preferences.[3] Once

---

[2] Later in this section, I show that this is merely an impression and that, when analysed in depth, Neoclassical Consumer Theory requires N, which it surreptitiously slips into its analysis.

[3] This very naive view contrasts sharply with the Marxist conception of the interrelations between production and N, which I analysed in chapter 9 of *Broadening the Look*, where I broach both Marx's view in the *Introduction to the Critique of Political Economy* (1857) and the analysis by J.P. Terrail et al. (1975/1977), who explore this view in depth. The

welfare economics abandoned the direct measurement of utility and adopted the satisfaction of wants as its basis, it came very close to *sustaining the equivalence between WB and opulence (real income)*,[4] holding that the subjective satisfaction of wants can be scientifically measured and used to evaluate conditions or policies.

The idea that individuals are the only authority to judge how right their wants are, Doyal and Gough continue, comes under severe questioning once the limits of knowledge and rationality are admitted. 'Wants based on ignorance are epistemically irrational', says G. Peter Penz. But Penz's most devastating critique is that of 'circular evaluation': wants are shaped by the same institutions and processes that must be evaluated based on the satisfaction of these wants (Penz, 1986, p 87). From the catalogue of problems and inconsistencies of NCT, Penz draws two additional conclusions that complement what was said before.

First, 'want satisfaction is a principle that cannot be made measurable without *additional normative judgements*' (emphasis added).[5] Second, if these external normative judgements are developed, 'their insertion into the want-satisfaction principle subverts the principle's fundamentally open-ended and subjective character. Yet not to insert them leaves it open to the problems of ignorance and irrationality, of evaluation circularity, and of non-comparability. This dilemma quintessentially reflects the shortcomings of the want-satisfaction principle and of the sovereignty conceptions that are based on it' (Penz, 1986, pp 132, 136; cited by Doyal and Gough, 1991, p 24).[6]

The following discussion is based on Bryant (1990) and Deaton and Muellbauer (D&M) (1980/1991), works specialising in the NCT. I will show that this theory ambiguously eliminates the concept of N, which is afterwards reintroduced through the back (or even front) door and cannot endure the introduction of HN and poverty thresholds in its most basic analyses.

In the NCT, 'the demand for goods and services is the result of the interaction between household preferences, synthesised in a *utility function* ... its possibilities, represented by the budgetary restriction' (Bryant, 1990, p 17), and an 'assumption or hypothesis of behaviour: that *households attempt to maximize satisfaction or welfare*' (Bryant, 1990, pp 18, 27, emphasis added).

Introduction, published many years before the *Grundrisse* has been included as the first text in the edition of the *Grundrisse* (Marx, 1857/1973, pp 81–111).

[4] As we shall see in Section 2.5, without the 'very close', this is what orthodox economists do when they study poverty: in actual fact, they equate utility with opulence or people's income.

[5] Ravallion admits this very explicitly, as we shall see in Section 2.5.

[6] This dilemma also affects Sen's CA, as one can see from the critiques presented in Section 2.5. His approach would lose its open, pluralistic nature if he introduced external, normative judgements. But failure to do so means that his proposal ends up being a non-operational, sterile approach.

Once these three elements are placed next to each other, the best solution (from which the demand equations are derived) follows algebraically.

D&M define a set of choice axioms 'the acceptance of which is equivalent to the existence of a utility function' (1980/1991, p 26). The axioms are: 1) *Reflexivity*. Any bundle of goods is at least as good as itself. D&M add that this is trivial but mathematically necessary; 2) *Completeness*. 'This axiom says that *any of two bundles can be compared; the consumer can judge between any two bundles [of goods]*'; 3) *Transitivity or consistency*. If bundle *a* is preferred to *b* and *b* to *c*, then *a* should be preferred to *c*; 4) *Continuity*. The meaning of this axiom coincides with the intuitive understanding of this word; 5) *Non-satiation*. The utility function is *non-decreasing* in each of its arguments (goods) and *increasing* in at least one argument; 6) *Convexity*. The meaning of this axiom is intuitively understood geometrically. These axioms, the budget linear restriction and the maximisation of utility provide the solution (1980/1991, p 26–30).

In the formal explanation of the NCT, *N are nowhere to be seen. And yet*, as we shall see, *they are everywhere*. In chapter 1, called 'The Limits to Choice', D&M state:

> The emphasis in the discussion is commonly placed on *preferences*, on the axioms of choice, on utility functions and their properties. The specification of which choices are actually available is given a secondary place. ... Unlike preferences, the opportunities for choice are often directly observable. ... It is our view that much *can be so explained [by opportunities]* ... [*while*] *the part played by preferences in determining behavior tends to be overestimated.* (1980/1991, p 3, emphasis added)

In their first diagram, in addition to budgetary restrictions, the authors include the '*survival constraint*' for the first and only time in the entire book. The axes measure amounts of food and lodging, indicating the survival minimum for each: together, both survival constraints define Point C. D&M conclude that, by introducing this additional restriction, choice is reduced to part of the space situated above B and to the right of A, and that HHs with a budget that only enables them to purchase at minimum survival levels will have to do this or cease to exist (1980/1991, pp 4–5). Introducing a survival restriction is equivalent to introducing HN and poverty.[7] However, the authors' ambiguous attitude is reflected in the fact that instead of fully

---

[7] Some laws of consumer behaviour that have been verified worldwide, such as the diminishing share of food expenditure in total household expenditure as the latter increases, known as the Engel Law, leave NCT speechless. Worst of all, these statistical regularities do not provide feedback to NCT.

assuming the survival restriction, they present it as a contingency: '*if there is a basic survival constraint*', they say. The presence of this constraint reinforces the conclusions of the above-cited paragraph. *When budget and survival restrictions leave the consumer with a zero degree of choice, preferences become inapplicable or irrelevant.* This evinces that *preference-based consumer theory must be revised*. But even more important – because of its generality for non-poor consumers, those whose budget is, by definition, larger than the required minimum – is the fact that freedom of choice only exists with respect to the surplus.[8] Despite the above, which would point to the recognition of N, the authors maintain that the amount demanded for a good depends solely on prices and budgetary constraints, once again denying HN.

When the authors introduce the Engel curves (which show the expenditure proportions that consumers allocate to a group of goods) and point out that they serve to *identify necessary or basic goods and distinguish them from luxury items*, they introduce *necessary* as an attribute of *goods* even though individuals have been defined as *free of N*. This creates a striking case of commodity fetishism since goods assume qualities which human beings have been stripped of. Because of its empty formal nature and its rejection of N, the NCT cannot predict or explain any statistical regularity in consumers' behaviour.[9]

D&M wonder (1980/1991, p 21) whether preferences are a crucial element in the description of consumer behaviour and answer 'probably not'. They add, 'the presence of indivisibilities, kinks, and other nonlinearities may limit choice *to the extent that only very mild additional assumptions are required to describe behaviour completely*' (emphasis added). Despite this awareness, D&M obviously defend NCT.

Other examples of how needs slip in through the back door in other authors' explanations are in chapter 10, subsection 10.2.2 of *Broadening Our Look*. But let us examine one in which N *come back through the front door*. To compare welfare levels between HH of different sizes and demographic structures (using the so-called equivalence scales), D&M *openly resort to HN*:

> equivalence scales are based on the assumption *that the only differences in tastes between households are because of variations in observable characteristics*. … In many contexts, it is important to know how well off the members

---

[8] When one introduces the interdependence of consumers and thereby patterns of consumption by class and social stratum (something that should be unavoidable), even this freedom of choice is highly restricted, if not eliminated.

[9] Some laws of consumer behaviour that have been verified worldwide, such as the diminishing share of food expenditure in total household expenditure as the latter increases, known as the Engel Law, leave NCT speechless. Worst of all, these statistical regularities do not provide feedback to NCT, since it is absolutely deductive.

of one household are relative to those of another ... one way [to do this] is to compute and compare the *per capita* budget levels. ... However, **this ignores the variation of need** with age: babies need less than adults. ... Households equivalence scales are deflators ... by which the budgets of different household types *can be converted to* **a needs-corrected basis**. (1980/1991, p 192, emphasis added)

Ignoring variations in N according to age cannot be wrong if, at the same time, it is right to ignore HN throughout the development of the theory. But the surreptitious introduction of concepts of N amid neoclassical discourse is not exclusive to D&M. It is an inevitable phenomenon. In chapter 10 of *Broadening Our Look*, I show how this is expressed in Bryant, who in describing HH notes that, 'without choice, a unit cannot pursue its own WB and therefore its conduct cannot be classified as goal-oriented behaviour' (Bryant, 1990, p 2). Bryant tends to illustrate indifference curves by placing food on one axis and all other goods on the other. In this context, he confronts one of the *inconsistencies of the axiom of non-satiation* and tries unsuccessfully – which is not shown in the quotation – to emerge from the corner into which he has got himself:

it is assumed that *the household prefers more to less:* more food or more 'all other goods' or more of both. You may wish to argue with this assumption, correctly pointing out that *there are many things, in amounts above a certain limit,* including food, *which the family prefers less to more*. (Byrant, 1990, pp 17–18)

What Bryant has just accepted, *the fact that non-satiation is false* and that many HN have absolute limits, demolishes the NCT. This 'over-the-top' restriction led original NCT theorists to conclude that not only do specific goods have a diminishing marginal utility, but money (and income) does too, from which egalitarian conclusions were derived. Bryant says that a HH is in equilibrium 'when it has no incentive to change its spending patterns' (1990, p 30). *The poor can never be in equilibrium.* NCT cannot say anything about their behaviour.

After analysing the evidence associated with four empirical models developed on the basis of NCT, D&M conclude that: 'a) ... models produce a conflict with theory. The restrictions of homogeneity and symmetry, basic to the assumptions of a linear budget constraint and *the axioms of choice,* are consistently rejected by data'; and b) there are important explanatory variables other than prices and total expenditure (1980/1991, pp 79–80, emphasis added). In other words, *some variables have been omitted.* These unfavourable conclusions for NCT force D&M into what I call the *inconsistency syndrome*:[10]

---

[10] This is a common syndrome among those that are led to something by impulses unrelated to the rationality of the issue in question. In this case, the impulse might be the need to

'We do not believe that … it is necessary to abandon the axioms of choice in the face of the results of this chapter. Ultimately, of course, given sufficiently convincing evidence, we should be prepared to do so' (1980/1991, p 82, emphasis added).

When one acknowledges that the consumer is not a robot but rather a biological and social being, and *HN are explicitly introduced,* the amount of a specific good demanded by a HH/individual will not only depend on the price of the good and the HH/individual's budget, but also on the consumer's inescapable requirements of the good (which may have a zero or positive value). We can therefore express the total budget (X_T) as the sum of the necessary budget (X_N) and the free budget (X_F). Increasing the price of one of several basic goods reduces X_T in real terms, and since the consumer will keep the X_N level unchanged as long as possible, X_F will diminish. The amount demanded of each basic good will be a constant with respect to changes in its own prices in all HH in which X_T is greater than or equal to X_N, up to the point where $X_F = 0$. Conversely, the amount demanded of non-basic goods will diminish when the prices of both types of goods increase.

Let us see what happens with axioms 2) *completeness,* 3) *transitivity* and 5) *non-satiation* when HN are introduced (the survival constraint). I begin by identifying the nutritional N of an adult male of average weight, height and type of activity: between 2,600 and 2,940 kilocalories and between 57 and 63 grams of ideal protein. Within these ranges, the adult male is in an ideal situation. Below both minimum levels he will suffer from malnutrition, and above the maximum ones he will be obese. Thus, in terms of proteins and calories, *consumers have very little margin of choice* to remain within an *optimum objective* (which is different from the subjective optimum of neo-classical theory). This is consistent with the 'vitamin model' (Warr, 1987), which holds that as the amount of a characteristic to which a person has access increases, WB initially increases until it reaches a level after which it remains constant, even if the amount of the characteristic increases and, finally, if the latter continues to increase, WB will start diminishing. This draws a WB curve in the shape of a mountain (climbs, stabilises and decreases). Although this model, *which contradicts the axiom of non-satiety* (above certain levels of a given characteristic, *the function of objective WB will be decreasing*), may not be applicable to all HN (education may be an exception), we can intuitively assert that it must be applicable not only to food but to many other N.

For *the completeness axiom* to be valid at income levels below the minimum requirements, HH would have to be capable of arranging several baskets that leave one or more N unmet from best to worst. Here is one example

---

belong to the 'mainstream economics club'.

of the terrible choices the 'rational' consumer would have to face: on the one hand, a basket that fails to buy half the food yet includes the householder's insulin, versus, on the other hand, one that covers the HH's nutritional requirements yet does not include insulin. In the first choice, all HH members will lose weight and could die of illnesses due to their weakened immune system and after a while will die of starvation. In the second, the householder will die soon. The axiom is pointless. No one can have the prior experience to be able to undertake this sort of evaluation. Whatever provisional 'decision' the HH makes, its members will be in a state of acute disequilibrium, contrary to the happy world of NCT's optimums and equilibriums. *The axiom of completeness does not apply below poverty thresholds.*

The axiom of transitivity is equally invalid for the poor. In order to appreciate this, let us add a third choice to the previous example. Let us assume that the HH can relieve its resource shortage if the teenage daughter starts working at a brothel. Since this option has not been adopted to date, the NCT would indicate that it is the least favoured one (option C of the transitivity axiom). In the following period, however, after the householder has had a diabetic crisis, the teenager may decide to work in a brothel. The least favoured option may end up being the chosen option. *Orderings are not transitive* below the PL.

Likewise, looking at the upper class, we might wonder whether a millionaire who has never had a yacht will know whether he prefers a yacht to a new house in the countryside. These types of decisions, at both the top and bottom of society, are made without previous experience, so that consumers can in no way know the meaning of these *ex-ante* choices. The middle class, located above minimums yet with restricted resources, is the only class eligible to act as a consumer based on an optimisation model. However, interdependence between consumers leads one to posit the hypothesis that choices, rather than being individual or familial, end up being determined by one's stratum or class as a whole due to the pressure to live like others do. The vast majority of HHs from these social strata end up adopting the same lifestyle and spending their income in a similar fashion.

In short, what I have said shows that *the axioms of completeness and transitivity do not apply in conditions of poverty and that the axiom of non-satiation does not apply for some types of goods. I have argued, as well, that the exercise of optimisation is pointless for upper class HH which, by definition, do not need to optimise their expenditures since they have no active resource constraints. These invalidated axioms are crucial in NCT. Without them, the theory collapses.* Another way of expressing this conclusion is that *whereas NCT might be valid for creatures without N, like robots, it is not valid for biological N-driven creatures.* In Broadening Our Look, I advance a tad towards the formulation of an alternative consumer theory based on the concept of a hierarchy of N.

2.3 Sen's and Nussbaum's capabilities approaches: a critique

Once utilitarianism and the NCT have been refuted by the critiques of Sen and Rawls, and of the other authors and myself presented in the previous section, it would seem that Sen's capabilities and functionings approach (CA) points in the right direction. Since the concept of *capabilities* appears at first glance as equivalent to capacities, and in my new approach I have posited *capacities and N* as the constitutive elements of the human flourishing axis (HFA), the latter would seem to be (at least partly) redundant. In order to be able to justify its need, I had to distinguish it from Sen's CA and explore the CA of Martha Nussbaum (MN), which provides an (apparently) similar answer to Sen's. Some of the conclusions I reach (among others) in *Broadening Our Look* (chapter 8, especially section 8.6) regarding Sen's CA, are: this approach does not regard the N-capacities unit as the constitutive element of the HFA; it directly and exclusively broaches the living standard axis, for it only considers the functionings associated with access to G&S; and it only considers *capabilities* associated with the person's purchasing power rather than human capacities as such.

In this and the ensuing paragraphs I present a summary of my critiques, and those of other authors, of Sen's CA. Bernard Williams (1987/2003) once told Sen, in essence, that his *theory was empty, that it had to be specified* (by defining a set of basic, corealisable *capabilities*, which Nussbaum has done, but not Sen) and that it needed theories of human nature and social conventions as foundations (which Sen has not done and Nussbaum claims to have done on the basis of Aristotle and Marx). Williams also showed that not all capabilities have to do with choice, by questioning the association between capability and freedom of choice, which is central to Sen's CA.

Gerald A. Cohen (1993/2003) maintains that Sen achieved a conceptual revolution by introducing two changes of approach: from actual state to opportunity, and from goods (and utility) to functionings. However, he also maintains that Sen's exposition suffers from a severe discursive obscurity due to the use of the word capability to describe both what a person is capable of doing *and what goods do for them*, but for the latter the word capability is inappropriate. Cohen highlights the passive side of human beings that the CA appears to have totally forgotten and criticises Sen's insistence on presenting what a person *achieves doing or being* as the constitutive element of his theory, for the type of life someone leads cannot be identified with achievements only, since there are many benefits that individuals do not achieve (such as not suffering from malaria). Cohen notes that the result of eating food is the capability to engage in valuable activities, but this is not the capability that Sen associates with food; he rather associates it with being well-nourished and being able to entertain friends. He criticises Sen for giving the term capability an athletic connotation, which in my view is the result of Sen's attempt to turn N into capabilities, which require that the person be an active subject. In the end, Cohen appears to accept functionings as dimensions of doing and being yet rejects the centrality of the expression *ability to achieve*, which ignores the passive side of human beings and overestimates the role of freedom and activity in WB. Sen has ignored Williams's and Cohen's critiques, giving the impression that he sees others as implementers of the new and unassailable paradigm.

John Rawls also strongly criticised Sen's CA. Sen himself narrates Rawls's belief that conversion rates of primary goods to capabilities cannot be compared between individuals who have different aims. *This would imply,* he suggests, *that the CA has no support basis as it is formulated* (Sen, 1992). This is very damaging, as Sen's assumption that everyone chooses their own set of capabilities implies that no two sets are the same. Sen's examples of the different conversion rates of goods to functionings are always based on the same functionings (such as being well nourished) between different individuals. Rawls's critique can be paraphrased with questions such as: 'Is it possible to say that Antonio's rate of converting bread into nutrition is lower than Pedro's rate of converting income into self-esteem?' In chapter 7 of *Broadening Our Look,* I provide a detailed analysis of Sen's attempt to demonstrate that such a comparison is possible and argue why it is, in my view; fruitless.

Frances Stewart (1996) identifies two problems in the CA. First, the *capability set* is *unobservable by nature*, which leaves the evaluation of functionings as the only option. Second, by failing to incorporate any form of value judgement, the CA is unable to order (from best to worst) two consumption sets for the same person, which coincides with Crocker's critique (1995) that the CA is *unable to categorise any* capability *as not valuable, or to distinguish it from pernicious ones*. Likewise, Des Gasper (2004, p 180) sarcastically notes that the key in the CA 'is what "people have reason to value". But unless we both interpret this as "good reason to value" and add a richer picture of human personality, with categories concerning skills and empathy, confidence and shame, habit and addiction, we will be liable to conclude that an American or European consumer stranded in front of her television set for five to six hours every day represents a fulfilment of reasoned freedom'.

Sabina Alkire (2002) has defended Sen from the critiques regarding the CA being non-operational by pointing out that its open nature means that there is no single way to operationalise it, but that this can be done in each specific application, therefore establishing *the theorists' refusal to theorise.*

In their efforts to implement the CA, both Alkire (2002, p 163, original italics) ('a basic *capability* is the *capability* to meet a basic need') and Meghnad Desai (1994) – who, in order to derive G&S requirements from his list of five basic capabilities for measuring poverty, finds it necessary to introduce N as an intermediate level – highlight the *CA's dependence on the concept of*

N, *showing that the CA cannot be set up as an independent approach*. A similar thing happens with MN's CA. However, when Alkire notices the difference between the verb *to need*, which is not intentional, and *the choice of capability*, which is intentional, she discovers that *the realm of N is eliminated in the CA*; that the replacement of N by capability eliminates the differences between food and dyeing one's hair blue.

Based on the formalisation (which has the advantage of precision) of the CA that Sen presents in *Commodities and Capabilities* (Sen, 1985), I show that it is a mechanistic approach. From the first equation presented in this book (1.1), one can deduce that the functionings achieved by a person are *only a function of their income (or entitlements) and of the personal characteristics that govern the transformation of goods into functionings*, this second element being the only one that distinguishes the CA from approaches that measure WB on the basis of income (for example, OA). Sen also introduces subjective (individual) evaluation functions of the functionings that replace utility functions. In doing so, he indulges three vices that he shares with utilitarianism (the second of which he himself has criticised): the function introduced is a mere artifice and the evaluation ends up being carried out on the basis of income alone; just as the resigned poor are extremely efficient converters of access to goods into utility, they value the same set of functionings more highly than an impoverished former member of the middle class; and the approach fails to exclude either expensive or offensive tastes.

As one can see, Sen's CA is subjectivist and mechanistic and could lead to the unacceptable result that the only satisfiers are G&S, a feature it shares with the most conventional PEP approaches. This CA leaves no room for capabilities such as MN's feelings, imagination and thought, or what Gasper (2004) calls *S-capabilities* ('S' meaning skill), but only for what the latter calls *O-capabilities* ('O' meaning opportunity). Sen conceives capabilities as *something derived from the possession of goods, as economic capabilities*. This is an alienated conception of human capacities, in which the only capacity is to possess commodities. Sen's failure to devise a law of diminishing returns to increases in income in terms of functionings and capabilities implies that the larger the income, the larger the capabilities (in a proportional way), whereby superfluous consumption is highly valued and inequality therefore justified, despite this author's important writings on *(in)equality*.

What Sen regards as valuable is WB freedom: the freedom of choice between viable sets of functionings, or *capability sets*, the breadth of which is determined by entitlements (or income). Sen leaves his CA intentionally incomplete because, in his eagerness to remain within 'mainstream economics', he needs to operate within the logic of preferences, which he would deny were he to formulate a list of basic capabilities. This is why Sen always speaks of the choice between states of being and doing, *considered valuable by the individual and not in terms of what is valuable per se*, which is why some of Penz's critiques of NCT are applicable to Sen's CA. As in NCT, according to Sen *what the individual chooses will always be optimal*, even if this means watching TV for six hours a day or torturing your neighbour.

Some authors believe that Sen's CA is extremely broad. But as one can perceive following the equations in *Commodities and Capabilities*, Sen proceeds mechanically from goods to functionings and then to capability. His universe is reduced to that which derives from the consumption of G&S, which excludes S such as relations and activities. This is a view of the person as a consumer (the opposite of what Cohen thinks), but who seems active because Sen festoons them with verbs.

Sen does not seek to found his conception on a vision of human essence or to lean on theories of N, because he does not need to. His CA has not been operationalised, meaning that no evaluations (of any type) can be undertaken on its basis. Despite this, Sen suggests that evaluations can take place in two spaces: achieved functionings and freedom (perhaps measured as degree of freedom, that is, breadth of capability set). In both cases, the result would depend primarily on the set of entitlements (or income) and marginally on the parameters for converting resources into functionings. In the absence of individual information about these parameters, the ordering of individuals (from better off to worse off) will be based on entitlements or income only.

MN identifies the following similarities and divergences between her version of the CA and Sen's: she defines a list of central human capabilities and a threshold for each capability (which he does not); Sen has never attempted to base the CA on the Marxist/Aristotelian idea of truly human functioning, which plays a key role in MN's; the distinction she makes between three types of capabilities has no parallel in Sen. These are *basic capabilities* (speech, love and gratitude, practical reasoning and the capability to work), which are innate; *internal capabilities*, which are a person's developed states; and *combined capabilities*, defined as internal capabilities combined with external conditions.

As MN argues, behind the identification of *certain central capabilities* and *a basic threshold in each capability* are the following intuitive ideas: certain functions are central in human life, in the sense that without them there is no human life, and there is a truly human (as opposed to not only animal) way of carrying out these functions. The central idea in MN's approach is that of a human being as a free, dignified creature who shapes their own life through the power of practical reason and sociability in cooperation and reciprocity with others. Her approach is radically different from Sen's and similar to the one adopted in *Broadening Our Look*. However, it is a naive approach insofar as it is not problematised, for example, with the notion of alienation.

The list of combined capabilities drawn up by Nussbaum identifies the key capabilities in any human life, and she considers that the list leaves room for a reasonable pluralism of specification.[11] It is a list of separate corealisable components. All are of central importance and have different qualities, which limits the trade-offs. Any condition below the threshold in any capability is tragic. When she says that certain human skills express the moral claim that they should be developed, MN attributes a moral force to capabilities that, according to Wiggins ([1987] 2002) and Doyal and Gough (1991), corresponds only to HN. When basic capabilities are deprived of the nourishment (satisfaction of N, including education) that would transform them into combined capabilities, they become sterile. MN points out that *flourishing is the development of human potentials and poverty their denial.*

As one can see, there is an enormous proximity between the ideas of MN and the central theses of *Broadening Our Look*. Note, however, that a sizeable proportion of the elements on the list are simply rephrasings of HN (which is obvious in 'being able … to be adequately nourished', 'being able … to have adequate shelter'), which disqualifies them as human capacities. Some refer to genuine human capacities. Some are not combined ('being able to have property … and movable goods'), since they do not constitute attributes of the person. This shows that the attempt to reduce all the features of the good life to a single category is inevitably flawed and that we need to talk at least about developed and satisfied N, developed and applied capacities, negative freedoms, and rights and opportunities if we wish to understand, measure, and foster human flourishing.

2.4 Synthesis of my New Paradigm of Human Poverty and Flourishing

1. I define *the good* as human flourishing and understand by it the *development of the human essential forces* (development and satisfaction of N, and development and application of capacities).
2. The final goal of public policy should be (in an ideal society) the full human flourishing of all.
3. I distinguish human wealth/poverty from economic wealth/poverty. Within each pair I distinguish two dimensions: their structural being

---

[11] Here is a highly simplified version of MN's *combined capabilities*: 1) *life*; 2) *bodily health* (includes adequate accommodation); 3) *bodily integrity* (includes reproductive opportunities and opportunities for sexual satisfaction); 4) *senses, imagination and thought* (includes pleasurable experiences); 5) *emotions*; 6) *practical reason*; 7) *affiliation*; 8) *other species*; 9) *play*; and 10) *control over one's environment.*]

(*ser* in Spanish) and their circumstantial being (*estar* in Spanish); *ser*/being and *estar*/being rich/poor. I distinguish the *ser*/being (structural quality of being) wealthy/poor from the *estar*/being (circumstantial/contingent quality of being) wealthy/poor. The *ser*/being of human wealth/poverty characterises those who need much/little and have/have not developed their capacities in depth and extension. The *estar*/being of human wealth/poverty is defined by the degree of satisfaction of human beings' effectively developed individual N and the degree of application of their effectively developed capacities.

4. To flourish, human beings must go beyond the satisfaction of *deficiency N* (physiological, security, love, and belonging N, following Maslow) and, through work and/or love, realise themselves as human beings who share the essence of the species: their potentials for universality, liberty, creativity, consciousness and relatedness (that is, satisfy their *growth N*). Following Marx and György Márkus, human flourishing can be conceived as the realisation of the human essence in concrete individual existence, the measure to which the individual freely and multilaterally unfolds through the development and expansion of their N and capacities, both of which tend, as do the individual's consciousness and social being, to universality.

5. However, during the prevalence of alienation and the spontaneous social division of labour, the growing universality of the human being, that is, social multilateralism, can coexist with growing individual unilaterality. It is thus necessary to carry out evaluations both at the societal and individual levels, subdividing the conceptual HFA into these two levels. The first can be called *social progress* and the second *development of the human essential forces*. Social progress can be conceived of as the *constitution of the social conditions for an unrepressed and rapid development of the human essential forces*.

6. Following the distinction established in paragraph 3), at the societal level I distinguish the constitution of the *conditions for the development of N and capacities* (*ser*/being dimension) and the constitution of the conditions *for the satisfaction of N and application of capacities* (*estar*/being dimension). These two dimensions are also distinguished at the individual level.

7. When the HFA is trimmed to keep its economic perspective only, the *conceptual standard of living axis* (SLA) – where *economic poverty/wealth* can be found – is delimited. The SLA is the economic perspective of the HFA. While in both axes we deal with the complete human being with all their needs and capacities, *in the SLA we look at them only from the economic perspective*: from the point of view of resources and economic conditions. The SLA also distinguishes both dimensions of being.

8. In economic poverty/wealth we can also distinguish the dimensions of *ser*/being and *estar*/being. Economic poverty is only the first obstacle

to be overcome to achieve human flourishing. But this obstacle has not yet been overcome by the immense majority of human beings. There are further obstacles, the most important of which is *alienation*. If the person, in order to survive, is forced to sell their only possession – their body and mind, and the capacities and knowledge they have been able to develop – so that someone else can use it; if in that external use of their capacities the person does not feel realised, does not feel their essential forces transforming the world and transforming themselves; if they only feel tired and bored; if they feel the product of their work as something alien, then this person is experiencing what Marx called alienation. The hope of many individuals who live to survive is laid upon FT.

9. We can thus distinguish four concepts of wealth/poverty (W/P): human *ser*/being W/P, human *estar*/being W/P, economic *ser*/being W/P, and economic *estar*/being W/P. These categories are different from the usual poverty concept, which despite coming close to the economic *estar*/being concept does not coincide with it for two reasons: first, because the usual concept is not the result of trimming the HFA but is rather constructed by broaching it directly as part of the SLA; second, because even in the broadest applications it only incorporates HN partially (in contrast with all HN in economic *estar*/being poverty) and leaves out human capacities.

10. By introducing capacities and creating the unity N-capacities, and by making explicit that the SLA derives from the HFA, the research of these topics (poverty, standard of living, human flourishing) is radically transformed. The interaction between N and capacities comes to the fore. Satisfaction of N makes the development and application of capacities possible. However, in capitalist societies, individual capacities have to be sold to be applied. This is valid both for a survival job (Kafka performing the bureaucratic job he hated) and a self-actualising job (for example, scientific research). In the first case the individual only applies some of their minor capacities, while in the second case the person applies their fundamental capacities and thus develops them. In the first case the driving goal is survival; in the second, human flourishing. But capacities must be sold not only to be applied (and thus further developed) but to make it possible to make ends meet, which in turn makes the reproduction of capacities possible. This synergistic interaction of N and capacities is lost in dominant approaches that only see one side of this dual unity.

11. We are used to thinking about N only in terms of satisfaction, but not in terms of development; in static terms, it is as if a new-born had the same N as an adult. One sense of the development of N is their extension (horizontal development). Not all adults have developed, for example,

Maslow's seven (groups of) N (physiological N, security, love and belonging, esteem, self-actualisation, cognitive and aesthetic N). Some individuals are dominated by physiological (and/or affective) N, while their superior N remain latent. A second sense of the development of N is their *qualitative development, their growing humanisation, or their deepening*. Many people cling to the religious education they have received and take the need for understanding for granted. For others, it is an endless search. Whoever has discarded the biblical myth of Adam and Eve can passionately seek to understand the origin of human beings in depth.

3

Critique of the Political Economy of Poverty, Part 2: conceptual maps and definitions

3.1 Critique of the dominant definitions of poverty in the PEP: comparison with the definitions of poverty in my New Paradigm

In Section 3.2 below I examine the predominant conception of needs (N), satisfiers (S), and resources or WBS, which as a whole I call *the conceptual map of the PEP*. I do this in a general fashion without referring to specific authors, with the purpose of highlighting the implications of directly dealing with the SLA, without considering the HFA. I call *critical thesis* the critique of an SLA built without deriving it from the HFA. The conclusions of this section, in which I examine several authors' definitions of poverty, underpin the generalisations I arrive at in Section 3.2. As will be seen in the analysis of specific definitions, the distinction between primary and secondary WBS is lost, as well as the entire dimension of S. Both analyses are complementary and should be jointly regarded as central to the CPEP.

According to the 'official' Spanish dictionary DRAE, poverty is 'the condition of lack of what is necessary to sustain life'. I have standardised the ten definitions of poverty included in Table 3.1 in line with the basic structure of the DRAE's phrasing, identifying the terms with which each author defines 'what is necessary' (the *means*) and how they phrase what follows after 'to ...' (the *end*). By doing so we can see how they identify the object of poverty studies.[1] The first column of Table 3.1 contains the authors' literal definitions, which are rephrased in the second column following the DRAE format, while the last column contains observations. The definitions have been classified in two groups: those incorporating the concept of N (definitions 1 to 5) and those based on different concepts, whether or not they explicitly reject the concept of N (definitions 6 to 10). The first group includes Altimir's definition, Foster and Sen's first definition, and Boltvinik's three definitions. The first three can be classified under the *conventional needs approach to poverty*, while the last two belong to the approach I developed in *Broadening Our Look*. The

---

[1] This is similar to the divergence found between diverse theories of inequality by the way they complete the phrase 'from each according to ... and to each according to ...'.

second group, which also includes five definitions, has in turn been divided in two sub-groups: Townsend's definition and Foster and Sen's second definition (6 and 7), which I have qualified as *failed searches for a new approach (FSNA)*, and the remaining three, which belong to the *dominant economicist approach* (definitions 8 to 10). These groups and subgroups are not homogeneous; there are stark differences within each one. The conventional needs approach, the FSNA and the dominant economicist approach comprise the PEP, the object of critique in this section. A quick way to compare the definitions is to read the standardised definitions in the second column of Table 3.1.

From his literal definition, we can infer that Altimir (1979) thinks the variable to be measured is WB, whose constitutive element he defines as the *satisfaction of basic N*. However, he doubly restricts the concept of HN; he only includes *basic* N (not all HN) and *not all basic needs, only those that are indispensable*. After examining the poverty measurement procedure adopted by Altimir, one concludes that he identifies 'a level of HH's current income' as 'what is necessary', implying a high degree of reductionism, which he shares with other authors included in Table 3.1.[2] Thus, his standardised definition is: 'lack of *current income* to *satisfy some basic needs*'. However, 'some basic needs' are restricted to food N when reaching the stage of measurement,[3] revealing further reductionism. Nevertheless, since Altimir's definition *incorporates at least one HN, it is not tautological,* unlike that of many economists.

Foster and Sen's first definition (1997) is almost the same as Altimir's, except that instead of 'basic' they qualify the N included as 'elementary and essential', illustrating them only with food and lodging throughout their examples, which suggests that they are indeed thinking of something extremely elementary and essential.[4] As for the contents of what is necessary, although at first glance they appear to be *opportunities*, once they are critically analysed (*deconstructed*), they turn out to be 'income adjusted to take human diversity into account' (see the observations column in Table 3.1), meaning that this definition can correctly be interpreted as '*the lack of income adjusted by human diversity to satisfy certain essential, elementary needs*'. Altimir takes human diversity into account via nutritional requirements that vary according to

---

[2] However, in the conceptualisation prior to measurement, Altimir has a much broader perspective. In Chapter 13 of *Broadening Our Look*, I conduct a detailed analysis of the concepts of poverty put forward by Altimir, Sen, Townsend and Hagenaars on the basis of ten additional issues for the definition.

[3] This is not totally evident. The NFB method used, as I have proved algebraically in various publications (see e.g. Boltvinik, 1999, pp 94–97), identifies only food poverty. For a more detailed discussion of this method, see Chapter 6.

[4] It is striking that in 1997 (in his work with Foster) Sen should continue to talk about N, as he appeared to have replaced this concept with capabilities and functionings since the first half of the 1980s.

age, sex, and occupation, something that further highlights the similarity between the two definitions, which I have therefore classified under the *conventional approach of restricted needs* in the study of poverty.

The definition used by Boltvinik (1992a) in the IPMM (definition 3), 'lack of WBS to satisfy human needs',[5] although *apparently* similar to the two previous ones, is *broader* in two respects: satisfaction of all HN, as opposed to basic/elementary/essential N, on the side of purpose, and all WBS as opposed to just one of them (current/adjusted income), on the side of means. This last difference is by no means small: it involves, among other things, the incorporation of available time, knowledge and skills, and has served as the basis of the broadest internal critique I have made of partial methods (which I call *partial* precisely because they only consider some WBS), which rank HH incorrectly by their living standard and measure poverty inaccurately.

At the end of this section I will broach the remaining two definitions of economic poverty (definitions 4 and 5) associated with the NAPHF (or NP), developed in *Broadening Our Look*. For now, let us move on to the authors that replace N with other concepts, beginning with Townsend and Sen, two fundamental authors in this subject who do not overtly reject the concept of N. Instead, they adopt close but clearly distinct concepts. As we shall see, however, replacing the word *needs* can never be an innocent choice. Peter Townsend replaces 'satisfying N' with 'participation in ordinary patterns of life (*types of diet, living conditions and amenities,* customs*, and activities*)'. One can argue, along with Wiggins (see Section 1.3), that the term N cannot be substituted by desires, wants, or preferences. Could it be replaced by 'participation in lifestyles', as Townsend suggests? Let us see how far his approach moves away from the concept of N. Out of the five elements constituting the purpose (the *what for*), the four I have italicised in the previous quote are S of N. Customs give rise to activities, diets, and perhaps facilities, meaning that they are (at least partly) redundant. Thus, we can rephrase Townsend's uniformed definition so that it reads as follows (this change is not included in Table 3.1): 'Lack of resources for acquiring the usual satisfiers', showing (as in the following quote) that the author has not in fact abandoned the sphere of N and their S:

> Any rigorous conceptualisation of the social determination of *need* dissolves the idea of 'absolute' need. *And a thorough-going relativity applies to time as well as place.* The *necessities of life are not fixed.* They are continuously being adapted and augmented as changes take place in society and in its products. (Townsend, 1979, pp 17–18, quoted in Sen 1983/1984, pp 327–328; emphasis added)

---

[5] The concept of WBS is similar, but broader, than the concept of resources, as explained in detail in Chapter 1.

Table 3.1: Dominant definitions of poverty: critique and comparison with the two definitions of economic poverty in my NP

Author	Definition (poverty is ...)	Reformulation of definition	Observations
1. Altimir	A value judgement regarding the identification of minimally adequate levels of WB, which basic N are indispensable to satisfy and what degree of deprivation is intolerable (Altimir, 1979, p 7).	Lack of current income ... to *satisfy some basic N*.	*Some N*, since he asks what basic N must be satisfied. In measurement, he specifies *what is necessary* as *income* and reduces N to food N. The definition does not specify thresholds.
2. Foster and Sen (first)	Inability to meet some elementary and essential N (Foster and Sen, 1997, p 210).	Lack of income adjusted by human diversity ... to *satisfy certain elementary, essential N*.	The real opportunities that specify *what is necessary* are incomes adjusted to take human diversity into account. They do not specify thresholds.
3. Boltvinik IPMM	A household is poor when, given its WBS, and despite their efficient allocation, it is unable to satisfy its basic N (Boltvinik, 1992a, p 364).	Lack of WBS ... to *satisfy HN*.	The IPMM is a combined method (both direct and indirect). Thresholds are defined in each dimension. The income threshold is based on a complete normative basket.
4. Boltvinik Broadening (first)	*Economic poverty of structural being is* the insufficiency of WBS and/or lack of adequate conditions for the development of N and capacities (Boltvinik, 2005, vol. I, p 428).	Lack of WBS *and/ or conditions/ opportunities* ... for *the development of N and capacities*.	*Conditions or opportunities:* for education; for a job that mobilises and develops activities; a cultural environment that favours the development of N and capacities.
5.Boltvinik Broadening (second)	*Economic poverty of circumstantial being* is the insufficiency of WBS and/or lack of adequate conditions for the satisfaction of *effective N* and application of *effective capacities* (Boltvinik, 2005, vol. I, p 428).	Lack of WBS *and/ or conditions/ opportunities* ... for ... *the satisfaction of effective N and application of effective capacities*.	*Effective* = actually developed. This and the previous definition must be applied together to prevent those who need least to seem less poor in circumstantial being.

Table 3.1: Dominant definitions of poverty: critique and comparison with the two definitions of economic poverty in my NP (continued)

Author	Definition (poverty is ...)	Reformulation of definition	Observations
6. Peter Townsend	Individuals, families, and groups in the population can be said to be in poverty when they *lack the resources* to obtain the types of diet, participate in the activities, and have the living conditions and amenities which are customary, or at least widely encouraged or approved in their society. Their resources *are so seriously below those commanded by the average individual or family* that they are, in effect, *excluded from the ordinary living patterns, customs, and activities* (Townsend, 1979, p 31).	Lack of resources ... to *be able to participate in ordinary patterns of life, customs, and activities*.	By conceiving N as variable between societies, he replaces them with lifestyles. The relativist emphasis on divergence from average income turns the latter into the standard of reference, thus turning what *is* into *what should be* for everyone. Despite a broad conception of resources, he ends up equating them with income. Hints at (relativist) thresholds.
7. Foster and Sen (second)	'Deprivation of minimal capabilit*ies* and elementary *social* skills' (Foster and Sen, 1997, p 112).	Lack of *income adjusted by human diversity* ... to achieve *minimal capabilities and elementary social skills*.	This is their favourite definition. *Capabilities is* (almost) the same as N. As in the first definition, opportunities refer to income adjusted by human diversity. They do not specify thresholds.
8. Citro and Michael	Poverty as economic deprivation: lack of economic resources (monetary/near monetary income) for consumption of G&S. Resources deemed necessary to obtain a minimally adequate standard of living defined appropriately for the USA today (Citro and Michael, 1995, p 19).	Lack of *monetary income or quasi-monetary income* ... to *achieve the consumption of economic G&S to achieve minimally appropriate living standards*.	'[T]he focus of our work is on economic deprivation, narrowly defined. We are concerned with the concept, definition, and measurement of economic poverty or what many call material poverty.' They specify thresholds.

(continued)

Table 3.1: Dominant definitions of poverty: critique and comparison with the two definitions of economic poverty in my NP (continued)

Author	Definition (poverty is ...)	Reformulation of definition	Observations
9. Ravallion	I will define a PL as the monetary costs for a given person, in a specific time and place, for a referential level of welfare [or utility]. People that do not achieve this level of welfare are poor. The PL is the point of the function of consumer expenditure that minimises the cost of achieving the referential level of utility with given prices and characteristics of specific households (Ravallion, 1998).	Lack of *consumer expenditures* ... to *achieve a referential level of utility* (U_z).	Ravallion admits that the theory does not help the definition of U_z and that the required expenditure function cannot be identified on the basis of observed consumer demand. *He concludes that external normative judgements (and information) are needed to define the PL.*
10. Hagenaars	Poverty is a situation where HH welfare, derived from its availability of resources, falls below a certain level of *minimal welfare,* called the *poverty threshold* (Hagenaars, 1986).	Lack of what is needed *(resources in a broad sense)* ... to *achieve a minimal level of welfare (utility)*.	N are replaced by utility, which 'can be measured in surveys'. Resources are equated with economic status. She does not specify thresholds.

Although he did not abandon the realm of N, when using the term he moved radically away from the notion of universal HN. Townsend has been ambiguous about the breadth or narrowness of his approach. On the one hand, he has maintained a much broader vision of the universe of S and N than the predominant one (although he does not use these terms but rather 'life patterns'). He has also maintained a far more extensive conception of resources than that of current income alone. In *Poverty in the United Kingdom* (1979) he used a set of 60 deprivation indicators referring to extremely varied aspects of life, ranging from food, clothes, fuel, and electricity to working conditions, health, education, children's playing areas, housing conditions, and domestic equipment. However, despite this breadth, he has demonstrated a stark degree of reductionism on at least two key occasions. He took the *first reductionist step* when he concluded from his statement that the basic S of life are not fixed, and that to update the thresholds (which he calls *sufficiency standards*) it does not suffice to record 'changes in prices, for that would ignore changes *in the goods and services consumed* as well as new obligations and expectations placed on members of the community. Lacking an alternate criterion, *the best assumption would be to relate sufficiency to the average rise (or fall) in real incomes'* (Townsend, 1979, pp 17–18, quoted in Sen, 1983/1984, pp 328; emphasis added). In his research project with Abel-Smith,[6] this led Townsend to use 50% and 60% of average HH income as PLs, which has become (with minor variations) the official PMMs used by the Organisation for Economic Cooperation and Development (OECD) and the European Union. This is a case of extreme relativism that ends up confusing poverty with inequality. Moreover, *resources have been reduced to current income,* thereby also reducing S to those that can be purchased with money, in contrast with the broad range of deprivation indicators mentioned earlier, in which there are certain areas (education, health, social interaction, cooked food) that do not depend on income or at least not only or mainly on it.

The second reductionist step taken by Townsend involved reducing the broad range of resources (drawn up in the same book) to income. In his search for an objective poverty line,[7] he associated household income (HHY) with the deprivation scores obtained by the same HH (in an illustrative calculation built using 12 out of the 60 direct indicators of deprivation mentioned earlier) with regard to the dominant lifestyle:

> In descending the income scale, it is hypothesized that, at a particular point for different types of families, a significantly large number of families reduce more than proportionately their participation in the community's style of living. *They drop out or are excluded. These income points can be identified as a poverty line.* (Townsend, 1979, p 249; emphasis added)

Through these reductionist steps that contradict his broad view of resources, Townsend shares the *reductionist view of means* of (nearly) all the other authors listed in Table 3.1.

In their second definition, Foster and Sen (1997) replace 'elementary and essential needs' with 'minimal capabilities and elementary social skills'. Note the symmetry of the adjectives. As in their first definition, what is necessary turns out to be income adjusted by human diversity referred to conditions, requirements and the ability to transform G&S into *capabilities*. And so, we arrive at a standardised definition: *lack of income adjusted by human diversity to achieve minimal capabilities and elementary social skills,* which leaves the first part of the sentence unchanged. As examples of minimal capabilities, the authors refer to avoiding hunger and avoiding living on the streets, which

---

[6] Abel-Smith and Townsend, 1965.
[7] See Chapter 2 for a succinct explanation of the measurement method proposed by Townsend, which I have called the 'objective poverty line'; for a more detailed explanation and critical analysis, see section 17.1 of *Broadening Our Look*.

are nothing more than an obvious rephrasing of the N for food and housing. As for examples of elementary social skills, the authors mention 'appearing in public without feeling ashamed' and 'participating in community life', which can also be seen as the mere rephrasing of HN such as self-esteem and belonging. Or, if we accept them as *capabilities*, then the critiques presented in Section 2.3 would be applicable, since both would be mere economic capabilities depending on the person's resources. All of Foster and Sen's examples fall within the concept of HN or, at best, develop the concept of *economic capabilities*. Thus, they fail to get rid of the concept of N, but in the attempt to do so they obscure it and remove the force that makes it irreplaceable. Their two definitions amount to only one.

Townsend and Sen, the leading authors on poverty, unsuccessfully attempt to develop original approaches and keep away from the concept of N, which is why I have classified them as *failed attempts to develop a new approach to poverty*. Both of them remain trapped in the dominant PEP and have contributed to shaping its current aspect.

Let us now move on to the analysis of the last subgroup: the *dominant economicist approach*. The definition adopted in the collective study edited by Citro and Michael[8] identifies what is necessary as merely a monetary or quasi-monetary income (food vouchers and similar items), revealing a high degree of reductionism in their conception of resources. In defining the purpose as 'to achieve the consumption of economic G&S', they exclude all S that are not economic G&S, thus making their reductionism explicit. Unlike other definitions, they add a second *to*: '*to* achieve the level of consumption required *to achieve* a minimally adequate living standard', which replaces N satisfaction. Their only answer to what the constitutive element of the SLA would be is 'the consumption of goods and services', something that can only be measured through the expenditures incurred. Therefore, *their definition of poverty is tautological,* since if we assume that savings – which are not included in the purpose – are equal to zero, then income and consumer expenditures are equal, and the resulting definition would be as follows: 'lack of consumer expenditures to achieve a minimally adequate level of consumption'.

As noted in the observations column of Table 3.1, although the authors are aware of the narrowness of their focus, they regard it as a virtue and use the terms *economic poverty* and *material poverty* explicitly: 'we focus on *economic deprivation, narrowly defined*. We are concerned with the concept, definition,

---

[8] Constance F. Citro and Robert T. Michael, 1995 (eds.). This collective book resulted from the efforts of a group of experts who worked for two and a half years, commissioned by the United States Congressional Joint Economic Committee, to thoroughly review the official US government poverty measurement method.

and measurement of economic poverty or what many call material poverty.' Proud reductionists!

Hagenaars (1986) replaces N (a concept that she paradoxically does not reject) with a minimum level of welfare (utility) which, following Van Praag, she holds can be measured through surveys. The result of the latter, which the author calls *utility*, is actually more like the respondent's view of their own situation. Hagenaars ignores Sen's and Rawls's critiques of utilitarianism ('cheap tastes' and 'expensive tastes', see Section 2.1). She also manages to replace N with something one would call *achievement of expectations*, whose place in the study of poverty is, however, extremely difficult to defend.

A more common view among the utilitarians is that of Ravallion (1998), who for a long time was considered the intellectual leader in this subject in the World Bank. If interpreted literally, these economists would postulate that the correct phrase in the DRAE should be 'lack of what is necessary (consumer spending or income) to achieve a referential level of utility'. However, they pretend to replace income with utility through the introduction of adjustments to income according to the characteristics of the HH (size, age, structure, etc.). Instead of descriptively referring to this change as such – that is, income adjusted per EA – they pretend to have achieved a shift from the space of income to that of utility.[9] Thus, critically interpreted, the phrase should read: 'lack of what is necessary (consumer expenditure or income) to achieve a referential level of consumer spending or income per equivalent adult', or more bluntly, '*lack of necessary income to achieve a referential income level*'. As shown in Table 3.1 (observations column), Ravallion admits that the NCT does not contribute to the definition of the referential level of utility, *meaning that external normative judgements are required to set the PL*. Considering the way in which the World Bank and, more generally, this type of economist operate, the determination of this referential level of income is *totally arbitrary*, which shows the kind of science they practice.

From my analyses, it is clear that Sen and Townsend's attempts to abandon the concept of N as a constitutive element of purpose in their poverty definitions of poverty are flawed. It is also clear that utilitarians turn out to be no such thing, since they have declared their concept to be

---

[9] This is borne out by a statement by Deaton and Muellbauer (1980/1991, p 192) which says: 'Equivalence scales are based on the assumption that the only difference in tastes between households are because of variations in observable characteristics'. In other words, utility functions per EA are identical for all persons/HH. But as I showed in Section 2.3, in order to maintain the imperative nature of calculating equivalent units, the authors must resort to the concept of N. This shows that although the latter has the front door slammed in its face, it re-enters through the back door of the NCT.

non-measurable and non-interpersonally comparable, replacing N either by 'meeting expectations' or by the tautological 'sufficient income to achieve a referential income level' definitions, in which income is both the means and the end. We must therefore *conclude that the indispensable character of the concept of N ends up enforcing itself.*

I will now contrast the two definitions of the concept of economic poverty (structural being (SBEP) and circumstantial being (CBEP)) developed in *Broadening Our Look* (definitions 4 and 5, Table 3.1), with the others. Although the concept of CBEP seems close to what I have called the *conventional N approach to poverty,* represented by Altimir's, Foster and Sen's first, and Boltvinik's IPMM definitions, there are two main differences: CBEP includes the application of effectively developed human capacities, and it refers to the satisfaction of effectively developed N.[10] Few people develop their needs extensively as to cover, for example, the whole range of N proposed by Maslow. For many persons, self-actualisation and higher cognitive N remain latent. For this and other reasons, the two dimensions of economic poverty (SBEP and CBEP) *must always be evaluated simultaneously and in conjunction with the two symmetrical categories of human poverty.*

I have identified the following differences between the new approach to economic poverty and the conventional N approach: the new approach does not imply a reduction of N; its *dynamic view (development)* of N opposes the static concept of the satisfaction of fixed N; by incorporating the *development and application of capacities* (C), this approach recovers the active side of human beings and reinforces the dynamic view of human flourishing through the dialectic unit of N and C; replacing a narrow view of resources with the broad concepts of WBS *and opportunities* (for work, study, etc.) widens the view of economic aspects related to human flourishing, thus overcoming the view of work as a mere means for obtaining income and incorporating its central role in the application (and subsequent development) of C; by shifting from a one-dimensional to a two-dimensional evaluation (CBEP and SBEP), the new approach enables one to record dynamic aspects that are obscured in the static approach; and the link between economic and human poverty radically transforms the referents of the concept while rendering more dynamic evaluations.

---

[10] Evaluating the situation of individuals who have not even developed the four basic N, which according to Maslow are driven by a deficiency motivation based on their effective N only, would appear to go against ethical principles and could lead to perverse results: the poor could end up in a better position than others who are less poor. However, as is stated immediately afterwards in *Ampliar la mirada*, CBEP should not be evaluated independently of SBEP, in which everyone is evaluated on the basis of the complete spectrum of HN.

3.2 The narrow conceptual map of the PEP compared with the broader one of my New Approach to Poverty and Human Flourishing (NAPHF) or New Paradigm (NP)

Needs and satisfiers

We must start by establishing suitable conceptions of each of the fundamental elements involved in the study of poverty: N, S, and resources or WBS. It is essential to distinguish *needing* and N, on the one hand, and *wanting* and *wants* on the other. To this end, it is useful to take up David Wiggins's statement that: 'I need [absolutely] to have *x* if and only if I need [instrumentally] to have *x* if I am to avoid being harmed' (1987/2002, p 10). The ensuing harm is what distinguishes what is needed from what is desired or wanted. Note that this is a very precise formal definition of what is needed (of the S) rather than of the N. This is defined by Wiggins himself 'as *states of dependency (in respect of not being harmed)*, which have as their proper objects things needed (or, more strictly, *having* or *using* things)' ([1987] 2002, p 16, original emphasis).[11] Earlier in the book, Wiggins says: 'Unlike "desire" or "want" then, "need" is not evidently an intentional verb. What I need depends not on thought or the workings of my mind (or not only on these) but on the way the world is' (Wiggins, [1987] 2002, p 6).[12]

In this reflection, we should begin with a precise concept of human beings as they actually are: natural, active, social, conscious beings distinguished from all other species in the animal kingdom. Human beings, like all living creatures, *require external objects* to reproduce their own lives, which, according to Marx, turns them into 'dependent, suffering beings'. *The human being, then, needs external objects (goods)*. But the human being is also an active creature who (as a species) can only satisfy their N through their vital activity, that is, work, which is directed (only) in a mediated way to N satisfaction. Since the human being is not such without work, work becomes their central N. The *human being needs their own activity*. The *human being also needs activities carried out by other persons that benefit them (services)*. But the human being is also a social creature. For Marx, 'man' cannot lead a human life or be a 'man' except in his relations with others and as a result of these relationships. The *human being therefore needs to relate with other human beings. They need relationships*. Lastly, the human being is also a conscious being, meaning,

---

[11] Although there does not appear to be any reductionism in the first part, since X can be an object, a relationship or engaging in activities, the second part does seem reductionist, since speaking of *having or using things* leaves out the N for relations with other people or the N to engage in certain activities.

[12] David Wiggins ([1987] 2002, pp 1–57). I analyse this essay in detail in chapter 1 of *Broadening Our look*.

among other things, that their own life is an object for them. According to Marx, *conscious vital activity* is what distinguishes man from animals' vital activity.[13] The *human being, therefore, needs to know and understand*; in other words, they *need information, knowledge, ideas, conceptual frameworks, theories and explanations*.

Based on this reflection, one can draw up a typology of S of human N: external objects (goods); other persons' activities that provide benefits for the subject (services); the subject's own activities; relationships (associated with which the subject carries out shared activities with the persons they establish relationships with); and information, knowledge, and theories. On the basis of the broad range of S identified by Max-Neef et al. (1986, p 42) in his 'matrix of needs and satisfiers', and following a critical examination of it, we can conclude that the previous typology should also include *capacities and institutions*. After adding both types of S and consolidating G&S into the category of objects, the typology of S is as follows: 1) objects (G&S); 2) primary and secondary relations; 3) subject's activities; 4) subject's capacities; 5) institutions; and 6) knowledge and theories.

In *Ampliar la mirada* I carry out a comparative analysis of the following authors' theories of HN: Marx (both directly and through the perspectives of György Márkus, Agnes Heller, and J.P. Terrail), Maslow, Fromm, Maccoby, Max-Neef et al., Doyal and Gough, and Nussbaum. One conclusion of this analysis is that one could posit, using rational arguments, that if one could interact with these authors in a process leading to the elimination of their purely taxonomic differences, although it would be impossible to reach a consensus on Maslow's theory of the hierarchy of N (1943, 1954/1987), there would be a consensus on his list of N, except for the aesthetic N. Therefore, in the rest of this section I will use Maslow's scheme – excepting aesthetic N – as a pattern for comparisons. His complete scheme of N comprises (see chapter 3 of *Ampliar la mirada*): *social freedoms* as a prerequisite for satisfying all N; a *hierarchy of N* consisting of five levels of 'relative prepotency' (Maslow, 1954/1987, p 17) – physiological, safety N, emotional (love, affection, belonging), esteem N (which can be divided in two: the achievements that form the basis of self-esteem, and reputation) and the N for self-actualisation; *cognitive N*, with their own hierarchy (knowing and understanding); and *aesthetic N*.

I defined the contents of the first two columns in Table 3.2 by grouping the N listed by Maslow in a slightly different manner and adopting the typology of six types of S obtained earlier. The cells in the first column show *four groups of N* in the following order:

---

[13] See chapter 2 of *Broadening Our Look*, which develops these ideas following György Márkus' superb interpretation of Marx's anthropological vision (1973/1978/1985/1988).

1. Survival *(or material)* N, which we can be roughly associated with the first two levels in Maslow's scheme – *physiological and safety (security)* N. The examples presented in this cell include food, shelter, and security.
2. *Cognitive N (knowing and understanding)*.
3. *Emotional N*, which include Maslow's N for *love, affection, and belonging*, the third level of his hierarchy, and the part of *reputation* within the N for esteem (which belongs to the fourth level of his hierarchy).
4. *Growth N*, among which I included the other part of the N for esteem, which Maslow calls the *bases of self-esteem* (comprising a person's achievements), and the N for *self-actualisation*.

On the basis of the typology of S presented earlier, the cells in the second column include the S identified for each group of N, classified into principal and secondary, according to the role they play in the satisfaction of a N. In order to avoid producing an over-complex chart, I have not tried to be exhaustive.

WBS or resources

In the third column of Table 3.2, we can use both the usual concept of resources and that of WBS. On the basis of this last notion, which I have been using for over two decades, I posited that the WB of individuals and HH depends on the following *direct sources*[14]: 1) current income; 2) basic patrimony (or basic assets), understood as the set of durable goods and assets that provide basic services for HH; 3) NBA and HH's borrowing capacity; 4) access to free goods and services (FG&S); 5) FT and time available for rest, HH chores and education; 6) individual skills and knowledge that are crucial to the performance of any activity, part of which bears on the performance of activities and part of which should be regarded as *direct S of human being's cognitive N*. Neither available time nor skills and knowledge are conceived of as means for earning income, but rather as direct S of N.[15]

---

[14] I originally formulated this in Boltvinik (1990a and 1990b).
[15] Although conceiving of capacities (and knowledge) both as a WBS and as a S seems to be an inconsistency in the taxonomy adopted, I believe this is not the case. The link between WBS and S does not always involve the mediation of the former to provide access to the latter, since current income is the means to acquire G&S as direct S of N. Indeed, specific basic assets, such as housing, furniture and domestic appliances, are goods that do not have to undergo the mediation of an exchange to be transformed into S; what they do have to go through is use: an uninhabited house, a refrigerator that is either empty or has been turned off or a sound system that is not played are WBS but not S (although they could be if they were inhabited, stocked with food or played). However, being S does not prevent them from being a WBS. Access to government services (which could have been

Table 3.2: The economic process of needs satisfaction: a totalising view

Types of needs (examples of each type)	Types of satisfiers principal/*secondary*	Resources (WBS) principal/*secondary*
Survival or material (food, shelter, safety/security)	1. Objects (food, housing, security services) 5. Institutions (family/insurance) *3. Family activities (buying, cooking, cleaning)*	Conventional economic resources: CY, BA, NBA, FGS* *Time; knowledge and skills*
Cognitive needs (knowing, understanding, education)	3. Subject's activities (reading, studying, researching) 6. Knowledge, theories *1. Objects (education, books)*	Time; knowledge and skills *Conventional economic resources: CY, NBA, FGS**
Emotional and esteem needs (affect, friendship, love, belonging, reputation)	2. Primary and secondary relations *3. Activities with partner/friend* *4. Capacities* *1. Objects*	Time; knowledge and skills *Conventional economic resources: CY, NBA**
Growth needs *(bases of self-esteem:* achievements as role fulfilment) *(self-actualisation:* realisation of potential)	3. Subject's activities 4. Capacities 3. Work *2. Secondary relations* *1. Objects*	Time; knowledge and skills *Conventional economic resources: CY, NBA**

* CY: current income; BA: basic assets; NBA: non-basic assets; FGS: access to free goods and services.

The first three WBS represent private economic resources (flows or stocks), whereas the fourth represents the flow of public economic resources (the so-called *social salary*).[16] Together, these four categories represent *conventional economic resources* (all of which can be expressed in monetary terms, although some of them cannot be turned into money). The fifth and sixth categories have their own measuring units and cannot be expressed in, far less reduced to, monetary values. These sources can evolve in diverse, even opposing ways,

---

    formulated as *right of access or entitlement to government services*) is similar to current income and available time: only if they are 'exchanged' for specific S, such as public education or time devoted to a specific activity, do they become S. Capacities effectively used for satisfaction are S, whereas effective available capacities are WBS. This is basically the same distinction as the one between stocks and flows. *WBS are potential S (some of them generic, such as income, some of them specific) and may be transformed into effective S.*

[16] Transfers received from philanthropic institutions must be conceived of as transfers within the private sector of the economy, in the same category as transfers from other HH.

since they are subject to different determining factors.[17] Living standards, poverty, and inequality depend on all six WBS. Thus, their study should take all of them into account.

The following hypothetical example illustrates the consequences of failing to do this. As a result of women's ever-increasing incorporation into paid work, monetary income increases in many HH. This is reflected in national accounts as an increase in GDP and as a reduction in the proportion of the poor when poverty is measured one-dimensionally through HH income. However, the apparent increase in WB could be partially or totally spurious. Despite the increase in market values, in terms of WB, need satisfaction, and capacity development, this improvement may be small or even non-existent. In terms of the six WBS, although income has increased, women's time available for housework has declined. It will be necessary to hire domestic help, pay for day care services or double the working days of one or more adults in the HH. More expenditure on transport and meals outside the home, among other things, will be required. The HH will have a higher monetary income but will also require more expenses *to achieve the same living standard*. The final balance may be positive, neutral, or negative regarding HH WB.

Although HH living standards depend on all six WBS, some of them (such as current income and NBA) act through the market, while sources 4), 5) and 6) (access to FG&S; FT and time available for rest, housework and the development of capacities; knowledge and skills) *act totally outside the market. Their importance is evidence of the limits of the market.* Measuring poverty (inequality or living standards) without acknowledging the multiple WBS and the limits of the market, as income-based methods do, *violates the principle of totality* (see Chapter 4), denies reality and leads to inaccurate results.

Some orthodox economists have developed an approach resembling that of WBS which acknowledges the insufficiency of current income as an indicator of the availability of resources and attempts to overcome this through *compound indicators of HH's economic status*. Although these approaches differ in several respects from the WBS approach, the main difference is the sharp contrast between these authors' reduction of everything to monetary terms and my position regarding both the irreducible nature of time and knowledge (which cannot even be expressed in monetary units or added together as though they were money), and the fact that, although for certain purposes the WBS's NBA, basic assets and access to free G&S can

---

[17] Beyond the logical possibility, this has happened in Mexico and other Latin American countries in recent decades. For an analysis of the radically different evolution of the WBS in Mexico and, therefore, of the incidence of human deprivation in different components, see Boltvinik (2003b). A summary of this study is included in chapter 19 of *Broadening Our Look*.

be expressed in monetary terms, for the HH and the individual they have degrees of convertibility ranging from total (indeed, certain NBA assume monetary forms) to impossible (I cannot exchange my right of access to free education for cash).[18]

Let us go back to Table 3.2. Column 3 shows the WBS (or resources) classified into dominant (or principal) and secondary. These are associated in each row with the N and S included in the first two columns. The table is now complete: the columns contain the N, S, and WBS, while each row contains one of the four groups of N identified in such a way that each cell in columns 2 and 3 identifies the S and resources associated with each group of N, particularly with the examples. Both S and resources are classified into principal and secondary.

The conceptual map of the NAPHF

Approaches to poverty may be characterised by the breadth or narrowness with which they conceive HN, the S that enable the latter to be met, and the resources (or WBS) that permit access to S; that is, by the breadth or narrowness of their conceptual map. Let us describe Table 3.2 in some detail to convey the idea of totality achieved through the three integral conceptions of N, S and WBS.

The first row shows that the principal S to meet survival or material N (exemplified by food, shelter, and security) are objects (G&S), exemplified by food, housing and security services, and institutions (such as family and insurance systems), while the secondary satisfiers are exemplified by family activities, such as buying, cooking, and cleaning. The principal WBS required to gain access to these S are the four I have grouped together under the name of *conventional economic resources*: current income (CY), basic assets (BA), non-basic assets (NBA) and access to free G&S. Meanwhile, I have classified (available) time and knowledge/skills as secondary WBS. Typically, (mostly raw) food is acquired with money derived from CY or NBA (for example, money drawn from savings), and cooked at home using available time and skills. Housing can be (as is usually the case in Mexico) a basic asset that one owns (sometimes paying a mortgage), or rents, in which case the rent (or the mortgage) is paid using monetary resources. Security services tend to be free public goods provided by the state, although some forms of insurance are private and acquired with monetary resources, or else are mixed and partly financed by the state.

---

[18] Aldi Hagenaars (1986) describes the 'economic status approach' which is applied by, among others, Garfinkel and Haveman (1977).

In the second row, the satisfaction of cognitive N (exemplified by Maslow's mini-hierarchy of knowing and understanding, to which I have added education – although it may be redundant) depends on two groups of principal S: the subject's activities (reading, studying, researching), and knowledge/theories. Objects (educational services, books), for their part, are regarded as secondary S. The principal WBS that provide access to these S are personal time (devoted to reading, studying and doing research), and knowledge and skills (which are previously acquired and essential for carrying out these tasks); monetary resources derived from CY and/or drawn from NBA (to purchase books, computers, and internet access, for example) and access to free G&S (such as educational services, libraries or internet access) play the role of secondary WBS. Classifying educational services as secondary S, and free G&S as secondary WBS is debatable, especially at young ages.

In the third row, the principal S to meet emotional N (affection, friendship, love, and belonging) and one aspect of the esteem N (reputation) are primary and secondary relationships (primary for affection, friendship, and love, secondary for reputation). I have identified the following as secondary S: activities with a partner or friend; emotional and socialisation C (to meet affection, friendship, and love N); 'professional' C (for reputation) and objects (for example, private space, contraceptives, restaurants, board games and sports articles to meet love, friendship, and belonging N). The principal WBS for relationships are personal time dedicated to their development, and knowledge/skills linked to these relationships and to the activities carried out as part of them. I have classified the conventional economic resources – especially income – that are required to obtain access to objects as S, as secondary WBS for these N.

Lastly, in the fourth row, to meet growth N (among which I have included achievements that form the basis of self-esteem, as well as the N that Maslow calls self-actualisation: becoming what one potentially is), the principal S are the subject's activities and C. In work-centred societies such as ours, work is key to self-esteem (since it enables one to obtain an income, perform the role of provider and play a role in society), although it often constitutes an obstacle to self-actualisation. Therefore, I have explicitly included it also as a principal S in Table 3.2. The activities associated with self-esteem and self-actualisation require certain objects that are secondary S: musicians require musical instruments and scores; writers and scientists require a computer and internet connection. The principal WBS are, once again, time, knowledge and skills, with monetary resources acting as secondary WBS. With this I conclude the description of the rows.

Note that, unlike survival or material N (excluding safety/security) – where the role of principal S is played by objects and that of the principal resource is performed by conventional economic resources – in the other groups of N the principal S are different – especially activities and relationships – and their principal WBS are time and knowledge/skills. When the principal S is an object (G&S), the principal WBS are what I call *conventional economic resources* (CY, BA, NBA, access to free G&S). Conversely, when principal S are the subject's relationships or activities, the principal WBS are time (devoted to cultivating a relationship or carrying out an activity) and knowledge/skills. All N, however, require the individual to invest personal time in them. In some cases, this time is of secondary importance, such as the time we spend eating or going to the doctor (although the time devoted to the provision and preparation of food is not so secondary). On the contrary, the time required by the subject to develop relationships and to carry out their own activities – which support self-esteem, self-actualisation, and cognitive development – is determinant. These associations are not coincidental: they involve a system of N-S-WBS that operate in a coherent, integrated fashion. If any of the elements is eliminated, the whole loses meaning.

Table 3.2 appears to be located on the HFA (see Section 2.5). This perception is derived from the inclusion of *non-material* N (cognitive, emotional and growth N) and, therefore, from the inclusion of S such as relationships. The first two columns are perfectly consistent with both the HFA and the SLA. But the inclusion after these two columns of a third (and last) one dedicated to WBS makes it quite clear that the table's main perspective is economic, which places the table in the SLA. To be located in the HFA, the table would need one or more additional columns dedicated, for example, to biological, psychological, or philosophical perspectives.

Table 3.2 draws the conceptual map of the SLA following my NAPHF or NP, originally developed in *Broadening Our Look*. It therefore confirms what I had proposed before: that the SLA of this approach comprises all HN, the entire human being, *but seen from an economic perspective only*. By incorporating Maslow's scheme of N, we begin, in column 1, with a complete human being and, therefore, all his N (except for the aesthetic ones, on which there is no consensus). This places us within both the HFA and the SLA. We remain on both axes in column 2, since the identification of S is a task shared by several perspectives. It was by adding column 3, and *no other column,* that I implicitly reduced and placed the table in the economic perspective (by eliminating the other possible perspectives) and, therefore, within the SLA.

This clearly suggests that the contents of the SLA that resulted from following this indirect derivative procedure are essentially different from what we would have constructed had we approached it directly: we would have implicitly eliminated N and S and reached a similar conclusion to that of the PEP's conventional needs approach. If this conclusion is deemed correct – and in my view it is – I would have shown that the path that deals with the problem of poverty directly on the SLA without taking the HFA into account (the only axis in which it is possible to identify all HN and C), the path taken by nearly all poverty researchers and which translates into a reduced universe of N (and therefore of S and WBS), is an inaccurate reductionist view.

This conclusion, which I call *the critical thesis*, becomes a powerful weapon to critique not only the conventional approaches to poverty, but also Sen's CA.

Both the conventional needs approach to poverty and the one involved in the FSNA (once the latter has been deconstructed), can be synthesised as *purely material needs satisfied solely with G&S (objects), for which only CY is required*. These approaches entail a partial conception that ignores immaterial N and are obviously mechanistic in that both regard human beings as robots or cattle. Except in the case of people who eat all their meals at restaurants or institutional canteens, which is extremely unusual, particularly in the Third World, eating does not only involve non-durable objects (food) but also cooking and related activities (such as buying food), as well as durable objects (stove, saucepans, table, chairs, plates, cutlery) and other non-durable goods (such as gas/electricity and detergent). Activities and objects other than foodstuffs are (nearly always) ignored in both currents of the PEP. The *dominant economicist approach*, which rejects the concept of N, is located in a conceptual vacuum that cannot be filled by the empty concept of utility. A summary of Sen's and Rawls's critiques of this concept is presented in Section 2.1.

Poverty measurement can adopt the *indirect* form of measuring HH resources or the *direct* form of observing unmet N. In both cases, it is possible to establish an explicit link with specific HN. In the second case, doing so is unavoidable. In the first one, it is possible to establish this link when the PL is being defined. If this definition is addressed by identifying complete normative baskets of S, as in the family budget method, establishing the link is also unavoidable, for it is necessary to explicitly define which N will be considered before proceeding to define and calculate the quantities of required S. In both these cases (direct procedure and indirect procedure using the family budget approach), we can identify the list of N included by an author as part of the exercise of measuring poverty, and we can show whether or not N have been eliminated by using any theory of HN. If, for example, based on the scheme of N of Max-Neef et al. (1986), we find that the list in question corresponds to these authors' N for subsistence, protection, and understanding, we can conclude that the other six N identified by them (affection, participation, leisure, creation, identity and freedom) have been eliminated.

However, when the PL is defined arbitrarily, as is done by the World Bank, this link is not established. When researchers use a single N – food – to establish a normative food basket (NFB) and multiply its cost by a factor to obtain a PL, as happens in the method I have called the standard food basket (SFB) used by ECLAC (see Altimir, 1979) and the US Government (Orshansky, 1965), the link is limited, for it is established on the basis of a single N. Since the method of indirect poverty measurement with no definition of complete normative baskets has predominated virtually worldwide, eliminating N has not become an issue, since virtually everyone who measures poverty does so implicitly by approaching the SLA directly without taking the HFA into account.

The argument is now complete. The CPEP leads us to conclude that conventional approaches include a partial and distorted conception of human beings. Adopting the NAPHF or NP enables us to overcome this distorted, partial vision, leading us to the complete person, with all their N.

The conceptual map of the PEP

In Table 3.2, I have highlighted the elements usually identified by the authors whose approaches I classified as *conventional N approaches* in the previous section: only part of the elements in the first and second rows. They only acknowledge material needs such as food, housing, and others whose satisfaction depends primarily on access to monetisable resources and whose S are objects. Some of them have an ambiguous position towards cognitive N, which they sometimes acknowledge as the N for education. Generally speaking, they perceive education more as a means for increasing human capital (and, therefore, expected income in the labour market) than as a form of satisfying human cognitive N. In other words, they excise the human being's heart, genitals and part of the brain, or else – which amounts to the same – they exclude the dimensions of the human being as a social, intellectual, spiritual, and artistic being, thereby violating the principle of totality as regards N (see Chapter 4). In order to distinguish the full identification of survival or material N and the biased, ambiguous acknowledgement of cognitive N by this group of conventional approaches, I have highlighted the latter N in dark grey and the former in light grey.

These approaches only acknowledge objects (G&S) as S and monetisable resources as the sole WBS (worse still, within the latter, they usually only acknowledge CY). Thus, even within rows 1 and 2, there is a general failure to acknowledge the fact that activities (such as cooking, buying, reading and studying) are also required, alongside G&S, to satisfy N such as food and cognitive N, and that therefore time and knowledge/skills WBS are essential. In failing to identify rows 3 and 4 – apart from row 1 – they end up omitting (almost) everything.[19]

The PEP is reductionist in three ways. First, conventional approaches to N only consider material N (although they sometimes include education) and usually fail to acknowledge the N for security and its principal S (institutions such as the family, the community, insurance, and the state). The dominant economicist approach ignores N and replaces them with utility. In both cases, Table 3.2 (except for those who acknowledge the N for education) becomes a vector. Second, all dominant approaches in the PEP (including the FSNA) reduce S (or 'utility suppliers') to objects, ignoring other types of S (relationships, activities, theories, capacities, institutions), thus violating the principle of totality as applied to S. Third, all dominant approaches in the PEP reduce resources to those that are monetisable and often to CY only. Time and knowledge and skills are WBS that are totally ignored by these conventional approaches, thereby violating the principle of totality as regards WBS.

Adherents of the dominant PEP approaches also fail to perceive that certain 'immaterial' N also require G&S as S and monetisable economic resources as WBS – as noted in the table (underlined or italicised words). This implies that they underestimate the PL, since they fail to identify part of the monetary requirements. Some examples of the objects that are omitted include the G&S associated with relationships (emotional N). Activities with one's partner involve the N for G&S (restaurants, shows, hotels, contraceptives, etc.). Subject activities require G&S (such as painting materials and canvas for painters; books, computers, and the Internet for writers, scientific researchers, and increasingly for people from nearly all walks of life).

This shows that the triple reductionism of conventional approaches (which acknowledge N or replace them with concepts that can be reformulated as N) is structurally interrelated, since the said approaches omit emotional

---

[19] One example is the set of recommendations presented by the panel on poverty and family welfare in the US National Research Council, the conclusions of which were published in Citro and Michael (1995). The authors say: 'We define poverty as economic deprivation. A way of expressing this concept is that it pertains to people's lack of economic resources *(e.g. money or near-money income) for consumption of economic goods and services (e.g. food, housing, clothing, transportation)*' (p 19). They only acknowledge certain N and S that correspond to the stereotype of material needs, thus adopting the narrow approach of the first row. Education, including complete cognitive needs, is excluded. The only explicitly acknowledged S are G&S, and only income is acknowledged as WBS (not even the set of what in Table 3.2 are called conventional economic resources). One could add several other examples, both academic and from international organisations, that confirm that this is the dominant approach among the economists that virtually monopolise the issue (see Chapter 6).

and growth (and often cognitive) N; all kinds of S except objects (relations, activities, etc.) associated with the N that have been omitted; and time and knowledge/skills, WBS associated with the omitted S.

Both the conventional approach to N and (once deconstructed) the FSNA – which can be expressed as *purely material 'needs' that are satisfied only with objects, for which only current income is required*, and which involve a partial conception even of so-called material N and ignore immaterial ones – are clearly mechanistic approaches in which human beings are seen as robots or cattle.

The main limitation of partial PMM (those that only take one or a few WBS into account), including the PL and UBN methods, is that they proceed as though N satisfaction depended solely on one or a few WBS; this produces partial, biased measurements. I departed from this insight to develop the original variant (OV) of the IPMM, which the UNDP applied in Latin America (UNDP, 1992).

4

Principles and good practices of poverty conceptualisation

4.1 Introduction

Poverty measurement must be multidimensional because HN are multiple. For example, Maslow's scheme (1943, 1954/1987) includes seven N, while that of Max-Neef et al. (1986) includes nine. Each N is met through various S (the typology of S presented in this book includes seven types; see Section 1.3) to which people have access through a range of resources or WBS (see my typology of six WBS in Section 1.2). This enormous diversity and complexity would not imply heterogeneity for the purposes of analysis if markets were unlimited, that is, if everything were bought and sold and had a price. But this is not the case. Markets have limits, and exchange values are not universal: many S cannot be acquired in the market. Money can neither measure nor buy everything. Some S and WBS cannot be expressed monetarily.

Therefore, the indicators we use to measure multidimensional poverty are either nominative indicators that can always be transformed into ordinal ones, or else cardinal indicators. This heterogeneity requires a solution to combine all the dimensions involved. Some solutions present in the literature are highly problematic and involve inconsistencies, and most of them lose much of the available information by adopting dichotomic indicators.

This chapter and Chapter 5 establish principles (Pr) and good practices (GP) that pave the way for better solutions to the problem of heterogeneity, as well as to many other problems I have found in PMM used worldwide. While this chapter broaches what I have called principles (Pr) and good practices (GP) of *poverty conceptualisation* (PPC and GPPC, respectively), Chapter 5 discusses *Pr and GP of poverty measurement* (PPM and GPPM). The boundary between conceptualisation and measurement is fuzzy, but the division seems quite useful. Although I had not stated them in written form, some of these Pr and GP have guided me in the multidimensional measurement of poverty I have been practising (and preaching) since 1990. Others, I have developed recently, partly as a response to a number of queries raised among some authors regarding my multidimensional measurement method, the IPMM.

4.2 Principles and good practices: a complete panorama

The problem with the apparent heterogeneity between dimensions of WB derives, as already stated, from the multiplicity of HN, and it is associated with the limits of markets, with the fact that exchange values are not universal, that not everything valuable for human WB can be bought, that not every valuable thing has a price. To address this and other conceptual/measurement problems, the following Pr and GP can offer a fundamental guide.

Table 4.1 holds the complete list of Pr and GP, classified in four categories: PPC, GPPC, PPM, and GPPM. The present chapter only broaches PPC and GPPC, while PPM and GPPM are analysed in Chapter 5. After discussing each PPC, the corresponding GPPC is analysed in the hope that this will render the narrative more clear.

PPC1: the principle of totality

The *principle of totality* is perhaps the most important and is expressed in the three fundamental conceptual elements of the study of living standards and poverty: needs (N), satisfiers (S) and WBS. *The Pr of totality applied to N* establishes that our study must be based on human beings considered as complete, complex beings with all their N, that we cannot excise humans' brain, heart, and social nature so that we are left with a creature – more akin to cattle than to human beings – that has been reduced to its stomach and genitals. To understand and measure poverty, we cannot reduce human beings to their biological dimension, thereby cutting off their emotional, social, intellectual, spiritual, and artistic dimensions. *The Pr of totality applied to S* (quality, diversity and quantity of the S required for each N) means that we cannot minimise N, degrading them to their animal nature or to precariousness and sub-minimal amounts. We cannot reduce food to cattle feed, nutritional requirements to calories, housing to shelter, health care to primary health care, etc. It also means that we cannot reduce S to G&S, excluding relationships, activities, and so on. These two forms of reductionism tend to go hand in hand, restricting human beings to a few N and operationalising the satisfaction of each N as the access to very few, precarious, and therefore extremely cheap S, which have in turn been reduced to G&S. This double reduction enables aberrations such as the International Poverty Line (IPL) of the World Bank. A detailed criticism of poverty measurement can be seen in Chapter 6. Lastly, the *Pr of totality applied to WBS* means that one should consider the access of HH to all WBS to identify the restrictions behind their unsatisfied N. I have classified the usual methods of measurement – PL and UBN – as partial methods whose results are therefore biased since

Table 4.1: Principles and good practices of poverty conceptualisation and measurement

Principles of poverty (PP)	Good practices of poverty (GPP)
Conceptualisation (PPC)	**Conceptualisation (GPPC)**
PPC1. Totality	GPPC1. Holistic
PPC2. Sensitivity	GPPC2. Sensitive to changes
PPC3. Comparability of objective well-being (OWB)	GPPC3. Based on an objective definition of poverty
PPC4. Entangled nature of the concept of poverty	GPPC4. Based on informed value judgements
PPC5. Dignity: central criterion for defining thresholds	GPPC5. Promotes human rights and optimal public policies
PPC6. Poverty as part of the SLA	GPPC6. Includes all dimensions of the SLA
Measurement (PPM)	**Measurement (GPPM)**
PPM1. Decreasing marginal OWB above thresholds	GPPM1. Applies PPM1 and PPM2 to measure P and to stratify the whole population
PPM2. Existence of an OWB maximum	
PPM3. Minimum error	GPPM2. Minimises errors
PPM4. Full and replicable cardinalisation	GPPM3. Uses information fully (cardinalisation) and is unbiased
PPM5. Symmetry	GPPM4. Full consistency of concepts and measurement procedures
PPM6. Full normativity	GPPM5. Full normativity

they only consider part of the WBS (see Chapter 1). In short, the Pr of totality establishes that in the study of P and of the standard of living one should consider all HN, all kinds of non-precarious S in sufficient amounts for a dignified life, and all WBS.

To understand this Pr, we must begin with suitable conceptions of N, S, and WBS. It is essential to distinguish needing and N, on the one hand, and wanting and wants, on the other, as I have done in Section 1.3. It is also necessary to rely on an anthropologically sound conception of the human essence, already synthesised in Section 2.4.

Approaches to poverty may be characterised by the breadth or narrowness with which they conceive N, S, and WBS. In Section 3.2, the idea of totality in the process of economic satisfaction of N was conveyed through a detailed description of the integrated conception of N, S, and WBS, and their interrelations displayed in Table 3.2. In the said table, this holistic approach was contrasted with the prevailing reductionist approach by highlighting the few elements in the table considered in the conventional N approach to poverty.

GPPC1: the good practice of adopting a holistic approach

Considering all WBS, all S and all N enables a holistic vision of WB and the application of a PMM which operationalises that vision. As we have seen, such a method must be multidimensional, a necessary but not sufficient condition for a good PMM.

PPC2: the principle of sensitivity

Both conceptualisation and measurement of P must be *context-sensitive* and *change-sensitive*. To be context-sensitive, the study of P must adopt a relative conception of P, as thresholds cannot be the same in a rich country like Denmark as in a poor one like Haiti. The adoption of the same absolute threshold(s) for all countries, or even for all developing countries – like the World Bank's IPL – is inadequate in that it applies the same evaluation standard (PL) to very different contexts. ECLAC, by contrast, considers the context and thus applies a different PL to each country in Latin America and the Caribbean. Change sensitivity requires that both the concept and the measurement procedure allow for external changes to be reflected in decreases and increases in P levels, both at aggregate and individual levels. In other words, we must acknowledge that individual/HH conditions can vary. There are some indicators, like levels of schooling, which once attained cannot be lost. They become, at the individual level, a fixed parameter, like eye colour. A PMM that relies only on this type of indicator is not change-sensitive. If there is an economic crisis, we expect poverty to increase. If it does not, it is likely that our PMM is not change-sensitive. A PMM that does not include indicators that express a deterioration of living conditions when there is a recession, earthquake, or any other type of disaster is not change-sensitive.

GPPC2: the good practice of adopting a context-sensitive and change-sensitive approach to poverty

Context-sensitivity requires overcoming biological approaches that do not consider the cultural and socioeconomic contexts of country or region. Therefore, a relative conception of P is required. To be change-sensitive (in the right direction), a P concept must not be built only with stock-type indicators that become fixed (like years of schooling); it should also consider flow indicators, like Y.

PPC3: the principle of the comparability of objective well-being

Human beings, as we have argued, are creatures with multiple N. Their N can be met – and indeed are – through diverse S, and to access these, a range of WBS is required. In light of this multidimensional phenomenon, natural indicators (for example, of weight and volume) are useless. The measurement of income P 'solves' this by assuming that prices are suitable weights for goods, so that poverty can be measured by comparing observed Y with a PL equal to: $X_1P_1 + X_2P_2 + ... + X_N P_N$, where X_i is the required amount of good i and P_i its price, acting as a weight. This approach is what I call the *monetary solution*, and it implies at least the following assumptions. First, only material N should be considered, ignoring Maslow's cognitive, emotional, esteem and growth (self-actualisation) N. Second, G&S are the only S, thus excluding relationships, activities, information/theories, institutions, and capacities. Third, Y is the only WBS, excluding assets (both basic and non-basic), access to free G&S, time and knowledge/skills. Fourth, markets are universal: everything is satisfied through them. Fifth, Y is a 'natural' indicator of WB. Lastly, WB is directly proportional to Y (this assumption is sometimes replaced by WB functions that assume a diminishing marginal utility of Y, although this rarely occurs in P studies). The first three assumptions, which constitute what I have called the *reductionism of conventional approaches to P*, show that the consequences of adopting the monetary solution are severe. For example, even within material N, this solution ignores the fact that most HH buy raw food and cook it, which means that activities such as shopping, cooking, and cleaning are also S, and that WBS other than income, such as time and skills (for example, for cooking) are also required. To avoid this reductionism, I have tried to follow one rule: to deal with the universe of HN, the full typology of S and the complete range of WBS sources, that is, applying the *principle of totality*. Regarding the fourth assumption, once market limits have been acknowledged – once we accept that not everything is money-like and therefore is not interchangeable for anything else – as in the IPMM (see Chapter 8), *it follows not only that all WBS are important but that their composition is too.* The point of view that income is a 'natural' indicator of WB (the fifth assumption) is rejected by Foster and Sen (1997, p 208): 'The metrics of exchange value ... was not devised to give us – and in fact, cannot give us – interpersonal comparisons of welfare or advantage.' The sixth assumption about the proportionality between Y and WB contradicts the old tradition of diminishing marginal utility of Y and the common-sense perception that an additional unit of Y is extremely important to a poor man and of no avail to a very rich one. Both Meghnad Desai (1991/1998) and I (Boltvinik, 1993 and 1994b) have adopted the following position: *below PL, deprivation decreases proportionally with the increase in Y, but above PL marginal well-being declines to additional increases in Y.* This means that Y (and consumption expenditures) cannot be used, unless adjusted, to evaluate WB.

As James E. Foster said in 2007,[1] stating that certain dimensions cannot be inherently comparable may mean one of two things: that they are not related, in the sense that they do not have the same purpose (for example, the purpose of one is WB and that of the other is not); or that they belong to different analytical spaces, in the sense that Sen construes this concept (for example, one belongs to the space of WBS, whereas the other belongs to that of G&S). If one wishes to construct an integrated, multidimensional index of WB, then one must define the appropriate set of WB indicators. Once we ensure that they are all WB indicators, they can no longer be regarded as non-comparable in the first sense. But while direct indicators (typically those of UBN) belong to the space of S, Y belongs to the space of WBS. They are therefore not comparable in the second sense; they belong to different analytical spaces. *But neither of these two spaces, be it WBS or S, is suitable for our purpose. Thus, in all cases, indicators must be transformed into indicators of another space:* the WB space. WBS are used to obtain access to S, which are then used to meet HN (or achieve functionings in Sen's CA), thereby producing objective well-being (OWB). Thus, whether we are in the space of WBS or S, we have to move towards the space of WB. In neither case can we interpret the original indicators and/or variables as a direct expression of WB. Thus, the apparent non-comparability of WB indicators is a result of the fact that their common nature, that is, being WB indicators, has not been made explicit because they have not been re-expressed as OWB indicators. *WB does not have obvious measurement units; we have to construct them.* One way to ensure a fully operational comparison is to define three conceptual reference points for each indicator: *the normative standard*, which separates deprivation from WB in the specific dimension; *the absolute or practical minimum*; and the *conceptual maximum*, which implies rejecting the non-satiation axiom of neoclassical economic theory (see the principle of the existence of this maximum in Chapter 5). The three are difficult and entangled concepts (see the principle of poverty as an entangled concept below), for which values must be made explicit. Once these three reference points have been defined, the scale of WB can be normalised in such a way that the range becomes the same in all indicators and the normative threshold is at the

---

[1] In a seminar organised by Coneval (Consejo Nacional de Evaluación de la Política de Desarrollo Social), the Federal Mexican Government office in charge of measuring P, and El Colegio de México, James Foster formulated this idea in his commentary to my paper. The seminar had three sessions and the papers presented by J. Foster, S. R. Chakravarty, D. Gordon, R. Hernández and H. Soto, and me, were published in Boltvinik et al. (2010b). Unfortunately, the debates were not recorded in any form.

same point. This standardisation is an initial step that is complemented by the first four PMP (see Chapter 5).

GPPC3: the good practice of adopting an approach that conceives poverty in terms of OWB

Besides what was just stated under PPC3, this GP implies rejecting what Sen (1981/1991/1992, pp 19–21) calls the *policy definition of P*, which only recognises deprivations that can be eliminated by current policy. The objective definition of P requires all existing P to be recognised, not only that part of it that may be eliminated by policy, that is, in Sen's words: 'the measurement of poverty must be seen as an exercise of description assessing the predicaments of people in terms of the prevailing standards of necessities' (1981/1991/1992, p 21, emphasis added).

PPC4: the principle of the entangled nature of the concept of poverty

P measurement cannot be entirely 'scientific' – for those who understand scientific activities as those without value judgements – because it involves comparing the conditions of observed HH (basically a descriptive task which can come close to this criterion of scientificity) vis-à-vis the normative levels (thresholds) which are either the researcher's value judgements, someone else's value judgements or explicit social value judgements (which are still value judgements) systematised through field research. Hilary Putnam (2002) has argued that the entanglement of facts and values becomes obvious when one looks at terms such as *cruel, crime* or *brave*, known as *thick ethical concepts*, which have normative and ethical uses and are counterexamples of the notion of an absolute dichotomy between facts and values. To use these terms in a discriminating way, says Putnam, *one must be capable of imaginatively identifying oneself with an evaluative point of view*. He adds that, in these cases, description itself depends on evaluation. *This is exactly what happens with the term P: the description of P cannot be carried out unless it has been previously evaluated (by comparing observed facts with thresholds), an activity in which values are inevitably present*. Putnam does not explicitly include P among the thick, entangled ethical concepts, but he argues that Sen's vocabulary in the CA is almost entirely made up of entangled concepts such as *valuable functionings*, while arguing that from Sen's standpoint, evaluation, and determination of facts are interdependent activities. The following statement by Putnam dispels any doubt: 'Welfare economics has found itself forced to recognize that its "classical" concern with economic WB (and its opposite, economic deprivation, that is, P, one might add) is essentially a moral concern and cannot be addressed responsibly *as long as we are unwilling to take reasoned moral arguments seriously*' (2002, p 57).

GPPC4: the good practice of basing the poverty concept on informed value judgements

Accepting the entangled nature of the concept of P and, thus, the inevitability of value judgements entails that one must try to minimise arbitrariness by basing decisions on value judgements that are as informed as possible. These value judgements should be based on HN, rights, history, and the perceptions and aspirations of the population.

PPC5: the principle of dignity as a central criterion for defining poverty threshold(s)

How can we determine the minimum living standard required not to be poor, namely, the P threshold(s)? Orthodox economists who dominate P studies pretend that the cut-off point is irrelevant and maintain that it is an arbitrary limit set by the researcher. This stance hinders a debate centred on this axis, thereby promoting the introduction of very low P thresholds that lead to the identification of a small fraction of the population as poor. This, in turn, reinforces the fiction that P is a minor problem of the existing social order and can therefore be solved through targeted cash transferences. In the simulation exercises performed in Boltvinik (2010b) and in Boltvinik and Damián (2020), we concluded that thresholds matter, and that they matter a great deal, inasmuch as the level of P incidence (H) is more dependent on the thresholds selected than on the measuring procedure adopted. Regardless of the method, virtually any H can be obtained by modifying the thresholds. But thresholds are not to be played with; they are not irrelevant. In countries like Mexico, where poverty-targeted cash transference programmes played an increasingly important role from 1997 to 2018, threshold levels determined the universe of people included in the target population (that is, identified as extremely poor). The lower the thresholds, the smaller the universe. Many lives may be lost due to the irresponsible reduction of certain thresholds to obtain measured poverty P levels that are 'acceptable' to the dominant elite. This is what Sen (1981/1991/1992, pp 19–21) wanted to prevent when he convincingly argued against what he calls the *policy definition of poverty*. The poor are not those people that a given political regime is able to or wishes to tend to; they constitute a reality independent of government's capacity/will. It is irresponsible to reduce reality to this capacity/will.

The orthodox stance maintains that the threshold level is an individual value judgement. Thus, Mollie Orshansky (1965, p 37), the creator of the official US PMM, pointed out that 'poverty, like beauty, lies in the eyes of the beholder'. This is also the position adopted by the World Bank: 'any cut-off point will reflect some degree of arbitrariness due to the subjective way in which poverty is defined' (World Bank, 1993, p 51). In contrast,

Karl Marx declares in *Capital* that, unlike other commodities, 'a *historical and moral* element intervenes in the determination of labour force value'. In a given country, at a given period, he adds, 'the average quantity of *means of subsistence necessary for the worker is a known datum*' (Marx, 1867/1976/1990, pp 275; emphasis added). Along the same lines, Sen (1981/1991/1992), argues against the view that P is a value judgement or a subjective exercise of some kind: he considers that researchers describe *prevailing social prescriptions (norms or standards)*, therefore implying that these prescriptions or norms have an objective social existence and can be observed and described by social scientists. In a famous passage in *The Wealth of Nations*, Adam Smith makes it quite clear that N go beyond what is essential for sustaining life and include what is required for keeping with the customs of the society in which one lives. Thus, to the biological dimension of N he adds the social dimension. The lack of the type of G&S involved in the social dimension does not endanger life, but it does drive the individual into social self-exclusion due to the shame that this lack provokes – an idea that reveals Smith's relative conception of necessary S (see PPC2 above). Sen appears to have changed his mind since *Poverty and Famines* (1981/1991/1992), or else allowed himself to be convinced by his co-author, since in the annexe to *On Economic Inequality*, he and James Foster qualify the cut-off point separating the poor from the non-poor as arbitrary (Foster and Sen, 1997, p 188).

Peter Townsend (1979) aimed for an objective definition of the P threshold when he sought a point in the Y curve below which deprivation indices (directly measured) increased rapidly. Later, Townsend and Gordon (in Townsend, 1993), pursuing the same objective, used the discriminant analysis statistical technique. Gordon et al. (2000) have stated that this is the scientific approach to P measurement. But what these authors have done is to classify a HH living in poverty as a function of whether what it does and has (in terms of consumption or lifestyle) is less than what others (or the majority) do and have (Townsend, 1979), or rather than what society regards as necessary (Gordon et al., 2000). Thus, norms are drawn from society; social prescriptions are described through the statistical compilation of people's perceptions and reality. This conception therefore assumes that norms have an objective, social existence, that – as Sen (1981/1991/1992, p 17) says – 'For the person studying and measuring poverty, the conventions of society are matters of fact'.

One could say that this controversy is about the validity of the concept of objective HN and their historically conditioned S. Thus, the controversy over the objective or subjective nature of the definition of the P threshold is also a controversy over the existence or non-existence of common HN, as well as the existence, in a certain geographical area and historical period, of a commonality of essential S associated with these N. This is a crucial controversy. If social norms lacked an objective social existence, then the concept of P would not be suitable for scientific research, and P measurement, as stated by Sen, would entail 'unleashing one's personal morals on the statistics of deprivation' (1981/1991/1992, p 17).

My position is that social norms that define minimum thresholds of HN satisfaction are active social norms that motivate and drive people to achieve them. People know these prescriptions (albeit vaguely, not systematically), which have a direct impact on their lives. Social research faces the challenge of apprehending the said prescriptions or norms in detail. The barrier to overcome is the role played by ideology in people's responses in surveys. Yet, despite these difficulties, the definition of thresholds can be an objective, scientifically based operation. The feeling of shame would be a significant indicator of whether certain satisfiers are basic.[2]

Social circumstances might determine that certain specific S become essential. For instance, cars were essential in Beirut in the 1990s, as the city had virtually no public transport; but around the same time, cars were not essential in London, where a good public transport system was in place.[3] In more general terms, social production and consumption conditions determine which S will be essential to satisfy a specific N. Another example: in several large Latin American cities, working hours, long journeys to the workplace, and women's participation in the LF have created the social N for day care centres and for the consumption of food prepared outside one's home.[4] In short, there are enough bases to construe the definition of thresholds not as an arbitrary act of a researcher, but rather as the result of systematic research on existing social prescriptions.

Following Maccoby (1988), who regards dignity as a HN (although instead of the word N, he uses the term *value-drives*), I would like to elaborate on the concept of dignity. One must note, he points out, the response of shame, pain, and anger when a child is ridiculed. Maccoby goes on to say that the drive for dignity appears to be fragile and easily crushed, but that this perception is disorienting. As adults, the pressure to survive or adapt to

---

[2] Unsatisfaction of the type of N derived from customs would lead, through shame, to ostracism or non-participation. In this case, the external penalty entailed by the norm would be self-exclusion. On the contrary, unmet biological N lead to sickness and death, while unsatisfied affective N (Maslow) or existential N (Fromm) lead to neurosis/psychosis.

[3] Sen (1983/1984, p 33), notes an inverse causality: '[I]n a society in which most families own cars, public transport services might be poor, so that a carless family in such a society might be *absolutely poor* in a way it might not have been in a poorer society. To take another example, widespread ownership of refrigerators and freezers in a community might affect the structure of food retailing, thereby making it more difficult in such a society to make do without having these facilities oneself.'

[4] For an in-depth analysis of this issue, see J.P. Terrail et al. (1977: 13–34), as well as a summary of his views in Boltvinik (2005: chapter 9).

a job may lead us to *swallow our humiliation*. But the drive to achieve dignity, even if frustrated, is never extinguished: it takes another form. It is often perverted into fantasy, revenge, and hatred. This frozen anger can explode into destructive violence. The drive to achieve dignity is a normal impulse, common to all societies. It develops naturally if a child is lovingly valued. In healthy children (and adults) the demand for equity and justice expresses the drive for dignity. Plato and Aristotle argued that the capacity to feel shame is what makes ethical development possible, since shameless persons are beyond the scope of the moral community.[5]

Let us now connect these ideas to what we described earlier. We have seen that Adam Smith associates the conversion of certain S into necessary ones due to the feeling of shame that their lack elicits. He also associates the terms *decent* and *creditable* with shame, all within the same family of meanings. The feeling of shame is defined in the *Collins English Dictionary* as 'a painful emotion resulting from an awareness of having done something dishonourable, unworthy, degrading, etc.'. The DRAE defines *vergüenza* (shame) as follows: 'mood disturbance usually accompanied by blushing, caused by consciously committing an offence or by a dishonourable, humiliating action (whether performed by oneself or others)'. When Smith says that no-one would dare appear in public without leather shoes, since the feeling of shame would prevent them from doing so, this is what he means. Smith explains the feeling of shame in correspondence with the dominant perceptions of his time (which explained poverty as an individual liability). This is why he associates the shame of being poor with the shame derived from an extremely dissipated behaviour. According to the DRAE, this type of behaviour leads to wasting money, but also to dissolution and moral relaxation. An individual would feel shame not because of the lack of leather shoes or a linen shirt but because this lack would reflect them morally. I think that if we remove the element of dissipated behaviour from Smith's text, which is moulded by the ideology of his time, we have an extremely clear view of the shame associated with P.

Shame, honour, decorum and honesty are also associated with *dignity*, one of whose meanings is defined by the DRAE as 'people's seriousness

---

[5] Agnes Heller (1985: 2–12) builds a general theory of shame. According to her, shame is an emotion to which all other emotions are linked. The feeling of shame leads us to conform to our cultural environment, since it results from the response to the fact (or judgement) that the person has not acted in keeping with the norms or has exceeded in his compliance with them. 'In regulation through shame, the norms, rules, and rituals of behaviour to which one should conform are not rational. But they are certainly not irrational. Still, their validity must be (and is) accepted without reasoning' (1985: 2–12).

or decorum in the way they behave'. The *Collins English Dictionary* defines dignity as 'the state or quality of being worthy of honour'. Dignified means: 'that which deserves something', as well as 'proportional to a person's merit and condition' (DRAE). Thus, when we speak of human dignity, we are referring to what people deserve by (proportional to) the fact of being human beings. In Abraham Maslow's theory of the hierarchy of HN (see chapter 3 of *Ampliar la mirada*), we find the N for self-esteem, which is clearly linked to shame, honour, and dignity. Maccoby (and Heller's) references to Plato and Aristotle show that shame is much more important than Adam Smith thought, since it is the feeling that makes people's ethical development possible. Shameless persons are morally childish beings with no dignity that could be wounded.

All of the above establishes the bases for enunciating the principle of dignity in the definition of the poverty threshold. Such a Pr seeks to make dignity a central criterion in establishing thresholds, which means not violating the dignity of those living at the level of the thresholds adopted.

GPPC5: the good practice of conceiving poverty concepts and measurement procedures as promoters of human rights and optimal public policies

P concepts and PMM should not violate but rather promote human rights. This can be achieved by using P criteria that seek to minimise the exclusion error (to exclude poor people from being recognised as such), rather than those that seek to minimise the inclusion error (including non-poor as poor); and also by including all HN and adopting dignified thresholds for each of them, instead of considering low quality S which deny human dignity.

PPC6: the Pr of P as part of the SLA

To present this Pr, I will begin by formulating an antithetical claim to that of Sen, who in addition to positioning his analysis on the SLA, in which he wants to include people's health status, proposes a special conceptual axis for P (different from the SLA), in which he includes only a few, elementary capabilities. This eliminates the possibility of having a coherent SLA. Sen would not be able to answer questions on the meaning of the lower part of the SLA and its link to P.

Foster and Sen (1997) argue in favour of the capabilities/functionings approach in P measurement by saying: 'Since we are ultimately concerned with the lives we can lead (and income is only instrumentally important in helping us to lead adequate lives), the case for taking the latter view of poverty [*inability to meet some elementary and essential N*] is quite strong' (1997, p 210; emphasis added).

Note the word *some*. In a footnote, the authors add:

> Important contributions have been made to the understanding of poverty in the literature on 'basic needs'. ... The focus on particular deprivations rather than just on the lowness of income has enriched the study of poverty. ... The 'basic needs' have, however, been typically characterized in terms of minimum amounts of commodities and specific facilities (such as food, housing, etc.), and *as a result this approach needs supplementation by the consideration of interpersonal variations in converting commodities and resources into functional achievements.* (1997, p 210, n271; emphasis added)

In the same text they conclude:

> If that view is taken, then seeing poverty as capability deprivation makes considerable sense. There is likely to be wide agreement that poverty exists when a person lacks the real opportunity of *avoiding hunger or undernourishment or homelessness*. These minimal capabilities and some elementary *social* abilities (such as the capability to 'appear in public without shame' and that 'to take part in the life of the community') were discussed [in some of Sen's previous works]. (1997, p 210; emphasis added)

The reader should note several things: on the one hand, in the third quote, Foster and Sen replace N with capabilities. On the other hand, P has been reduced, in the first quote, to the inability to satisfy 'certain elementary and essential needs', which raises several questions: Why 'some' and not all the elementary and essential needs? Does substituting the term *basic* for *elementary* and *essential* mean something? The reader should then note that, in the footnote (in italicised words), Foster and Sen reduce the difference between the basic N and the CA to considering or not the variability in the conversion of goods and resources into functional achievements. Thus, the CA appears here only as a basic N approach that also takes this variability into account.[6] Note the words in italics in the last phrase of the first quote, since Townsend's accusation that Sen is minimalist would seem to fit this text perfectly.

---

[6] Interpreted literally, this means that the CA is not a new approach, since all good studies on poverty take the variability of N into account and are therefore (at least for Sen and Foster) capabilities studies.

Were it not for Foster and Sen's attempt to deal with poverty P on a different axis from that of the SLA (with a smaller number of capabilities), stating this principle would be unnecessary. But Sen's enormous influence makes it necessary to formulate this Pr. The PPC6 can be formulated very directly: economic P should be conceived of as the portion of SLA located below the threshold(s) that identify it.

GPPC6: the good practice of including all relevant dimensions of living standards in the conceptualisation and measurement of poverty

In keeping with the Pr of P as part of the SLA, we can avoid the use of poverty-only measuring-sticks, which implies conceiving the poor as second-class citizens.

PART II

Measuring poverty

5

Principles and good practices of poverty measurement

5.1 Poverty measurement

In this chapter I explain the lower part of Table 4.1, which refers to principles and good practices of P measurement.

PPM1 and PPM2: principles of diminishing marginal WB and the existence of a maximum WB

In his major work on the collapse of the facts/values dichotomy, philosopher of science Hilary Putnam (2002) makes a radical criticism of neoclassical economic theory and its normative expression, so-called 'welfare economics'. He recalls that in the late nineteenth century, neoclassical economists (such as Jevons and Marshall) adopted the concept of utility, assumed that it could be quantified, and drew utility curves whose shape was determined by the Law of Diminishing Marginal Utility (LDMU), which holds that the utility derived from the consumption of the last unit of a given good diminishes as consumption increases. In *Welfare Economics* (1920), Putnam adds, Pigou argued that money and income (Y) are also subject to the LDMU. Based on this, Pigou formulated the thesis that the reduction of Y inequality increases social welfare, since total social utility (or happiness) would increase if one withdrew a thousand dollars from a millionaire and gave them to a destitute person.

Such a subversive thesis, however, could not last in academia (which tends towards an apology of the status quo). Putnam relates that, in 1938, Lionel Robbins convinced all mainstream economists that interpersonal comparisons of utility lack any significance. He maintained that rational discussion in the domain of ethics is impossible and that, therefore, ethical issues should be kept completely outside economic theory. Thus, in a single stroke, the idea that economists could and should be concerned with social WB in an evaluative sense was rejected. The dichotomy between facts and values was taken to the limit in Robbins' statement: 'It does not seem logically possible to associate the two studies [ethics and economics] in any form but mere juxtaposition. Economics deals with ascertainable facts; ethics with valuation and obligations' (Robbins, 1932, p 134, quoted by Putnam, 2002, p 54). Putnam goes on to say that economists, convinced by

Robbins's ideas, instead of abandoning the discipline of welfare economics, sought – however strange this may seem – a criterion of optimal economic functioning that was value-neutral and found it in the notion of the Pareto optimal. Since this optimal is based on the impossibility of comparing utility between people, one can only say that there has been a social improvement when, for example, some are benefitted but no-one is harmed. Therefore, Putnam states:

> Pareto optimality is, however, a terribly weak criterion for evaluating socioeconomic states of affairs. Defeating Nazi Germany in 1945 could not be called Pareto optimal, for example, because at least one agent – Adolf Hitler – was moved to a lower utility surface. … The upshot of this little bit of history is that if there is to be such a subject as welfare economics at all, and … if welfare economics is to speak to problems of poverty and other forms of deprivation, *then [it] cannot avoid substantive ethical questions.* (2002, p 56, emphasis added)

The LDMU runs parallel to the law of decreasing marginal productivity of neoclassical production theory; it refers to an increase in a factor of production when at least one of the other factors remains constant. The classic example is agriculture, where the fixed factor is land: when certain inputs (such as seed and fertiliser) increase, production grows but marginal productivity decreases. Although in the case of specific goods the LDMU could be based on the concept of satiation without resorting to the presence of a fixed factor, satiation does not support the validity of the LDMU for Y as a whole.

A little-known book by Staffan B. Linder (1970) sheds light on the subject. Linder points out that economists have always implicitly assumed that consumption occurs instantaneously, that it does not consume time (T), which is false. Once consumption T is considered, the consumption process is regarded as the result of the combination of personal T and G&S (enjoying a play involves both paying for the tickets and attending the performance, that is, devoting T to it). Thus, Linder finds that T is not only a resource for production but also for consumption. However, T is a very special resource: total personal T cannot be increased nor accumulated, and it is interpersonally distributed in an egalitarian fashion.

With economic growth or family opulence, some persons have access to more G&S: T becomes increasingly 'scarce' and G&S more abundant. Since consumption involves a combination of T and G&S, increasingly less T will be assigned to each consumer good/event while, conversely, the goods-intensity of consumption will increase. Thus, 'the yield on T' will increase while the 'degree of use of the capital stock represented by consumer goods' will decrease. Thus, the yield on goods will decrease alongside the return on the Y that serves to acquire them. Economic growth is mistakenly associated with total rather than partial opulence due to the lack of awareness that consumption requires T. In rich countries, the average employee – says Linder, discarding the alleged problem of growing leisure – lives under the pressure of T. They are a member of the hurried leisure class.

This is the foundation we had been searching for: the LDMU of Y is based on the existence of the fixed T factor, coupled with an increase in the access to G&S (hereafter referred to as goods). One of the consequences of this, notes Linder, is that traditional pleasures are under pressure. Eating becomes a lower activity that stops being a key pleasure with profound psychological dimensions and becomes a maintenance function. Hence the tendency towards the predominance of fast food, one might add. Sexual love, says Linder, takes time, and the pressure to save time means that sexual adventures – which require a considerable time – become less attractive, that less T is devoted to each sexual encounter, and that their frequency declines. Furthermore, this is tantamount to an increase in fast sex. Linder's subversive idea, which revives Pigou's thesis and properly substantiates it, has naturally been ignored by orthodox economics.

These arguments led me to posit the principle of diminishing marginal WB (DMWB), which applies above the poverty threshold in the face of successive increases in S. Given the finite nature of available T, S such as relationships and activities – that require a good deal of the T resource – can only be increased within narrow ranges. Conversely, the possession of objects appears to have no limits, even if they are not used or are used increasingly less. Applying this principle would imply using an adequate WB function, such as those developed by Atkinson.[1]

This principle is complemented by the derived (or associated) principle of the existence of a maximum WB level or point (both in each HN dimension and in the aggregated WB), beyond which marginal WB derived from the addition of satisfiers is zero, or in some cases – such as food – becomes negative. This means that WB functions should have a decreasing slope above the threshold and end in a maximum value.[2]

---

[1] Desai (1991/1998) applies an Atkinson-type (Atkinson, 1983) function in his proposal for the Achievement Set of the Social Progress Index. Following Desai's proposal, the Human Development Index used a similar function to calculate the index's GDP per capita component for many years, but it was subsequently replaced by a logarithmic function. In the IPMM, I have not used a suitable function for reflecting this principle fully (see Section 8.2).

[2] Despite not having used WB functions that are consistent with the principle of DMWB, in the IPMM I have limited the maximum value of the achievement indicator to a score of 2 in the cases where the original variable is metric – such as Y or years of education. To do so, I have defined a conceptual maximum (for example, an Y of ten times the PL), equated the values above it with the conceptual maximum, and proportionally rescaled the remaining

GPPM1: the good practice of applying PPM1 and PPM2

GPPM1 applies PPM1 and PPM2, thus converting the IPMM into the IPSMM (Integrated Poverty and Stratification Measurement Method).

PPM3: the principle of the minimal error

Some researchers argue that they do not include dimensions other than Y or that they do not cardinalise ordinal indicators (see below) in their poverty measurements (for example, Comité Técnico para la Medición de la Pobreza (Technical Committee for Poverty Measurement, Mexico, 2002) because they think their weights (and/or scores) are difficult or impossible to define. Thus, although they acknowledge the importance of other WB dimensions, they only measure Y poverty, ignoring the fact – or failing to acknowledge its importance – that in so doing they are assigning a zero weight to all other WBS. And this is (quite probably) the greatest possible error. Applying the principle of the minimal error involves overcoming these difficulties in all cases, since failure to do so implies (quite probably) committing the maximum error. Applying said principle involves an enormous amount of not-very-elegant work, as well as being bold enough to make value judgements when necessary (judgements that must always be made explicit). Including non-monetary dimensions in the multidimensional measurement of poverty and opting for its full cardinalisation are perhaps the main tasks to which this principle is applied.

GPPM2: the good practice of minimising errors

GPPM2 is the set of good practices that apply PPM3, thus minimising measurement errors.

PPM4: the principle of replicable full cardinalisation (generalised dichotomisation)

To be able to say 'Let's begin with a matrix of data x', as Foster (2010, p 342) does, one must ensure that all variables are expressed in cardinal numbers (metric scales). But many original dimensions are formulated in terms of alternative solutions to a N (water supply systems, materials used for housing construction, type of health service, etc.), so they are expressed in words rather than numbers. The first step is to arrange these nominal variables

---

range above the threshold (1 to 10) to reduce it to 1 to 2. As argued in the previous footnote, this practice can obviously be improved with an appropriate WB function.

from worst to best (in terms of the objective level of WB they provide), thereby converting them into ordinal variables. However, ordinal numbers (first, second, etc.) cannot be entered as such into a matrix, so the second necessary step will be to convert them into cardinal WB variables. Foster (2010) implicitly carries out the first step, and to accomplish the second one he opts for dichotomisation, a form of cardinalisation that entails an enormous loss of information. In dichotomisation, all intermediate solutions between the worst one (which obtains a score of 1 on the deprivation scale) and the normative one (which obtains a score of 0), are assigned a value of 1, even though they would deserve intermediate values (for example, 0.3, 0.5, 0.7). This shows that the solutions imply partial rather than total deprivation and that, in addition, as reflected in their arrangement, some solutions are better than others, or not as bad as the others. Solutions above the norm will obtain the same score as the norm; this implies losing additional information, since we know that they are better and should therefore be given negative values. These losses of information affect the final classification of certain HH as poor/non-poor and the measurement of P intensity (or degree of WB) of all HH, thereby denying the PME.

The procedure of full cardinalisation that I use in the IPMM has been criticised because it is perceived as difficult to replicate (in other words, for a lack of standardised procedures). This was James Foster's opinion, expressed in a video conference organised by Coneval-El Colegio de México in July 2007. Encouraged by Foster's commentary, I developed a standardised procedure for full cardinalisation, which I present below. This procedure provides scores not only for the intermediate options between the worst (0) and the norm (1), but also for values above the norm. It shows that full cardinalisation can be easily replicated using generalised dichotomisation (GD), which is almost as simple as usual dichotomisation. In section IV of Boltvinik (2010b), I apply this procedure to all UBN indicators that allow it and compare these results with those of the original cardinalisation procedure which I had been using in the IPMM.

Applying this replicable cardinalisation has enabled me to draw up some steps and rules to carry out the process (Table 5.1). The exercise consists in a GD which, instead of adopting a single threshold, adopts all the logically possible ones. With each threshold, a dichotomy is constructed, a score is obtained for each of them (0,1), the scores are added, and the sum is standardised through division by the sum of the 'authentic' threshold. This standardised value constitutes the final cardinal value of each solution.

The steps of this exercise are as follows. 1) Order the solutions to the N (arrangements to provide for it), for example, water provision or housing materials, from worst to best in terms of the OWB they provide. 2) Define $n-1$ dichotomies by using a different solution as the standard or threshold in each case (the worst solution must be excluded, or else the entire population would be not deprived). 3) Define which solution represents the 'authentic threshold' that expresses the minimally satisfactory solution separating deprivation from satisfaction in culturally determined conditions of dignity. 4) Obtain the matrix of 0,1 achievement scores for each of the n solutions (rows) and $n-1$ dichotomies (columns B to G): a matrix of n by $n-1$, where solutions below the threshold are assigned a score of 0 and solutions equal to or better than the threshold, a score of 1. 5) Add (horizontally) all the scores obtained for each solution in each of the dichotomies. The penultimate column of Table 5.1 shows that in the hypothetical example the sums range from 0 to 6, while the sum for the authentic threshold is equal to 3. 6) As noted earlier, in order to standardise the sum of the scores for all indicators, it is useful to assign value 1 to the true threshold. In Table 5.1, this is achieved by dividing the sum of scores by 3 (which is the sum of scores of the true threshold solution, as seen in the penultimate column). The values of the standardised scores now range from 0 to 2, and the true threshold is located at score 1. 7) These standardised scores are the cardinalised values of the achievement indicator for each solution, which we will call A_j. Achievement indicators in HHj in indicator i can be identified as A_{ij}. These values can be used to perform all kinds of mathematical operations. If the true threshold were also the best solution (which in the example of Table 5.1 would mean eliminating solutions E to G so that no solution is better than the true threshold), the achievement indicator would vary from 0 (for the worst solution) to 1 (for the best solution and true threshold). This would be a truncated scale, and the cardinal scale would therefore only vary from 0 to 1. By contrast, the example in Table 5.1 reflects an ideal symmetrical situation where the number of better-than-the-threshold solutions is equal to the number of worse-than-the-threshold solutions (three). This situation enables the unfolding of the complete scale in the desired range from 0 to 2. If the maximum cardinalised value were higher than 2 (which is uncommon, yet still possible given the qualitative variables involved), the values above 1 would have to be rescaled from +1 to +n to the range of +1 to +2 (see above the discussion of the principle of the DMWB and the associated principle of the existence of maximum WB in each dimension).

This procedure and its rules, as well as its full application to the databases from the 2005 National Income and Expenditure Household Survey (ENIGH) in Boltvinik (2010b), show that the full cardinalisation of an ordinal indicator can be obtained as the quotient between the sum of values (0,1) obtained for each solution and the corresponding sum obtained for the solution representing the authentic threshold. This implies that the use of all the logical dichotomic variables, or GD, is equivalent to full cardinalisation. In addition, the result obtained is an equidistant cardinalisation, which has a long tradition in the social sciences, as pointed out by Sen (1981). The replicable procedure will be preferred by those who place a greater value on replicability than on flexibility

Table 5.1: Procedure for generalised dichotomisation (replicable full cardinalisation)

Solutions arranged from worst to best in terms of OWB	Alternative standards or thresholds used to dichotomise (all except for the worst) Dichotomic scores (0,1) obtained for each solution when the standard (threshold) used is:						Sum of scores for each solution Σ	Standardised score (=Σ/3) Cardinal score sought
	B	C	D	E	F	G		
A (the worst)	0	0	0	0	0	0	0	0.000
B	1	0	0	0	0	0	1	0.333
C	1	1	0	0	0	0	2	0.666
D (authentic threshold)	1	1	1	0	0	0	3	1.000
E	1	1	1	1	0	0	4	1.333
F	1	1	1	1	1	0	5	1.666
G (the most luxurious)	1	1	1	1	1	1	6	2.000

Note: See text for a full description of the procedure. The data in the cells show dichotomic achievement scores in the six dichotomies.

of judgement. However, the empirical results of both options in this case are virtually identical, and there is no reason to think that this will not be the case in general. Lastly, replicable cardinalisation does not entail eliminating all normative judgements: one must still establish the 'authentic threshold', in other words, one must identify the correct normative standard.

Thus, we can conclude that full cardinalisation can be easily replicated and has enormous benefits. Once all achievement indicators are expressed in cardinal units (some indicators, for example, Y, do not undergo this cardinalisation process), the deprivation indicator score or gap (G_{ij}), which equals $1 - A_{ij}$, can be calculated. The data matrix of this normalised gap (in dimension i for household j) is the central matrix for poverty measurement. If A_{ij} has the full desired range from 0 to 2, G_{ij} will vary from -1 to $+1$. The weighted average of all gap or deprivation scores G_{ij} of HHj over all individual (i) gap indicators, can be regarded (in simple cases) as the definitive, central indicator of P in each HH and may be called P_j. Therefore, $P_j = \Sigma k_i G_{ij}$, where k_i is the weight of indicator i, and $\Sigma k_i = 1$. If P_j is positive, the HH is poor; if it is zero or negative, the HH is non-poor. Moreover, the value of P_j allows a full stratification of HH from the poorest to the upper class. Using an extremely simple procedure, fully replicable cardinalisation or GD enables a shift from an extremely precarious measurement procedure to a fully developed one in which all the APM can be calculated. (APM are analysed in Chapter 9.)

Replicable cardinalisation was applied in section IV of Boltvinik (2010b) as an alternative to the original procedure. Both procedures, as well as their empirical results, are then compared in the same section. This process confirms that replicable cardinalisation is a practical and feasible option. The empirical results are virtually the same in both procedures.[3] As compared with standard dichotomisation, GD always reduces the errors involved. To show this, let us imagine that four solutions are arranged from worst to best and that we determine that the authentic threshold is solution D (see Table 5.1 and mentally eliminate rows E to G). If we apply standard dichotomisation and calculate achievement scores, solutions A, B and C will have a score of 0, whereas solution D will have a score of 1. Solutions A, B and C will obtain the same score even though – since we had already arranged them from worst to best – we know that the WB derived from solution C is higher than the one derived from solution B, and that the latter is higher than the one corresponding to solution A. We can therefore know that we are committing an error by assigning the same score to the three solutions. If we apply GD in this example, we will obtain the following scores: 0, 0.333, 0.666 and 1.0 for solutions A, B, C, and D, respectively. This allows us to prevent the error of giving the same score to solutions we know must have different scores. We have thus avoided this qualitative error, but have we also reduced the quantitative error? We know that the real achievement score for solution B (SB_{RS}) is higher than the one for solution A, yet lower than the one for solutions C and D, so we can write (assuming that 0 is a correct value for the worst solution and 1 for the true threshold): $0 < SB_{RS} < SC_{RS} < 1$. This is still too broad and vague, but we can make it slightly less so by assuming that we cannot distinguish between solutions unless their values differ by at least 0.1. Thus, in arranging the four solutions, we have assumed that solution B deserves a score of at least 0.1 and that solution C has a ceiling of 0.9. Therefore, both B and C will have to be assigned scores within the range of 0.1 to 0.9, separated by a distance of at least 0.1; this we can write as $0.1 \leq SB_{RS} \leq 0.8; 0.2 \leq SC_{RS} \leq 0.9$. Considering our ignorance as to where the real values for these intermediate solutions lie (within the expressed ranges), the most reasonable route is to proceed as though they were normally distributed among the ranges identified above. Thus, both their medians and means would be 0.333 and 0.666, which are the scores assigned by replicable cardinalisation. This is, then, the correct path to minimise error in the light of ignorance. If ignorance is not total, then the

---

[3] The incidence of integrated poverty using IPMM with a 2005 database was 77.9% applying the usual cardinalisation (which is more flexible) and 78.3% applying replicable cardinalisation, a difference of 0.4 percentage points which, as one can see, is quite small.

scores for each solution must be assigned through specific estimates, which is the path of my usual cardinalisation procedure.[4]

GPMM3: the good practice of cardinalising indicators

GPPM3 is the practice of fully cardinalising indicators (applying the PPM4), thus avoiding the loss of information and the biases involved in dichotomisation. It implies the leap from dichotomisation to GD.

PPM5: the principle of symmetry

This principle maintains that when adopting truncated PL that only reflect the cost of a few HN, or only one of them (for example, food), this cost should not be compared with total HH CY, but only with that portion of Y that is actually available for the HH to meet the N considered in the PL. When a truncated PL is compared with total HH CY, one violates the principle of symmetry and incurs the error of asymmetry, which consists of comparing the partial cost of satisfying some HN with the totality of HH resources. In the following paragraphs, I illustrate this error with the example of the method defined by the Mexican Government (2003–2008) with the assistance of the Technical Committee for the Measurement of Poverty (TCMP), designed for this purpose by the Secretaría de Desarrollo Social (Sedesol, Ministry of Social Development), during the period 2002–2006. This method explicitly excises HN (in its three PL), so that the error of asymmetry can be seen more easily. This error is shared, as stated, with ECLAC.

The highest PL of the three adopted by Sedesol is the so-called patrimonial poverty line (PPL), originally called PL_2 by the TCMP. The highest PL defined by the TCMP, called PL_3, was rejected by Sedesol. PL_3 was the result of the coherent application of the NFB methodology, with the peculiarity that a group of extremely poor HH was chosen as the stratum of reference to calculate the Engel coefficient (E): the PL is obtained by dividing the cost of the NFB by E. The PL_3 – unlike the PPL – is a full concept of poverty in the sense that it refers to the G&S 'required' to satisfy all HN, despite being a SN method which only handles food normatively (which is why I wrote

---

[4] The best way to carry out this scoring is by means of a panel of experts, where each expert's initial individual judgement is refined as a result of a collective discussion. One would expect that in an exercise of this nature the variation range between individual scores after the collective discussion would be smaller than the pre-existing range. Thus, even if a consensus is not reached, the smaller range would allow the mean, median or mode to reduce the degree of error, in other words, the application of the PME.

'required' in inverted commas). Conversely, the PPL and Sedesol's two lower PL – the so-called food PL (FPL) and the capacities PL (CPL) – are truncated. According to the TCMP/Sedesol, the PPL measures a HH's capacity to satisfy only six N: food, clothing, housing, public transport, health, and education; the FPL measures this capacity regarding only one N (food), while the CPL does so for three N (food, education, and healthcare). Each one of these PL completely excludes the N not included in their corresponding subsets of reduced N. As I have already stated, the procedure adopted for measuring P using the three truncated PL suffers from what I have called the problem of asymmetry; moreover, it violates the principle of totality regarding N.

Let us start with the following general P criterion: HH_J is poor if $Y_J <$ PL. If the right side of this inequality is disaggregated into the PL's food and non-food components, the adoption of a fully normative PL approach – namely, that of the normative generalised basket (NGB)[5] – is made explicit; the resulting P criterion is $Y_J < [CNFB + CNnFB] = CNGB$ (where CNFB is the cost of the NFB, CNnFB is the cost of the normative non-food basket, and CNGB is the cost of the normative generalised basket). A similar disaggregation can be made by dividing the total cost of needs satisfaction into any n subgroups. If we consider the six needs included in the PPL for this purpose, then the P criterion can be written as follows: $Y_J < [CN6NeB + CNONeB]$ (where CN6NeB is the cost of the normative six-N basket and CNONeB is the cost of the normative other-N (or excluded N) basket).

The stated P criterion, which expresses the insufficiency of HH Y to purchase the NGB, can be interpreted as the HH's economic inability to meet the whole set of N. The first implication of this criterion is that every partial economic capacity to satisfy (any) partial set of N must be derived from this general inequality. There are no partial economic capacities except for those that depend on or are derived from this general capacity. This implies, for example, that the criteria for food P and for the six N PLs must be derived from one of the two disaggregated general inequalities presented above. Since we only want to have CNFB or CN6NeB on the right side of the equation, we will have to subtract CNnFB or CNONeB from this side of the equation and, therefore – to respect the rules of algebra – do the same on the left side. Thus, we will arrive at the concept of available Y to spend on food (Y_J – CNnFB) or on the six needs (Y_J – CNONeB) and

---

[5] Whereas the NGB method constructs full standard baskets that include all the G&S a HH requires to meet all its N, the NFB method only constructs a (raw) food basket and obtains the PL by dividing the cost of the NFB by the Engel coefficient observed in the chosen stratum of reference. For a fuller discussion, see Chapter 6.

obtain the following P criteria: $Y_J - CNnFB < CNFB$ and $Y_J - CNONeB < CN6NeB$.

According to these two P criteria, what can be compared, with algebraic consistency, with the truncated PL expressed on the right side of both inequalities, is not total Y but rather available Y for the corresponding purpose. An alternative procedure for achieving consistency – a logical rather than an algebraic procedure – is to subtract from the left side not the normative cost of non-food or other needs to obtain the available Y but the observed expenditures (in non-food G&S or in other N in household J). In the first procedure (expressed above), one obtains the normative available Y, whereas in this second one, it would be the observed available Y.

One can conclude that TCMP/Sedesol's truncated poverty lines (FPL, CPL and PPL), or ECLAC's extreme PL would have to be compared with available Y after deducing the corresponding expenditures, rather than with total current Y. Comparing truncated PL with total current Y constitutes the error of asymmetry, which invalidates the use of the PPL and of ECLAC's extreme PL, unless they were compared with available Y, which does not happen.

We can thus rephrase the principle of totality as follows:

> HH's economic capacity to satisfy HN is unitary and indissoluble. It is Y as a whole (when this resource alone is considered) that provides the capacity to satisfy N. Partial economic capacities to satisfy N (for example, food) cannot be formulated as independent economic capacities but should be expressed instead as capacities derived from the unitary, indissoluble economic capacity. HN also constitute an indissoluble system, with which Y is compared in a unified fashion. This is how the neoclassical consumer theory addresses Y and its allocation between different goods. The budget line expresses the purchasing power of Y as a whole. If we compare Y as a whole with a fraction of the cost of satisfying HN, we not only violate the rules of algebra and/or logic but also those of the system of HN.

GPPM4: the good practice of full conceptual and measurement consistency

Since the formulation of the GPPM4 comprises not only full consistency of poverty measurement procedures but also full conceptual consistency, it could also have been classified as a GPPC. Together, the GPPM4 and the GP of full normativity (see below) constitute general guides that complement the principles of totality and dignity.

PPM6 and GPPM5: the principle and good practice of full normativity

The dimensions and thresholds included in each indicator must be defined on normative bases, not empirical ones. The use of observed parameters as norms reflects the rejection of the principle that P is an entangled concept that cannot possibly avoid evaluation. 'Ought' is not equal to 'is', nor does it derive from it. Empirical procedures assume an uncritical stance towards reality and can act as defences of the status quo. Norms are to be derived, essentially, from a conception of HN which, in turn, should be founded on a theory of human essence (see Section 2.5). Human rights are the highest collective expression of such standards, especially when inscribed in laws which are or can be enforced. P and human rights violations tend to become synonymous, especially if the human rights involved are internationally recognised, in which case the norms guiding the study of P become universal. The relative conception of this principle can, however, maintain its validity in the space of S, where differences based on climate, history, culture or perceptions/expectations may exist.

The practice of defining thresholds based on observed parameters is present in both the OECD and the EU, whose PMM define the PL as a certain percent of the observed median or average HH Y. It is also present in the NFB PMM, officially applied by the US PMM and by ECLAC in Latin America, according to which the PL depends, in principle, on the observed value of the Engel coefficient (percentage of HH Y spent on food) which, in turn, is a function of Y (see Chapter 6).

6

A typology of poverty measurement methods: a critique of direct and indirect poverty measurement methods

6.1 A systematic typology: comparison with Gordon et al.'s and Ringen's views of poverty measurement methods

The typology I present here classifies PMM, in the first place, into normative (No), semi-normative (SN) or non-normative (NN) methods. I consider normative those PMM that define the threshold(s) separating the poor from the non-poor based on a notion of the acceptable minimum level of life or on a conception of the N that must be satisfied, and the S required to meet them. No and SN methods are additionally classified on the basis of two characteristics: the direct or indirect nature of the measurement of WB (or deprivation)[1] and the use of one or various indicators in one or various dimensions. This gives rise to the further classification of methods into the categories of direct and indirect, and one-dimensional and multidimensional. The methods that use both direct and indirect indicators I call combined.

In the following pages I compare this typology with Ringen's (1995), as well as with the methods described by Gordon et al. (2000). I include a critique of direct and indirect methods, leaving the critique of combined methods for Chapter 7.

I have not included Sen's CA in the typology, since it has not been made operational to measure P or the standard of living. Neither have I included the measurement of social exclusion, for this concept is different from that of P, regardless of the serious difficulties encountered for its definition and measurement.

Table 6.1 presents a synthetic typology of PPM. The typology is built on three axes: the first axis (displayed in the columns) is the one-dimensional or multidimensional character of each method; the second (displayed in the rows), the indirect, direct or combined nature of each method; and the third

---

[1] Direct measurement is based on observed HH living conditions. Indirect measurement identifies whether available HH resources (most usually reduced to CY) are enough to meet N, regardless of whether these are met or not. Another way to distinguish both procedures is to call them *factual* and *potential* N satisfaction or factual and potential attainment of a certain living standard.

(also shown in the rows), the No, SN or NN character of the methods (the first two categories have been grouped together in the table). All the NN methods included are indirect. With these simplifications, a matrix with potentially 18 cells was reduced to an eight-cell matrix where three cells remain empty. Thus, all of the analysed methods end up grouped in five categories: indirect one-dimensional NN (cell 1.1); indirect one-dimensional SN and No (cell 2.1); indirect multidimensional normative (cell 2.2); direct multidimensional normative (cell 3.2); and combined multidimensional SN and No (cell 4.2). These category names are cumbersome and, given the fact that all direct and combined methods are multidimensional, they can clearly be simplified, so that we can obtain the following (name-simplified) PMM categories: NN, indirect one-dimensional, indirect multidimensional (in fact bi-dimensional), direct, and combined. In Table 6.1, the distinction between SN and No methods has been identified by writing No or SN after the name of each specific method when necessary (cells 2.1, 2.2 and 4.2). I have included the names of some prototypical authors for each method.

The PMM that combines Y and time – which belongs to the third of our five groups of PMM (indirect multidimensional) – is rarely used, and the references in Table 6.1 are almost the only available ones. Nevertheless, the possibility of measuring P indirectly by combining current income (CY) and time (two resources) is implicit in all conceptions that regard HH not only as consumption but also as production units. In modern neoclassical theory as developed by Gary Becker (1965), as well as in feminist thought – where HH are regarded as producers of G&S (transforming raw food into cooked and served food, dirty clothes into clean and ironed clothes, etc.) – it becomes evident that the HH members' WB level depends not only on CY but also on available time (among other things necessary for domestic production). If a HH lacks time for, let us say, cooking, its members will have to eat at restaurants or buy cooked food, spending a larger proportion of CY on food and thus reducing available Y to meet other N. Beyond domestic production, education and sheer enjoyment of life (interactive and ludic activities) also require time. In this chapter I will not be able to broach these methods in detail,[2] but I will briefly describe all the direct and indirect methods included in the typology.

Stein Ringen's (1995) typology of 'measures of well-being' involves two criteria: direct–indirect and narrow–broad. The first would seem to be the same as mine (although it will become apparent that it is not), except that

---

[2] For a detailed and informed discussion on this subject, see Araceli Damián (2003, 2014). IPMM includes time, CY and UBN indicators. When considered on its own, the income–time poverty dimension of IPMM corresponds to this third category in the typology. Damián explains and evaluates how time is addressed in the IPMM. See also Chapter 8.

Ringen does not include the combined category. The second criterion is similar to my one-dimensional vs multidimensional criterion, although I use it as a dichotomy (because I regard methods with two or more components as multidimensional), while Ringen construes it is a continuum. He does not include the normative vs non-normative criterion. He obtains six categories and classifies them in his two-dimensional matrix (Table 6.2) as follows (direct–indirect in the columns; narrow–broad in the rows): in cell 1.1 (indirect and narrow) Ringen includes two categories, the 'income approach' and the 'resource approach'; in cell 1.2 (direct and narrow) he includes the 'expenditure approach' and the 'consumption approach'; in cell 2.1 (indirect and broad) he includes one category, the 'capabilities approach'; lastly, in cell 2.2 (direct and broad) he includes one category, 'the way of life approach' (see Table 6.2).

Appendix 1 of *Poverty and Social Exclusion in Britain,* Gordon et al. (2000, pp 72–75) included a table that describes the following methodological approaches for the measurement of P: 1) *Consensual/social indicators.* This category includes two of the approaches I have classified as direct (cell 3.2): Townsend's deprivation index and Mack and Lansley's ELSPN. It also includes the two approaches called the 'truly poor' (Nolan and Whelan; Halleröd), which I have classified as combined (cell 4.2). 2) *Subjective measures or subjective PLs*, which I have classified, under the second name, as indirect one-dimensional (cell 2.1). 3) *Income thresholds.* This category comprises both the use of CY and of expenditure as observed HH variables, which coincides with my view and disagrees with Ringen's. Three approaches of income thresholds are identified depending on how the PL is determined: a) the PL is equal to an official standard (this I would classify as a non-normative approach, unless the official standard has been determined normatively); b) it is calculated as 50% or 60% of the average Y of all HH (this is a NN approach that I have called purely relativist); and c) the *objective PL.* 4) *Budget standards.* This approach leads to establishing a PL. I have called it – alongside its English name – the GNB (Table 6.1, cell 2.1) to distinguish it from the NFB, which I consider SN. Gordon et al. do not distinguish partial budget approaches from the full budget approach.

Ringen's distinction between the expenditure approach and the Y approach evinces that his interpretation of direct and indirect methods is different from mine. I include the expenditure approach – which according to Ringen's definition employs only one indicator, HH consumption expenditure – together with what he calls the Y approach – which, again, following this author's definition, uses a single indicator, HH income – as two variants of the same PL or indirect one-dimensional approach. Ringen separates these and regards the expenditure approach as a direct method. He defines direct measures as those based on 'information that describes **the outcome** of the choices people *have* made' and indirect as those that 'make use of information that describes the choices [people] *can* make' (1995, p 7; italic emphasis in original, bold added). Ringen follows Sen's distinction in *Poverty and Famines* (1981/1991/1992) between the direct and the Y methods. According to Sen, direct methods are based on information regarding the satisfaction of specified N, whereas the indirect or Y method compares Y with a PL previously identified as the minimum Y required to meet all specified N. In what sense can a single figure on HH expenditure describe the outcomes of choices? Does it describe the (un)satisfaction of each specified N? No, it does not. At most, if the income figure is also available, we could calculate the savings figure and learn something about the choice made between consumption and saving. In Sen's opinion, which I share, the expenditure method is simply a slight variation of the Y approach, but its thrust is the same: potential satisfaction of basic N and not actual or factual satisfaction of them, which is the essence of direct approaches. Ringen states that 'the expenditure approach rests on two strong assumptions, namely that *what* we buy is a valid expression of *what we consume* and that what we consume is a valid expression of well-being' (1995, p 8; emphasis added). However, in the expenditure approach (HH expenditure compared with PL) we do not know what is bought. We only know how much money has been spent. Direct approaches require and emphasise information on the quality of S, which is almost impossible to obtain via expenditure data. Even if we move from the expenditure approach to the consumption approach, we might not get a direct approach unless we have defined norms for each N or lifestyle dimension. The same holds for Ringen's way of life approach.

Within the indirect approach, Ringen goes from Y to a broader concept of resources and then to capabilities. The first step is quite clear. Nevertheless, for the indirect approach to remain as such, everything must be expressed in monetary terms, that is, the calculation of the economic status of HH (or similar concepts). The second step does not seem a broadening of information but, as Sen would say, a change of space. This brings us back to the question of whether the CA constitutes a measurement method (of WB and/or P). I have expressed my opinion at the beginning of this section: I regard it is a conceptual stand that has not been made operational for measurement (see also Section 2.4).

6.2 On non-normative Poverty Measurement Methods

Among the NN methods (cell 1.1 in Table 6.1), we find the purely relativist ones, which define the poor as the population of certain deciles of the Y distribution, or else define the PL as a fraction of the mean (or median) of current observed HH Y. The forerunner of the latter approach was Peter Townsend (1962), who declared that 'individuals and families whose resources, over time, fall seriously short of the resources commanded by the average individual or family in the community in which they live ... are in poverty' (p 225). Abel-Smith and Townsend (1965) established PL of

Table 6.1: Typology of poverty measurement methods

		One-dimensional (1)	Multidimensional (2)
Indirect	Non-normative (NN) (1)	Poverty line (PL) * Purely relativist (EU, OECD) * Other NN PL (Wolf Point) * Other (for example, Engel coefficient) (1.1)	
	Semi-normative (SN) and Normative (N) (2)	* Normative food basket (NFB)[1] (SN) (Orshansky; ECLAC; Mexican Govt) * Food expenditure vs NFB cost * Generalised normative basket[1] (GNB) or budget standards (N) (Rowntree; COPLAMAR; Bradshaw) * Subjective PL (Hagenaars)[1,2] * Objective PL (Townsend and Gordon) (N) (2.1)	* Income-time (Vickery; Douthitt; Boltvinik and Damián) (N) * Income-assets (suggested by Townsend) (N) (2.2)
Direct	Normative (N) (3)		* Unsatisfied basic needs (UBN) Original variant (INDEC; UNDP; RLA/86/004) (N) Improved variant (Boltvinik; UDAPSO) (N) * Deprivation index Original variant (Townsend) (N); Improved variant (Desai and Shah) (N) * Enforced Lack of Socially Perceived Necessities (ELSPN) (Mack and Lansley) (N consensual) Acute Poverty Index (OPHI-UNDP) Individual Deprivation Measure (IDM; Wisor et al.; Pogge and Wisor) * UBN revealed norms (Progresa/Oportunidades) (N) (3.2)

(continued)

Table 6.1: Typology of poverty measurement methods (continued)

	One-dimensional (1)	Multidimensional (2)
Combined Semi-normative (SN) and Normative (N) (4)		*IPMM original version (OV-IPMM; UNDP, RLA/86/004) (N) *IPMM, improved version (IV-IPMM; Boltvinik) (N) *Social Progress Index-Lifetime Deprivation (SPI-LTD) (Desai) (N) *'Truly poor' (Nolan and Whelan; Gordon et al.) (SN) *'Consensual truly poor' (Halleröd) (N consensual) *Double cut-off counting (Alkire and Foster; Foster) *Modified truly poor (Coneval, Mexico) (4.2)

[1] In any of these methods, PL can be compared with Y or expenditure.

[2] When the procedure is based on the minimum Y question for any HH, it can be considered normative consensual, but when it is based on the question about the Y adequacy for the specific HH interviewed, as is the case for the Leyden and Hagenaars procedures, it is non-normative.

Notes on Table 6.1

Cell 1.1 According to the Wolf Point, those HH whose savings are zero or negative are poor. The Engel coefficient method selects a value of this coefficient (percentage spent on food) as its poverty threshold; those above it are poor. For the references on these procedures, see Boltvinik (1999 and 2000 or 2001) and Lidia Barreiros (1992).

Cell 2.1 For the procedures of the NFB, see Section 6.3 and Boltvinik (1999 and 2000 or 2001a). The original work (Orshansky, 1965) has become, since then, the official PMM in the United States. The original version of ECLAC's procedure can be found in Óscar Altimir (1979) and CEPAL-PNUD (1992). For the GNB or budget standards methodology as applied in Mexico, see COPLAMAR (1982a and 1983), as well as Boltvinik and Marín (2003). One of the main variants of the NN approach to the subjective PL is known as the Leyden PL, as it was developed at the University of Leyden (Netherlands). The NN variant, in which the PL is the average Y of people who consider their own Y as sufficient, was developed by T. Goedhart et al. (1977). For an excellent review of the story and an application of the Leyden PL, see Aldi Hagenaars (1986). The normative variant of the subjective PL has been applied, among others, by L. Rainwater (1974). (See text for the reasons why I classify some variants as N and others as NN.)

Cell 2.2 For the references on income-time poverty measures, see text. The combination of Y and assets was suggested by Townsend (1979) but has not been applied. Nevertheless, see Teresita Escotto (2003), where the relation between resources (conceived as assets, both human and non-human) and poverty is analysed systematically by looking at the relationship between poverty (as measured by the IPMM) and resources instead of by properly incorporating assets into the measurement exercise.

Cell 3.2 The original (restricted) variant of UBN was applied for the first time by the Planning Office of Chile (ODEPLAN, 1975). However, the method became generalised after its application, guided by Altimir, at the Institute of Statistics and Census from Argentina (INDEC, 1985). This approach was promoted by the Regional Project to Overcome Poverty (RLA/86/004), UNDP, Latin America. A collection of results is brought together in Luis Beccaria, Julio Boltvinik, Óscar Fresneda and Amartya Sen (1992). For the references for other methods, see text.

Cell 4.2 See text.

Table 6.2: Ringen's typology of approaches to the measurement of well-being

	1. Indirect	2. Direct
1. Narrow	Income approach Resources approach	Expenditure approach Consumption approach
2. Broad	Capabilities	Way of life

Source: Ringen (1995)

50% and 60% of the median Y to measure P in Great Britain. This method is currently one of the most widely used, especially in Europe: it is applied by both the OECD and the EU.[3] According to Nolan and Whelan (1996, p 44), this method's main problem is that 'it does not provide any basis for selecting one threshold instead of another'. The main problem, however, is much more serious: by lowering everyone's income during a recession, far from increasing, P could decrease.[4] The problem with the approach that classifies the population of the lowest deciles as poor is that poverty incidence (H) can never change. Both approaches confuse poverty with inequality. One way to distinguish between both concepts would be to define inequality as a dimension that results from comparing the condition of one HH with that of others but to define P as the result of comparing the condition of HH with a No/threshold or set of No/thresholds. When we qualify people whose Y is below x% of the mean or median Y of the population (which we call the PL) as poor, we appear to be measuring P, but what we are really measuring is inequality, since the mean or median are summary expressions of the whole population's condition. Applying a proportion of this average only serves to identify those who are well below said average.

The Wolf Point or equilibrium point method can also be considered a non-normative PMM. It identifies the PL as the Y level where HH savings are equal to zero. This method relies on the argument that the consumer distributes his budget rationally. I share Barreiros' (1992: 370) opinion that 'this method seems very rudimentary for the analysis of poverty'.[5]

Other authors, such as H.E. Oshima and D. Nanto (cited by Barreiros, 1992) and Watts (cited by Hagenaars, 1986) have proposed identifying the

---

[3] For the OECD procedure, see OECD (2013). For the EU procedure, consult EAPN (no date).
[4] Amartya Sen stated that 'a general decline in income that keeps the chosen measure of inequality unchanged may, in fact, lead to a sharp increase in starvation, malnutrition and obvious hardship; it will then be fantastic to claim that poverty is unchanged' (1981/1991/1992, p 15).
[5] Barreiros quotes M. Bronfenbrenner, *Income Distribution Theory*, Aldine, Chicago, 1971, as a reference for this method.

poor based on the value of their Engel coefficient (E), which equals the proportion of expenditure allocated to food. Watts identified the cut-off point where E reaches a maximum; this would indicate that the HH has reached a point where most urgent food needs have been satisfied. Barreiros found that in Ecuador the PL resulting from this procedure equals less than 50% of the cost of a minimum diet, and for this reason dismissed the method as useless. In the procedure proposed by Watts, the E threshold can be set at any level. As Hagenaars comments, if the E observed among the poor is something one can choose, the method results in a circular definition; if it is chosen based on the median of E, it results in a relative PL. This method, says Hagenaars, assumes that the WB of two HH that spend the same proportion of their Y on food is the same (1986, p 25).

The Wolf Point procedures and those based on the value of E try to identify a pattern of HH behaviour that would indicate that food or all basic N have been satisfied. They could therefore also be called *revealed PL* procedures.

6.3 Description and critique of normative (and semi-normative) direct and indirect methods

I will now briefly describe and appraise each one of the direct and indirect, No and SN methods included in the typology presented in Table 6.1 (cells 2.1, 2.2 and 3.2). Methods in cell 4.2 are broached in Chapter 7.

PL: NFB

This method is SN, for it combines a normative stand on food with an NN (empirical) position on all other N. All variants of the NFB method define a NFB, whose cost is divided by the observed parameter E (which can vary from close to zero to close to 1) to obtain the PL. In some applications (for example, ECLAC and Government of Mexico), the cost of the NFB is considered the extreme PL. The main difference between most variants is the procedure to select E. Some authors select the E observed among the poor (Shari, 1979, quoted by Barreiros, 1992; World Bank, 1990; TCMP, México, 2002). Others select the observed E in the whole population, for example, Mollie Orshansky (1965), who can be considered the designer of the NFB method. A third option is selecting the observed value of E in a reference stratum identified as satisfying its nutritional requirements with minimal expenditure. This was suggested by Townsend[6] and has

---

[6] Townsend (1954, p 135) suggests selecting from among all HH that are able to satisfy their nutritional requirements the fourth part (25%) that attains this with the lowest income, and to interpret average expenditure in this group – minus some fixed costs – as the PL.

been adopted by ECLAC as its official methodology (see Altimir, 1979; CEPAL-PNUD, 1992). I call this the orthodox procedure. As I have shown in Boltvinik (2000), this variant measures food poverty (that is, identifying HH that are unable to buy the NFB due to insufficient Y). This is not the case at ECLAC, among other things, because it has applied the same E to all countries and maintained the absolute value of E since the 1960s (despite enormous variations in observed E values).

Food expenditure vs NFB cost

This is the obvious alternative to the NFB method. It compares the amount spent by a HH on food with the cost of the NFB considering its size and composition. Although I have not come across this method in the literature, it has been applied in Mexico by Boltvinik and Damián (2001) and Damián and Boltvinik (2003), with surprising results: it identifies the largest proportion of P when compared to all the other PMM applied in Mexico.[7] Whether to classify this method as direct or indirect is a difficult question. It could be conceived as a direct one-dimensional poverty measure, arguing that the only expenditure identified is the one allocated to food. Nevertheless, what the method identifies are HH that are potentially capable of meeting food N given the amount they spend on food; however, there is no direct observation to ascertain, for instance, whether the expenditure composition allows the HH to meet their nutritional N as well. These are the reasons why, for the purposes of the typology, I have classified this method as indirect one-dimensional.

PL: GNB or budget approach

This wholly normative approach is the oldest but seldom used PMM. A complete normative basket of G&S is defined and its cost is established as the PL. Developed by Rowntree (1901/1902, 1937, 1941, 1951), this approach has been broadly applied in Mexico under the name of NBES.[8] In the United Kingdom, Bradshaw and Yu (1993) have defined budget standards but have not used them to measure poverty. This methodology prevailed up to World War II. Many countries used it to define minimum wages. The arguments against this method are, in my opinion, very weak. Let us take

---

[7] This would not have been the case, perhaps, if food and overall consumption expenditures had been adjusted to national accounts, and if a similar adjustment (of Y) had been made in methods comparing Y with the PL.

[8] The details of the NBES can be seen in COPLAMAR (1983: Annex II). The PL defined in this way has been used to identify poor HH in Mexico by Hernández Laos (1992), Levy (1991), Alarcón (1993), Lustig (1990), Boltvinik (1996, and many other later works), Damián and Boltvinik (2003), Boltvinik and Damián (2016) and Evalúa CDMX (2022).

shoes as an example. Everybody agrees that in almost all existing societies walking barefoot is shameful (and potentially harmful). Thus, expenditure on shoes should be included in the GNB. With the argument that defining the quality and quantity of shoes is very difficult – or arbitrary, in Atkinson's words[9] – these analysts end up including a total amount of expenditure (Y) for all non-food items, and no one can be sure whether this black box includes any expenditure for shoes at all. In my opinion, these criticisms and the practical alternative lead to greater errors than those made by trying not to avoid 'difficult' or 'arbitrary' decisions. Moreover, applying the principle of the minimal error, explained in Chapter 5, leads to the adoption of the GNB or budget approach.

PL: subjective PL

In sharp contrast with all other PL variants but similar to the ELSPN and the 'truly poor' methods (see below), the variants included under this heading define the PL based on the perceptions of the interviewed population. There are two procedures. The first is the minimum income question, addressed in terms of the Y necessary for any HH of a given size and structure. The average response to this question defines the PL. The second procedure, as described by Hagenaars (1986), requires the interviewed population to qualify a series of Y levels, according to their own specific conditions, as *very bad, bad, insufficient, sufficient, good,* and *very good*. Interviewees are also asked about their CY. From this point, two lines of action can be followed. The most transparent one is to estimate the media of all those who consider their own CY as sufficient. The second line of action estimates sufficient Y as a function of current Y. The point on this function where both current and sufficient Y are equal is the PL. The procedure recognises the positive correlation between CY and people's perception of sufficiency. Although I have classified both lines of action as normative, only the first– the minimum income question – really classifies as such (Rainwater, 1974). The second course of action captures opinions about the necessary Y level to fulfil one's expectations, which increase the higher our CY is. Thus, the so-called PL is really an average of those who have their expectations fulfilled. The number of people below this threshold has nothing to do with H.

---

[9] When analysing absolute poverty, Atkinson says: 'Where precisely the line is drawn depends, therefore, on the judgement of the investigator, and the idea of a purely physiological basis for the poverty criterion is lost', adding, 'In the case of non-food items, there is an even greater degree of arbitrariness' (1983, p 226).

'Objective' PL

Townsend (1979) uses his deprivation index to establish the 'objective PL' that will be used to measure poverty. Townsend adjusted two straight lines to a scatter diagram depicting the deprivation index (y axis) and CY (x axis) of his surveyed HH. The threshold is found where deprivation starts growing faster per unit of decrease in Y, thus revealing said level of income as the threshold. This I have listed as the last PL method (cell 2.1). Poverty is measured based only on Y, and the threshold is identified using the observed association between Y and deprivation, where deprivation is measured using direct indicators only. It could therefore be said that this PL constitutes a potential poverty concept (or resource-based or indirect poverty measurement). Townsend and Gordon (1993) did a similar exercise using the statistical technique of discriminatory analysis to identify the PL. This illustrates the search for an objective poverty threshold that avoids value judgements, something that Piachaud (1981) called the search for the Holy Grail.

Income–time poverty

Under this heading, Table 6.1 (cell 2.2) includes two methods: the one developed by Vickery (1977) and applied by Douthitt (1992), and the one developed by Boltvinik as part of the IPMM and appraised and applied – on its own and combined with Y – by Damián (2003, 2005, 2014). Vickery's approach defines two interrelated poverty thresholds: $Y(M_0)$ and available adult hours for HH management (T_0). If the HH is at M_0, it will require a higher availability of time (T_1), while at T_0 it will require a higher level of $Y(M_1)$. The line uniting points M_0T_1 and M_1T_0 is the income–time poverty threshold. In the first case all domestic work is carried out with the HH's own available time, while in the second all domestic work is carried out by hired persons or replaced through G&S purchases, reducing T to its minimum (time required for personal, mental, and physical maintenance and overall HH management tasks). Vickery identifies substitution possibilities for both resources as well as their irreducible minimum levels. She establishes time requirement norms (for domestic work as an inverse function of Y and for other types of physical and mental maintenance) based on a 1967 time-use survey. Vickery uses the official USA PL – defined by Orshansky (1965) – that, as stated above, is the NFB variant of the PL. This author sets a very low level of normative FT for adults (10 hours a week), thus leaving a huge amount of time (86.6 hours) available for domestic and paid work. Establishing the M_0T_1–M_1T_0 line and calculating income–time H can be done for each HH. As Damián (2003) has argued, Vickery's parameters and norms are set too low.

While developing the IPMM, I included a procedure to identify time poverty and combine it with Y to obtain an income–time poverty measure. Now this combination has been discontinued (see Chapter 8). Time poverty was previously identified with an index of excess work (EW). The norm on the number of hours an available person can work domestically and/or extra-domestically, or the sum of both, was set at 48 hours a week based on Mexican law, and only 28 for students. All adults (15 to 69 years) are considered available for both types of work, except for disabled persons. Students count as $28/48 = 0.5833$ available persons. The total weekly available time in a HH can be obtained by multiplying 48 by the number of available adults. Time required for domestic work was calculated as dependent on three variables: number of persons in the HH, presence of children under 10 years old and an index of intensity of domestic work. This index is calculated based on three indicators: the need to carry water, unavailability of domestic labour-saving equipment and lack of access to day care or schools for children. Total weekly available time minus domestic net work requirements (domestic work performed by paid personnel is subtracted from estimated requirements) equals available time for extra-domestic work, which is then compared with observed weekly work hours to obtain EW. EW was defined in such a way that it varied from 0.5 to 2, with the norm at 1. Values above 1 indicate time P, while values below 1 indicate time availability above the norms. CY is divided into EW to obtain a new concept of Y: *without excess work and performing the required domestic work*. This operation is not performed when the HH is Y poor and has an EW < 1, since 'underwork' in poor HH is considered forced labour. The new concept of Y is then compared with the PL to identify income–time P. Damián carried out a thorough evaluation of the parameters employed in this methodology using time-use and income–expenditure surveys. She concluded that said parameters are 'in orders of magnitude consistent with social practices and that the methodology allows us to identify the HH with higher time deprivation' (2003, p 160; also in Damián 2014). This author introduced some changes to parts of the methodology that we both applied until very recently.

As can be seen, there are some similarities in the methodologies developed by Vickery and myself. When I developed and started applying the IPMM, I was not aware of Vickery's writings, so both developments must be considered independent of each other. The main similarity lies in the fact that we both consider Y as only one WBS and time availability as another important one, although Vickery does not include or perceive the other four WBS. One main difference lies in the normative parameters. While Vickery establishes ten hours a week as the norm for FT, I consider 44 hours a week (six daily hours from Monday to Saturday plus eight hours on Sundays is a distributional option). An additional difference is that I consider weekly work (whether domestic or extra-domestic, or their sum) to be at a maximum of 48 hours per week, while Vickery considers nearly twice as much: 86.6 weekly hours. These differences reflect something more profound, namely that Vickery is looking for available time for domestic work to complement available Y, while I – like Damián – am looking for available FT.

UBN: restricted original variant

Each of the included dimensions (which are very few in this variant) is evaluated for every HH, so that one can get a horizontal panorama of each HH's WB condition. The procedure in this method is identified as follows: a threshold is defined for every dimension; each HH's observed condition is compared with the corresponding threshold and a dichotomy is built; when the observed condition is on or above the threshold, it is qualified as a satisfied basic N (zero score), and when it is below the threshold, it is qualified as a UBN, receiving a score of 1.[10] Any HH with one or more UBN is considered poor. If the sum of scores is equal to or higher than 1, the HH is considered poor. This is a union approach criterion of P. The approach allows us to calculate the relative headcount or H index. However, because of the dichotomised indicators and the absence of an explicit weighting procedure, this variant does not allow us to estimate the relative P gap or poverty intensity index (I)[11] or, for that matter, any of the more elaborated APM. Something more damaging is the fact that the P criterion that identifies as poor all HH with one or more UBN, turns H into a function of the number of items (N) included in the exercise: the larger the number of items, the higher the incidence.[12] This is a perverse

---

[10] This is also how Townsend (1979) scored his dichotomic-type indicators (see his index of deprivation below). Desai and Shah (1988) formalised his procedure, but in the Latin American UBN tradition, scores are not used explicitly.

[11] Naturally, one could consider that all indicators have the same weight and calculate I (see Chapter 9) as the quotient of dividing the number of UBN (items) by the total number of N (items) considered. This form of calculation would still be quite limited because of the dichotomic nature of the indicators, which grades a N as equally unsatisfied whether the HH is near the threshold or very far from it. For instance, if the norm adopted for availability of space in the dwelling is two persons per dormitory, the dichotomy classifies a HH with 2.5 persons per dormitory and a HH with 10 persons per dormitory as being in the same condition.

[12] The reason is very simple: if one adds one indicator to a given procedure – originally having, for instance, five indicators – some HH that had previously not been found to be deprived, will be found deprived after the sixth indicator has been added: they will now be classified as poor whereas before they were non-poor. However, HH that had previously been classified as poor cannot be reclassified as non-poor even if they meet the threshold for the sixth indicator.

and unacceptable feature for any PMM and might explain why the method uses such a reduced number of items (indicators). I therefore call it the restricted UBN variant. The usual indicators include adequacy of housing materials, space availability in the dwelling, adequacy of water provision and excretal disposal system, and school attendance by children of certain ages. Since all indicators are absolute measures, with fixed thresholds over time, P always shows a downwards trend as society modernises. This approach has been extensively applied in Latin America (though not in Mexico) to build P maps. (See UBN empirical studies in Latin America in the references.)

UBN improved variant (UBN-IV)

The features that distinguish this IV from the OV are the following: this variant allows the proper calculation of the P gap for every HH as well as the aggregated poverty gap; H is not a function of the number of indicators included; it operates with a wider list of indicators (both in number and scope); and a mechanism of expectations is introduced as an additional element in the definition of the thresholds for each indicator. This implies a relative conception of P, for each specific threshold becomes related to achieved modal levels in a society. In order to attain these features, the following was done: dichotomy indicators were transformed into numerical multilevel indicators,[13] thus building fully cardinalised scales, and indicators were combined using weights based on each item's share in the total normative costs to obtain the overall index for each HH (this is not the only possible reasonable weighting procedure). Conceptually, the purpose of poverty measurement is to express the OWB level implied in each alternative solution to a N. For non-metric original variables, the WB associated with each solution is expressed by a numerical value (a multiple or fraction of the threshold's numerical value), implying a qualitative WB function. In metric variables (already expressed as threshold fractions or multiples), a rescaling procedure is performed for values above the threshold, rendering an implicit WB function. Here, WB is proportional to the variable's level up to the threshold; between the latter and the conceptual maximum, WB

---

[13] This procedure sometimes requires an ordinal scale to be transformed into a cardinal one. Let us imagine, for instance, that a series of alternative solutions for water provisioning are ordered from worst to best in an ordinal scale. The latter is transformed into a cardinal scale by imputing a WB positional score (in a standardised scale running from 0 to 2, where 1 is the threshold), which is not a welfarist (utilitarian) scale (that is, dealing with subjective feelings of happiness, pleasure or utility) but an objective scale (dealing with objective conditions of WB). This standardisation transforms all scales (given in different units of measurement) into a unique WB scale. Although the latter implies a judgement, it can, and should, be an informed judgement. This is what the PPM4, 'full and replicable cardinalisation', is about.

is less than proportional but linear; above the maximum, marginal WB is zero. This rescaling procedure is also applied to Y in the IV-IPMM (see Chapter 7).[14] This function can be improved. The UBN-IV for poverty measurement was applied on its own in the development of the Poverty Map of Bolivia (UDAPSO, 1994). It has also been extensively applied as one of the three components of the IPMM (alongside Y and time) in Mexico. The procedure to build the integrated UBN index for HH_J involves the following steps after the non-cardinal variable X_{IJ} for HHJ in dimension I has been assigned a cardinal WB value:

1. An achievement indicator A_{IJ} is built for dimension I and HHJ: $A_{IJ} = X_{IJ} / X\star_I$, where $X\star_I$ is the threshold in dimension I; A_{IJ} varies from 0 to n; values at the threshold are scored as 1; n will be 2 for ordinal variables (except in truncated variables, where conditions above the threshold are not captured or not captured fully in surveys), but will usually be higher than 2 for original cardinal variables; A_{IJ} is standardised by dividing X_{IJ} by $X\star_J$, so that it will be expressed in multiples/fractions of the threshold (normative value).
2. In the case of original cardinal variables (for example, years of schooling or rooms per person), values of A_{IJ} above the threshold (1 or more) are rescaled with the double purpose of transforming them into a WB indicator (which at this point they are not) and adjusting their range to the standard range 0 to 2: $A'_{IJ} = [(A_{IJ} - 1) / (\max A_{IJ} - 1)] \mid A_{IJ} > 1$. With this formula, the range 1 to n of A_{IJ} is reduced to 1 to 2; max A_{IJ} is the conceptual maximum previously referred to, where marginal WB is zero. In the range 1 to max, WB increases less than proportionally with S. Only values above 1 are rescaled because, as already stated, below the threshold (norm) the implicit WB function entails decreases in deprivation (increases in achievement) in proportion to increases in S.
3. A deprivation indicator is obtained as follows: $D'_{IJ} = 1 - A'_{IJ} = I_{ij}$, which varies from −1 to +1 (except in truncated variables). Values at the threshold are equal to 0. We now have fully cardinal indicators, normalised with the threshold and with a homogeneous range (except in the case of truncated indicators).
4. The HH UBN_J deprivation integrated indicator is obtained as follows:

$$D(UBN_J) = I(UBN)_J = \Sigma_I k_I D'_{IJ},$$ where k_I is the weight of indicator I defined in terms of the relative participation of dimension I in

---

[14] This rescaling is the practical form of applying PPM1 and PPM2 in the IPMM: 'Decreasing marginal OWB above thresholds' and 'existence of an OWB maximum'.

the social costs of satisfaction (at the threshold level) of the UBN package of N/S.

UBN-IV overcomes the two main limitations of UBN-OV in two ways. First, H, as a function of the number of indicators, is overcome by making all indicators vary from −1 to +1 and adopting the weighting procedure to obtain $D(UBN)_{IJ}$, which implies that introducing more indicators can mean both increasing or decreasing H. Second, the inability to calculate poverty intensity (I) (and hence all other more elaborated APM), is overcome in steps 2) and 3), through which I_{IJ} is obtained.

Townsend's deprivation index

In Chapter 6 of *Poverty in the United Kingdom* (Townsend, 1979), Townsend calculated a deprivation index which can be interpreted as an approximation to a direct method. He did this based on 12 indicators that he chose for heuristic purposes from 60 he had built beforehand. Although Townsend did not identify P on the basis of this index, this could be done by devising a P criterion (for example, a deprivation score of 3 or more).

Deprivation index, improved variant

Desai and Shah (1988, reprinted in Desai, 1995) propose using a continuous measure for each HH, adequate to calculate APM, thus overcoming some of the limitations of Townsend's index. In other words, they propose full cardinalisation, beyond dichotomies, but they do so by expressing all consumption experiences as events. The frequency of these events can be obtained by applying a questionnaire. Subsequently, the modal frequencies become the normative values. Having frequencies below the norms due to lack of resources is a sign of deprivation. Lack of resources is distinguished from tastes through econometric analyses. As a weighting procedure to combine specific deprivation indicators into a global HH indicator, the authors suggest weighting each item against the proportion of the population that is able to satisfy said item. This would reflect the subjective feelings of deprivation, which are more intense when one belongs to a deprived minority than when the majority is deprived. Desai and Shah's proposal was stated in the context of the Townsend–Piachaud debate about the objective Y threshold (see objective PL above); it is therefore not clear whether they did figure out an intrinsic poverty criterion or were using Townsend's idea of finding the point in the Y scale where deprivation starts increasing rapidly. This index has not been applied.

Enforced Lack of Socially Perceived Necessities (ELSPN)

The emphasis of this approach is on lifestyle. In order to avoid Piachaud's criticism (1981) regarding Townsend's work in the sense that many of his indicators reflect tastes or preferences and not necessarily deprivation, Mack and Lansley (1985) introduced the concept of *enforced lack*. This concept considers that deprivation is present in a socially perceived necessity when its lack is due to an inability to pay (when the interviewee states that they lack a certain item because they cannot afford it). This course of action assumes that restriction in CY is the only possible cause of deprivation. It begs the question on the WBS. The fact that Mack and Lansley's work is the point of departure for a whole generation of combined methods left a 'birthmark' in all these combined procedures, which reproduce this interviewing procedure. This method includes many more indicators than the restricted original UBN method and requires a different poverty criterion. Mack and Lansley adopted three or more enforced lacks (from their list of 26 socially perceived necessities) as constituting P. Because of the dichotomic character of the indicators used, the procedure does not allow analysts to calculate the intensity (I) of deprivation, or each HH's gap (distance) vis à vis the threshold. Given this restriction and the fact that the method does not include the calculation of an overall index for every HH, the P intensity or gap cannot be adequately calculated at the individual or aggregated levels,[15] nor can the more elaborated poverty aggregated measures be estimated. It shares with UBN-OV the very damaging feature that H becomes a function – if the poverty criterion is fixed–, of the number of items considered. In contrast to most previous approaches, which depend on expert judgement or on expectations, but with some similarity to subjective PLs, the definition of thresholds is here defined by a democratic procedure based on a subjective majority.[16]

Acute Multidimensional Poverty Index (AMPI)

This index applies the 'double cut counting' methodology developed by Sabina Alkire and James Foster (2009) (see Chapter 7). As recorded in the

---

[15] As in the case of the original version of UBN, the ELSPN leaves the possibility open for dividing the number of enforced lacks by the total number of items to obtain a precarious measure of the individual gap.

[16] Socially perceived necessities are, according to Mack and Lansley's classification, those items considered necessary by more than 50% of the interviewees. Gordon et al. call this approach 'consensual', which would be an appropriate designation if these necessities were defined as those identified by, say, 75% or more of the interviewees.

Human Development Report, no. 20, 2010, the UNDP decided to apply the AMPI to 104 developing countries. The base document was prepared by Alkire and Santos (2010). Unlike the original approach by Alkire and Foster (2009), the AMPI does not include the Y dimension, which is why I classified it as a direct multidimensional method rather than a combined one.

The AMPI defines three dimensions: health, education, and standard of living. Each dimension has the same weight (1/3) when combining all the indicators for the identification of poor HH. The established thresholds are an example of extreme minimalism, which is more evident in the indicators for education, water/sanitation and durable goods. In education, for instance, an illiterate HH is considered no longer deprived if a child member finishes grammar school. The only thing that matters regarding water is the liquid itself, not the form of supply, so that carrying water up to half an hour (each time it is needed) is tolerated. Moreover, classifying as non-deprived people who only have two durables out of a given list is evidently quite minimalistic. One way to fully appreciate the minimalism of the thresholds is by observing the deficiency levels for each indicator in Mexico. These can fluctuate between 0.6% in electricity and drinking water up to 2.8% in cooking fuel. Education and health, which are among those with the greatest weight, range from 0.7% in nutrition to 2.1% in years of schooling.

Once the deficiencies are established for each indicator, the poverty criterion is as follows: poor HH – including all their members – are those that have the equivalent of three or more standardised deficiencies out of a possible total of ten; in other words, those whose sum of deficiencies (each multiplied by its weight) is higher than 0.3 (or 3 if multiplied by 10). Thus, the very low (minimalist) thresholds in each indicator, complemented by the minimalist criterion of the low number of standardised deficiencies, are almost leading to the disappearance of poverty in Latin America and even more clearly in East European countries. Mexico, with a poverty rate of 4%, Ecuador with 2.2%, and Brazil with 8.5% could entrust their small poverty problem to private philanthropy and dedicate government resources to other causes. Mahbub ul Haq, creator of the Human Development Report, would be quite unhappy to see that the institution he created to offer an alternative vision to that of the World Bank is now competing with the latter to see who minimises world poverty the most. Aware of this situation, the authors – and the institutions that support them – affirm that AMPI reflects 'deprivations in very rudimentary services'.

Individual Deprivation Measure (IDM)

Based on participatory research in poor communities in six countries, the IDM (Wisor et al., no date; Pogge and Wisor, no date) replaces the usual HH measures of P with an individual one. Although it includes a 'proxy' indicator of income/consumption, it does not combine it with the 15 deprivation indicators considered in the first dimension to obtain a single final measure but handles both as separate dimensions (as Townsend does). I have therefore classified IDM as a multidimensional direct method. It includes many uncommon deprivation indicators, such as control of decision in the HH, experience of violence, access to contraception, exposure to environmental harms, and status of respect in work. Like the IV-IPMM, IDM rejects dichotomic indicators and opts for cardinalising ordinal ones. It also includes (again, like the IPMM) the diminishing marginal value of successive improvements in S to value HH conditions. It could be argued that many additions are alien to the concept of poverty; for example, in a violent society all social groups are exposed to violent actions, or rich families can be very authoritarian. The proxy indicator of income/consumption (or asset index) is inadequate to capture sudden changes (due, for instance, to a depression or a pandemic) in P (contrary to the income indicator, which has this ability as one of its salient positive features), since assets might have been acquired years before.

Revealed or objective UBN thresholds

As Gómez de León (1998) points out, the 'central aspect of discriminatory analysis consists in identifying existing differences in multidimensional profiles (on the discriminant variables) between provisionally poor families and those who are not', and in establishing a rule which allows a reallocation of each family to one of the two groups on the basis of the multidimensional profile.[17] In other words, this method – as applied by *Progresa* (later *Oportunidades* and finally *Prospera*, which disappeared in 2018) – consists in dividing the population into two groups on the basis of an extreme PL (which is equal to the cost of a food basket and assumes HH can spend 100% of their income on said basket), and then correcting the initial grouping using discriminatory analysis. The use of only one PL instead of a set of PLs – which is what statistical methods suggest – has implications that are analysed later. As Gómez de León explains (1998, p 19–20), a linear combination of the discriminatory variables is estimated for each of the preliminary groups of poor and non-poor. This renders a new one-dimensional variable Z, which is a weighted average of the selected variables, where weights are determined internally by using the model to maximise the standard distance between the means of the poor, Z_p, and those of the non-poor, Z_{NP}. These means are multivariate 'centroids that typify the profile of the two groups of families'. Finally, 'a family is classified in the group from whose centroid

---

[17] This paragraph is based on Boltvinik and Cortés (2000).

it is less distant, or which has greater probabilities of having been extracted as a random selection' (Gómez de León, 1998, p 20).

The procedure adopted by *Progresa* can be seen as the inverse of the one adopted by Townsend and Gordon. While these authors employ the direct deprivation scores (regarded by them as based on people's participation in a style of living, as opposed to UBN deprivation scores) to define the objective PL, *Progresa* uses the PL to define the objective set of UBN poverty thresholds, the Z_{PL} separating the poor from the non-poor. Nonetheless, this is done by *Progresa* in a non-conscious and contradictory way. First, the extreme PL (EPL) is selected without any discussion, in deep contrast with Townsend (1979) and Townsend and Gordon (1993), who conform a system of scores based on a highly elaborated conception and a very rich intellectual history. While deriving a PL on the basis of a deprivation scoring system with such a solid base seems defensible (although certainly disputable), deriving a UBN profile based on an arbitrary (and very difficult to defend) PL is, on the contrary, not defensible.

In this case, the orthodox procedure in discriminatory analysis would use a set of EPL to classify, as a first step, people who are undoubtedly extremely poor or undoubtedly non-extremely poor. This leaves an intermediate group to which discriminatory analysis would then be applied to further classify its members in their corresponding groups. The undoubtedly extremely poor would be those who have an income below all the EPL and, conversely, the undoubtedly non-extremely poor would be those who have an income above all the EPL. A number of doubtful cases would remain: those who are above or below some, but not all, the EPL. As *Progresa* uses only one EPL instead of a set, and as this is the lowest used in Mexico, HH identified as extremely poor in the first step can be regarded as such without any doubt. However, the same does not apply to the non-extremely poor, since many among them would be identified as extremely poor with other EPL. If the orthodox procedure were followed, the undoubtedly extremely poor and Z_p would be the same as in *Progresa*, but the undoubtedly non-extremely poor would have a higher average income and their Z – let us call it Z'_{NP} – would be farther from Z_p than Z_{NP}. Therefore, while the distance from any intermediate HH to Z_p would remain unchanged, its distance to Z'_{NP} would always be greater than its distance to Z_{NP}. Consequently, the number of cases classified as extremely poor would increase were the orthodox procedure used. In other words, Z'_{PL} would be higher than Z_{PL} and thus the number of extremely poor would be larger. In a nutshell, the way *Progresa/Oportunidades/Prospera* applied discriminatory analysis minimised extreme poverty.

7

Combined methods of poverty measurement

7.1 Description and critique of combined methods included in the typology

IPMM, original variant (OV-IPMM)

Two separate explorations carried out by Beccaria and Minujin (1987) and Kaztman (1989) enquiring whether the UBN-OV and PL-NFB methods identified the same HH as poor, and obtaining negative answers, became a model for the simultaneous application of both methods. The result was a contingency table (matrix) in which HH and population were classified in four categories: poor on both; non-poor on both; poor only by UBN; and poor only by PL. To this, Boltvinik (1990a) added a poverty criterion and identified a new method: OV-IPMM, which was adopted and broadly applied by UNDP's Regional Project to Overcome Poverty in Latin America (RLA/86/004). The method has a number of interesting features, one of which is that in certain circumstances it allows the distinction between a recently impoverished population (strongly associated with the poor only by PL in countries going through a recession or economic crisis) and a more structural type of poverty (poor on both methods). OV-IPMM also allows analysts to *identify poverty of publicly provided goods*. The newly adopted poverty criterion, derived from the notion of the complementary nature of both original methods (PL and UBN) and the conception of WBS explained in Chapter 1, is that only those identified by the union of both sets are poor, which means, in turn, that only HH identified as non-poor by both methods are non-poor. Nevertheless, this method has various limitations. First, it identifies only food P, as it incorporates the NFB variant in the Y dimension; second, the incidence of UBN P is not independent from the number of indicators; third, it cannot calculate the HH poverty gap I_j nor, in consequence, any other APM, except for the incidence or proportion of poor people in the population; fourth, it does not consider two WBS: FT and knowledge/abilities; and lastly, the poverty criterion is difficult to uphold: a millionaire HH not sending its child to school, for example, is considered poor.

IPMM, improved variant (IV-IPMM)

Designed to overcome the limitations of the original variant,[1] this method combines the UBN-IV with the PL budget approach and the time poverty indicator explained in previous chapters to obtain an integrated P index for each HH. In doing so, this variant overcomes all the limitations of the previous method. By including the budget approach or GNB in the Y dimension, it goes beyond food P. The second and third limitations are overcome by adopting the improved variant of UBN, thus allowing the calculation of all APM and preventing the level of P from being a function of the number of indicators. It overcomes the fourth limitation by including educational level in UBN and incorporating time poverty as a third dimension. Lastly, it adopts $I(IPMM)_j > 0$ as the P criterion, a very good criterion inasmuch as, among other things, it incorporates compensations so that the millionaire not sending their child to school will not be classified as poor. The index can be disaggregated into its components to obtain a truly detailed and dynamic deprivation profile. We can also estimate the contribution of each dimension and component to the P integrated index and build contingency tables in two, three, or more dimensions. The method has been applied mainly in Mexico, but Y. B. Guillén Fernández (2017) has also used it for UK data.

Social Progress Index – Lifetime Deprivation (SPI-LTD)

In many aspects, this seminal contribution of Meghnad Desai[2] is similar to the IV-IPMM (for a comparison of both methods, see Boltvinik, 1993

---

[1] The seminal contribution to the IPMM is Boltvinik (1992a); very detailed empirical applications can be found in Boltvinik (1994b, 1995, 1996, 1999, and 2012), in Boltvinik and Damián (2016), and in Evalúa CDMX (2022); in Boltvinik (1993 and 1994) IPMM is compared with Desai's approach (1992).

[2] Desai's SPI-LTD, conceived as an *achievement set* (that is, as a measure of the *aim* of development) evolved alongside Boltvinik's *opportunity set*, conceived as a measure of the *process* of development. Together they form the Social Progress Index (SPI). As there can be 'unequal development' between both sets in a given society, countries can be classified according to their efficiency in transforming opportunities into WB (see Meghnad Desai, Amartya Sen, and Julio Boltvinik, 1992). In the cited publication, Desai's index is presented in chapter 3, 'Well Being and Lifetime Deprivation: A Proposal for an Index of Social Progress'. Amartya Sen wrote chapter 1, 'Progress and Social Deficit. Some Methodological Issues'. Boltvinik wrote chapter 2, 'Towards an Alternative Indicator of Development', and the 'Introduction', which provides an overview and presents both elements synthetically: the opportunity set and the achievement set. The achievement set has not been empirically applied. In chapter 2 a simplified version of the opportunity set was used to rank 143 countries, and also to assess Colombia through time (in yearly figures) from 1970 to 1988.

and 1994b). Still, there are some important differences. First, the SPI-LTD does not include FT, as the IPMM does. Instead, it includes *quantity of life* as a third dimension, separate from UBN and PL. Second, the weighting procedure for specific UBN indicators is different: instead of participation in social costs, Desai considers the proportion of the population meeting each item.[3] Third, UBN and PL indicators in SPI-LTD are combined using a multiplicative format instead of the weighted average used in IPMM. Fourth, SPI-LTD uses an explicit WB function (Atkinson type) to transform the global satisfaction index into WB, while in IPMM this transformation is implicit when applying two processes for each indicator: first, equalising their range (all deprivation indicators are adjusted within a range from −1 to +1) by re-escalating the values above the norm for those indicators that are originally cardinal, and second, giving scores in that range to those which are originally ordinal. Desai's quantity of life indicator – called 'proportion of life potential realised in capable conditions' – cannot be calculated for individuals but only for groups; it therefore requires a previous classification of individuals in terms of their condition in the quality-of-life dimension (UBN and PL). Once this is done, the proportion of lifetime potential realised is calculated for each group of individuals, grouped by age and WB stratum. Each individual will then receive the value of the proportion of life potential realised from the group to which they belong.

The truly poor

Nolan and Whelan (1996) and Gordon et al. (2000) are based on Townsend's definition of poverty and on the distinction, introduced by Mack and Lansley, between two causes of non-participation in an event (or consumption activity): tastes and resource constraints, which leads them to adopt the concept of 'enforced lack'. Nolan and Whelan show that the correlation between below-PL Y and enforced lack is not as high as one would expect. These authors operationalise 'exclusion due to lack of resources' as a condition in which a HH has at least one enforced lack item *and* is below a purely relativist PL (less than 40%, 50%, or 60% of median HH Y), which I have classified in the typology as NN. As a result, they consider only those HH in cell 1.1 of Table 6.1 (first row and first column) as poor. In the matrix version of the IPMM, these HH are called the *total or chronic poor*, labelled as *consistently poor* by Nolan and Whelan. Gordon et al. also regard the HH in cell 1.1 as poor but

---

In Boltvinik (2003b) an improved version of the opportunity set is empirically applied to Mexico from 1981 to 2000 (for years with available data).

[3] As I have stated before, the weighing procedure is not essential in a method and can be modified without affecting its essence.

identify them as those having two or more enforced lack items and being below a PL estimated statistically according to its association with enforced lacks.

Consensual truly poor

Similarly to the previous method, Halleröd (1995) only considers poor HH whose income is below a PL (in this case defined with the subjective or consensual approach) *and* who show a high deprivation index, although there is no defined threshold in this dimension. The author modifies Mack and Lansley's ELSPN procedure by considering all items when calculating the index rather than only those which the majority of the population finds necessary, as Mack and Lansley do. However, Halleröd weighs each item by the proportion of the population who considers it necessary.

Dual cut-off counting

This method (Alkire and Foster, 2009; Foster, 2010) uses the counting-based approaches that have appeared in the sociology literature. The identification of the poor is accomplished with the help of two types of cut-offs. First, the *domain-specific poverty cut-off*, which defines a person as being deprived in a specific dimension when the achievement falls below the cut-off. The second, a *cross-dimensional cut-off*, indicates the minimum range of deprivations necessary before a person is considered poor. Each dimension of WB is given a weight (usually equal weights), with all weights summing up to one. A person is considered poor if the sum of the weights in the dimensions where they are deprived exceeds (or equals) the specified cut-off, and non-poor if it amounts to less. This now highly fashionable procedure can be seen as a UBN-OV method in which the union approach has been replaced by an arbitrary number of deprivations (or sum of weights) that function as a threshold, and *where Y can be included* as one of the dimensions.

Modified truly poor

By law, P measurement in Mexico must be multidimensional and has to be carried out by a semi-autonomous agency, Coneval. The official method adopted by Coneval in December 2009 is a variant of the intersection or truly poor approach and thus underestimates P: to be considered poor, a HH has to be both below the PL *and* be deprived in one or more (out of a total of six) UBN dimensions defined in the law. However, within UBN the method adopts a union approach, in which suffering one deprivation is enough to be considered deprived, which leads to overestimating deprivation in this dimension. To compensate for this, UBN thresholds are set at a very low level indeed. Populations in cells 1.2 and 2.1 of Table 6.1 are considered *vulnerable* (not poor), so that the method creates a dual calculation of disadvantage: *poverty and vulnerability*.

7.2 Prevailing disagreement on the poverty criterion among combined methods

Out of the many conclusions that can be drawn from the typology presented in Table 6.1, I want to address two issues: on the one hand, the trend to move from direct to combined methods, both in the European tradition and in Latin America; on the other hand, the almost complete disagreement on the poverty criterion that prevails among combined methods.

Latin America moved from the PL and UBN methods to the IV-IPMM, adding FT. Europe went from the ELSPN to the combined methods known as 'truly poor'. In the same fashion, Desai moved away from the improved variant of the deprivation index – a direct method, as we have seen – to the SPI-LTD, a combined method. So combined methods are the baseline of the innovative direction, the new search undertaken in the last two decades of the twentieth century and in the twenty-first century regarding the measurement of P. But the new current of thought, as we might call it, does not derive its worth merely from being a novelty. What we should welcome from this new development is that, in its contradictions, as we will see, it reflects the importance of taking all WBS into account. Among combined methods (cell 4.2 in Table 6.1) there are enormous disparities – as is to be expected when new paths are being explored. When a direct and an indirect approach are combined (or at least used simultaneously), two differences appear: how each approach is used within the method (the role it plays) and the poverty criterion adopted (the criterion that identifies who is poor and who is not).

While both the objective PL method – which resorts to the direct measurement of deprivation (without establishing a poverty criterion in this dimension) to reveal an indirect threshold – and the method of the UBN revealed norms – which uses a PL to reveal the UBN norms – might be considered combined in a very special sense, all other combined methods included in Table 6.1 (cell 4.2) are combined in a more precise sense: they identify the poor *on both dimensions* as part of the measurement procedure.

Table 7.1 presents the matrix (or contingency table) formed when identifying the poor in both dimensions. Before the dual cut-off method was devised by Alkire and Foster, all methods identified the HH/individuals in cell 1.1 as poor by using the combined procedure, that is, poor on both the direct and the indirect procedures (from now on direct and indirect poor). But in dual cut-off counting, some HH/persons in this cell might be non-poor, as a separate account dividing the direct and indirect dimensions is not required. Apart from the seven methods classified as combined in Table 6.1, I have added the

Table 7.1: Poverty criteria in combined methods

	Direct poor (UBN, deprivation index, or ELSPN*)	Direct non-poor (UBN, deprivation index, or ELSPN*)
Indirect poor (PL or PLT)	*(cell 1.1)* 1. Objective PL (Townsend and Gordon) 2. UBN revealed norms (*Progresa*) 3. Pre-IPMM (Kaztman; ECLAC) 4. OV-IPMM (Boltvinik, UNDP-LA) 5. SPI-LTD (Desai) 6. IV-IPMM (Boltvinik) 7. 'Truly poor' (Nolan and Whelan; Gordon et al.) 8. 'Consensual truly poor' (Halleröd) 9. Dual cut-off counting (Alkire and Foster; Foster) (some HH*) 10. 'Modified truly poor' (Coneval, Mexico)	*(cell 1.2)* 1. Objective PL 3. Pre-IPMM 4. OV-IPMM 5. SPI-LTD 6. IV-IPMM (some HH*) 9. Dual cut-off counting (some HH*)
Indirect non-poor (PL or PLT)	*(cell 2.1)* 2. UBN revealed norms 4. OV-IPMM 5. SPI-LTD (some HH*) 6. IV-IPMM (some HH*) 9. Dual cut-off counting (some HH*)	*(cell 2.2)*

Note: Households in indicated cells are poor for each method.

* *Depending on the specific values.* IV-IPMM also includes the time dimension, which was combined with PL to obtain PLT in the recently modified version. See Chapter 8 for the latest changes to the IV-IPMM. The other methods do not include time, but SPI-LTD includes the quantity of life.

procedure followed by Beccaria and Minujin (1987), by Kaztman (1989), and by ECLAC. I have called the last of these the pre-IPMM; it consists in calculating both partial methods and putting them together in a contingency table without establishing a combined method. I have also included the objective PL and the UBN revealed norms. Out of the ten procedures included, nine consider HH in cell 1.1 as poor and those in cell 2.2 as non-poor. Procedures 7, 8, and 10 (the 'truly poor', the 'consensual truly poor', and the 'modified truly poor') only consider those in cell 1.1 as poor. All other methods consider at least those (or part of those) in one additional cell as poor.

If one looks at cell 1.2, which holds only the indirect poor (by PL), and at cell 2.1, which holds only the direct poor (by UBN, ELSPN, or the deprivation index only), disagreement looms large. Four methods always consider the indirect poor (cell 1.2) as actually poor: the objective PL, the pre-IPMM, the OV-IPMM, and the SPI-LTD. According to the IV-IPMM, a fraction of the HH in cell 1.2 will be poor, while the rest will not, depending on the values of the partial deprivation UBN and the PLT indices. The objective PL and the pre-IPMM methods consider all the HH in cell 1.2 as poor because these methods actually measure poverty indirectly (by Y); the direct indicators are used in the first method only to reveal the PL, and in the second to characterise the poor, who are identified only by PL. The OV-IPMM considers any HH below the PL or poor by UBN, or both, as poor. In other words, P in this method is defined by the union of the two sets. In the SPI-LTD, HH in this cell are always poor because the values of the UBN achievement indicators range only from 0 to 1 (where 1 is the norm and 0 the worst possible condition); when these values are multiplied by CY, modifying or correcting it before comparing it with the PL, we see that UBN indicators can diminish Y, but they can never increase it. Therefore, all those who are poor by Y will continue to be so by the combined index, but some who were not will become poor. Table 7.1 locates the IV-IPMM in its previous version, although the results may be applicable to the new version in which time, UBN, and PL are combined in a single step. In the IV-IPMM, in contrast to the SPI-LTD, since both indices can be negative or positive, a HH only poor by PLT (the same as one only poor by UBN) can turn out to be poor or non-poor when combined with UBN or with PLT.[4] In dual cut-off counting, some HH in this cell could be considered poor.

HH in cell 2.1 are always poor according to UBN revealed norms (*Progresa*) and by the OV-IPMM. In the first case, this is because the method really identifies the poor solely by UBN and uses the PL only to reveal UBN norms or thresholds.[5] In the second case, it is the union of both sets that constitutes the universe of poverty. In the SPI, the IV-IPMM, and dual cut-off counting, HH in cell 2.1 may or may not be poor: in the first case, because Y above the PL, when multiplied by a number smaller than 1, may result in a modified Y, which might (or might not) still be above the P; in the second case, for the reasons already explained for cell 1.2.

As we can see, all logical possibilities as to the cells where HH are to be regarded as poor have been adopted by at least one method. The disagreement could not be larger. Leaving aside the quasi-combined methods (objective PL and UBN revealed norms), there is a fundamental difference between the

---

[4] This also depends on the procedure and weights used to combine UBN with PLT. I have used a weighted average of both indices to obtain the integrated index for each HH. By having used the structure of social costs as weights, I had obtained a weight of around 2/3 for PLT and 1/3 for UBN. The weights can be modified without altering the essence of the IPMM.

[5] Naturally, revealed norms/thresholds depend on the PL selected when only one PL is used, as was the case in *Progresa*. This renders the process circular: if one selects a very low PL, one will get very low UBN thresholds. Therefore, *revealed* is very far from *objective*. The same comment applies to the so-called objective PL. If the items included in the ELSPN change, one ends up with quite a different objective PL.

Latin American methods (including Desai's SPI-LTD in this group) and the European ones. The methods employing the direct approach of ELSPN seek to identify deprivation enforced by Y restrictions. Enforced lack is identified as deprivation in items which the majority considers to be necessary for any HH and which the person interviewed wants to have (or do) but cannot because they cannot afford it. So, to use Halleröd's words, direct and indirect measurements are two sides of the same coin: Y limitations on one side (the indirect approach) and its manifestation as enforced deprivation (in the direct approach). In both measurements, the only WBS of a given HH is CY.

Nevertheless, the authors of these methods have not explicitly assumed the previous observations. For instance, when referring to socially perceived necessities, Nolan and Whelan point out: 'In assessing which of these items are suitable as indicators of deprivation, we are interested not only in whether they are regarded as a necessity or possessed by most of the sample, *but also their relationship with income*' (1996, p 80; emphasis added). The measure of deprivation they look for is, thus, enforced lack due to Y limitation. These authors consider the answer 'I cannot afford this expenditure (item)' as a self-evaluated enforced lack and assert that these subjective evaluations have to be regarded carefully. Previously, they stated: 'our own results confirm Hagenaar's suspicion that the indicators of deprivation related to housing and durables may be particularly weakly related to current income and may not be satisfactory as indicators of generalised exclusion' (1996, p 70). Nolan and Whelan classified their direct indicators in three groups on the basis of factorial analysis: *basic lifestyle deprivation* – food, clothes, doing without heating; *secondary lifestyle deprivation* – leisure activities, car, telephone, capacity to save, central heating, gifts for friends; and *housing deprivation*, which includes domestic durables, like TVs and the characteristics of the dwelling (except central heating and telephone, which are included in lifestyle. In a very ad hoc manner, which I have criticised extensively in Boltvinik (2000), they exclude the last two groups from their measurement with the following arguments:

> Here, given our objective, we concentrate on what we have termed *the basic dimension*. As we have seen, the items in the basic deprivation index clearly represent socially perceived necessities and are possessed by most people[6]. ... Most of the items in the secondary dimension, on the other hand, are not overwhelmingly regarded as necessities. ... The

---

[6] The argument is false. It can be reverted in favour of the housing dimension. No other item received such a high level of consensus. The same is true for the possession of the items: heating in the living areas when it is cold received the highest percentage (97%), followed by the refrigerator with 95%, an indoor toilet with 93%, and a bath or shower with 91%. The items in the basic list have lower percentages, especially a roast meat joint or equivalent, with 76%.

housing and durables items are possessed by most people and regarded as necessities by almost everyone (except for the TV). However, we have seen that that *they do not relate to current resources and extent of exclusion of the household in the same way as the basic items.* The fact that they do not cluster with the basic items itself means that *rather different households and causal procedures are involved.* Deprivation in terms of housing and related durables appears to be a product of very specific factors, *and so the housing items, though providing valuable information about one aspect of living standards, are not satisfactory as indicators of current generalized exclusion.* (Nolan and Whelan, 1996, pp 118–119; emphasis added)

What Nolan and Whelan understand by 'current generalised exclusion' is not at all clear. Persons already living in inadequate dwellings are *currently* deprived (mostly in an enforced way) of items such as a refrigerator, a television, a bath, or a washing machine. The few items included in the author's measurement – which is limited to food and clothing as well as heating in a very restrictive sense – end up conforming to a list of G&S shorter than the severely criticised Rowntree's subsistence list. Moreover, the items included by Nolan and Whelan do not even guarantee subsistence. Like many other researchers, they became obsessed with the relationship between direct indicators and CY. As becomes transparent when they exclude from poverty measurement their third group of indicators (housing), which depends on WBS different from CY (basic assets, mainly), they are interested in reducing direct indicators to the 'other side of the coin' of Y.[7] This constitutes yet another aspect of the reductionism that characterises most poverty studies, as I have already pointed out.

In stark contrast, both in the original and in the improved IPMM, as well as in the SPI, the baseline is the thesis that PL and direct poverty measurements (UBN) are complementary because they consider different WBS and identify deprivation in different dimensions. In the improved

---

[7] Gordon et al. (2000), who throughout their text use a broader spectrum of direct deprivation indicators compared to Nolan and Whelan (albeit without conceptual arguments and based only on statistical tests that cannot substitute theory and are quite questionable, as they rely on the links between the deprivation indicators and external variables such as health and the perception of poverty), eliminate six indicators of direct deprivation, arguing that they are not reliable, valid, or additive. Five out of the six items eliminated refer to domestic equipment (television, refrigerator, freezer, washing machine, beds, and bedding for everyone) and are related to WBS 2, basic assets, in the same way as the housing group eliminated by Nolan and Whelan. By doing so, Gordon et al. reduce their indicators to a subset that is very similar to those determined by low CY, thereby pushing their inquiry closer to 'the other side of the coin' of CY. Only two items remain in the group of basic assets considered necessities by more than 50% of the sample: carpets in living rooms and bedrooms, and a damp-free home.

IPMM, complementarity is achieved because UBN focuses on dimensions like housing and domestic equipment, whose satisfaction for most HH depends on WBS 2 – basic accumulated assets – and on dimensions like education and health services,[8] whose levels of satisfaction are strongly associated with WBS 4 – access to free or highly subsidised G&S. On the other hand, indirect P focuses on dimensions like food, clothing, personal and household hygiene, personal care, culture, and recreation, all of which depend for all HH on CY (monetary and non-monetary) and on the possibility of becoming indebted or dis-save.[9]

Therefore, there is a salient difference in the basic nature of the IPMM and the SPI-LTD, on the one hand, and the combined methods which are based on ELSPN (Nolan and Whelan, Gordon et al., and Halleröd), on the other. The IPMM approaches the conditions (satisfaction/dissatisfaction) of some HN directly and of other needs indirectly, while in European combined methods the same HN are measured by both direct and indirect approaches (like Y to buy food and direct diet indicators). In the IPMM, UBN and PLT are different dimensions not only because they are captured by a different procedure but also because they refer to different groups of HN, that is, different aspects of the human condition. Something similar could be said of SPI-LTD. Therefore, in the IPMM and the SPI-LTD, when a HH is above the norms in some dimensions but below the norms in other dimensions, the crucial question is whether the over-satisfaction observed in some dimensions compensates deprivation in other dimensions. One important baseline in the IV-IPMM is that there can be compensation in different dimensions and that, therefore, the problem is reduced to an empirical problem on the specific values of the indices involved in each HH for cells 1.2 and 2.1.

By contrast, in the 'truly poor' approach, consensual or not, to the extent that it attempts to measure the insufficiency of CY both directly

---

[8] Insofar as the public health system in Mexico (and in most poor countries) is segmented and insufficient, for those not entitled to social security, access to adequate health services depends mainly on CY. This is assumed in the IPMM, where satisfaction of HS and SS N (income maintenance mechanisms such as pensions, paid sick leave, and similar payments, excluding unemployment compensation which is non-existent in many poor countries) is verified through a mixed procedure: direct for those entitled to social security (which includes health services), and Y for those excluded from social security.

[9] To take these possibilities (depletion of savings and indebtedness) into account, the IPMM would have to use consumption expenditures instead of CY in the PLT dimension. In the IPMM's empirical applications to Mexican data, I and others who apply the IPMM have as yet not used consumption expenditure as the main variable, except in the food expenditure vs NFB cost method (cell 2.1. in Table 6.1).

and indirectly, the dilemma seems to become a purely methodological one related to the reliability of measuring methods and – as Halleröd has pointed out, quoting among others Amartya Sen – to the variability of the transformation rate from Y to achievements. Nevertheless, insofar as this search for the two sides of the coin is not conscious – neither in Nolan and Whelan nor in Gordon et al. – some inconsistencies arise. For Nolan and Whelan, I have pointed out such inconsistencies above and in Boltvinik (2000), while those of Gordon et al. were discussed in note 7 in this chapter.

Evidently, in the IPMM or the SPI-LTD it would be nonsensical to insist that to be poor, a HH must be deprived both in the dimensions verified by UBN and in those verified by PLT, since what constitutes poverty is the insufficiency of WBS as a whole considering the restricted level of substitutability among them. In this way, if a HH is below the PL in the income–time dimension of the IPMM but reaches the normative level in UBN (or vice versa), it will be poor; said HH does not have to be deprived in both dimensions to be considered as such.

The poverty criterion in the 'truly poor' methods of poverty measurement considers poor only those HH which fall in the intersection of both sets of poor, and therefore implies (speaking of the other side of the coin) that all HH that fall in the union of the non-poor sets are considered non-poor. For these authors, to be considered non-poor, it suffices to be considered as such in only one of the approaches (direct or indirect). In this way, the HH of our previous example, which is below the PL and on the norm in the direct dimension, will be considered non-poor despite the obvious insufficiency of its WBS.

With such a definition, the measurement error type II, or inclusion error (identifying someone who is not poor as poor), is minimised, but the exclusion error, or type I error (not identifying someone who is poor as poor) is maximised.

Scholars who developed this approach are conscious of the quite large measurement errors to which the indirect approach is subject, due to the low reliability of the income data (as Halleröd has solidly argued) and to the poor scope of the CY concept when referred to the resources pertinent for the measurement of P. Hence, their stance is asymmetric and tends to underestimate the incidence of poverty. This can be appreciated in Gordon et al.: they conceive as not poor both those with an income on or above the PL, but with direct deprivation in two or more items (something Kaztman (1989) had called *inertial deprivation*), and those below the PL but who have less than two enforced lacks (something Kaztman called *recently poor* in 1989). In figure A1 of their appendix 2, in which these categories are interpreted dynamically through time, it becomes clear that both those who are 'sinking into poverty' and those who are 'climbing out of poverty' are considered as not poor, even though in the graph the second group is below the poverty threshold.

Nolan and Whelan, Gordon et al., and Halleröd – the authors with whom the truly poor approach is illustrated and who depart from the work by Mack and Lansley, which was apparently attempting to cover all WBS but had in fact a birthmark in the other direction – end up reducing, mostly implicitly, all their field of inquiry to the consequences of a low CY. The hope I once placed in combined methods of measurement to open the door to a full recognition of all WBS has vanished as regards the truly poor approaches. The IPMM and SPI-LTD are the only operational approaches left which embrace a holistic vision. And, although the SPI-LTD does not include FT, it incorporates the quantity of life.

8

The Integrated Poverty Measurement Method (IPMM)

8.1 The genesis of the IPMM

In 1987 I presented a lengthy report on poverty in Mexico to UNDP Latin America. The report had been prepared by a small team of consultants that I headed and was well received at the headquarters of the Regional Project for Overcoming Poverty. As a result, I was soon hired. Shortly after that, the new head of the Mexican team, Antonio Suárez McAuliffe, wrote a comment severely criticising the structure of the report, particularly the lack of integration between the measurement of Y poverty (or PL method) and the parallel description of the levels and evolution of deprivation regarding some basic N. He was absolutely right. I had followed COPLAMAR's procedure and thus replicated its fragmentary and disintegrated character. My receptivity to this criticism changed my view of poverty. A few months later, I had the good fortune of coming across the research results by Beccaria and Minujin (1987) and Kaztman (1989), referring to Buenos Aires and Montevideo, respectively. These authors had been experimenting with the contrasts between the populations identified as poor by the two PMM applied at the time in South America: Y poverty (PL) and UBN, which were conceived as alternative methods. In its Latin American variants (that I call original or restricted, because of the very few indicators used), UBN conceives a HH as poor if it is poor (deprived) in one or more indicators, as described and appraised in Chapter 6. Both research papers looked simultaneously at UBN and PL, formulating a contingency matrix similar to the one presented in Table 8.1.

Neither Beccaria-Minujin nor Kaztman realised that they were witnessing the birth of a new PMM. However, my awareness had been sharpened by Suárez McAuliffe's critique, and I discovered that by adding a P criterion to these contingency matrices, a new method would ensue. This method, which I called the Integrated Poverty Measurement Method (IPMM), conceives PL and UBN not as alternative but as complementary PMM. The poverty criterion adopted defined the poor population as the union of both sets of poor, that is, the three italicised cells in the matrix: the poor by PL and by UBN separately (13.5% and 16.5% respectively) and the intersection of both (40.7%), totalling 70.7% (Boltvinik, 1990a).

Table 8.1: Contingency matrix: poor by PL and by UBN, Peru, 1985

	Poor by UBN (%)	Non-poor by UBN (%)	Sums (%)
Poor by PL (%)	40.7	13.5	54.2
Non-poor by PL (%)	16.5	29.3	45.8
Sums	57.2	42.8	100.0

Source: Boltvinik (1990a)

The rationale for conceiving PL and UBN as complementary methods is based on the insight that WB at the HH/individual level derives – as discussed in Section 1.2— – from the following WBS: 1) CY; 2) family patrimony (or basic assets); 3) NBA and borrowing capacity; 4) access to free or highly subsidised G&S; 5) free/available time; and 6) knowledge and skills. The evolution of WB at the social level depends on the evolution of the level and distribution of these six WBS.

The main limitation of partial methods (PL and UBN) is that they proceed as if WB depended only on some of these sources. PL only considers WBS 1 and implicitly WBS 3, when the variable observed is consumption expenditures and not Y (since consumption expenditures can be financed by NBA or by borrowing). According to the indicators used, Latin American applications of UBN implicitly consider WBS 2, 4, and partially 6.

The conclusions are obvious. PL and UBN are partial methods and, therefore, their results are biased, while the WBS they consider are different, making the methods complementary and not alternative.

However, the OV of IPMM, applied by UNDP in ten Latin American countries – whose results can be consulted in UNDP (1991 and 1992) – has serious flaws, which led me to develop the improved variant of the IPMM (IV-IPMM). Said flaws are related to the specific variants of PL and UBN that were uncritically incorporated into the OV-IPMM and that consequently characterise it. First, the method can only use the most elementary APM, that of H (proportion of poor persons in the population); second, H is not independent of the number of indicators used, but rather increases with them, which is a very serious defect; third, it has an structural tendency to generate a decreasing temporal decline in poverty, due to its fixed thresholds and stock-like variables; fourth regarding Y, it only measures food poverty; lastly, it does not consider FT as a WBS.

The IV-IPMM overcomes all these defects, but overcoming the third one requires an additional external task: the periodic review of indicators and thresholds. The way the IV-IPMM handles information – by transforming all non-metric indicators of UBN to metric scales (cardinalisation) – enables it to calculate all APM, including those sensitive to distribution. The number of items can be increased without necessarily leading to an increase in H because this improved method allows a compensation of deprivation in one N with WB above the threshold in another. The IV-IPMM incorporates a variant of PL based on family budgets that covers all HN met via the market or self-production, not simply food. Finally, it incorporates what constitutes its most important innovation (along with cardinalisation): time as a third dimension, in addition to PL and UBN.

After a few years, Suárez McAuliffe's critique was transformed into a new PMM that allowed me to overcome the schizophrenic feeling of parallel and disintegrated realities that prevailed in previous methods and to offer instead a holistic view that elevates our dynamic understanding of P.

The construction of indicators in the IV-IPMM reflects some improvements made by COPLAMAR, such as the establishment of normative thresholds in UBN variables and the use of a modified procedure to define PL, where the cost of items verified by UBN – for example, housing – was eliminated from the cost of the NGB (known as NBES in COPLAMAR).

In the IV-IPMM, TP was until very recently measured by the index of excess working time (EWT), which considers also required domestic work. Based on the analysis of the connection between Y and time poverty, Araceli Damián (2003, 2014) examined the theoretical and methodological implications drawn from the use of the EWT index. Damián employed the EWT index to verify the extent to which HH reacted to a fall in income with an increase in their work effort – a reaction postulated by many scholars in Latin America that would form the so-called *household survival strategies* school of thought. The author found that around 50% of Y-poor HH did not fully use their available human resources for extra-domestic work, and that this situation became more acute in periods of crisis, thus disproving the main thesis of the abovementioned school.

The first HH time-use module in Mexico was applied in 1996; this opened the door to verifying, for the first time, the normative parameters used in the EWT index. Damián (2005, 2014) found that most of the parameters used in the EWT closely resembled the observed social practices in Mexico. Damián (2014) compares the EWT methodology with other existing Y-TP measuring methods. Time poverty has important implications for HH's quality of life but, despite its huge relevance, has been insufficiently studied in Mexico and the world.

8.2 General description of the IPMM

In contrast to the OV-IPMM, the IV-IPMM combines the improved variant of UBN (IV-UBN), the budget standards approach to PL (BSA-PL), and TP to obtain $I(IPMM)_j$, the deprivation score for HH_j. This variant overcomes the first OV-IPMM limitation (see Chapter 7) by adopting the BSA, whereby

Figure 8.1: Components of IPMM and integration procedure

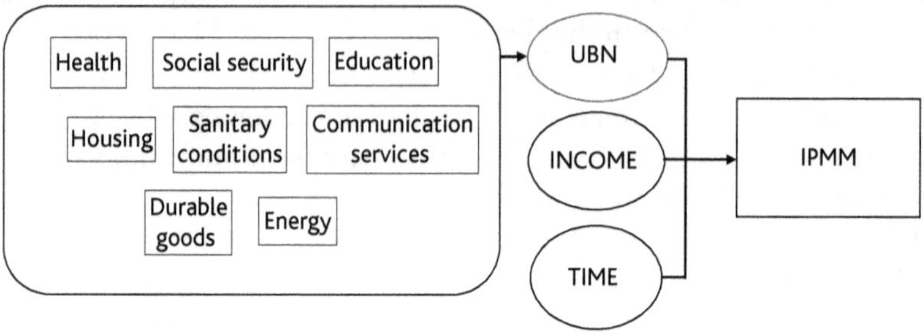

```
┌─────────────────────────────────────────┐
│  Health   Social security   Education   │      ┌─────┐
│                                         │ ───→ │ UBN │ ─┐
│  Housing  Sanitary     Communication    │      └─────┘  │
│           conditions   services         │               │    ┌──────┐
│                                         │      ┌────────┐│   │      │
│  Durable goods   Energy                 │      │ INCOME │├──→│ IPMM │
│                                         │      └────────┘│   │      │
└─────────────────────────────────────────┘               │    └──────┘
                                                 ┌──────┐ │
                                                 │ TIME │─┘
                                                 └──────┘
```

the PL measurement goes beyond food P; to overcome the second and third limitations, it adopts IV-UBN; to solve the fourth limitation, it includes educational level in UBN and incorporates time poverty; by adopting the expectations criterion, IV-UBN overcomes the static character of indicators and thus the inevitability of the declining incidence of UBN P; and by adopting $I(IPMM)_J > 0$ as the P criterion, it allows for trade-offs.

The general procedure of the IPMM is represented in Figure 8.1. Here it is shown that by combining UBN, PL, and time components, one obtains the IPMM. It also shows that UBN comprises eight components. Table 8.2 lists which needs are verified by UBN, which by a mixed procedure, and which by PL. It synthesises the time component methodology and, in the last column, describes that the PL used in the IPMM (IPMM-PL) is equal to the cost of the GNB – or NBES, the specific application of the BSA in Mexico – minus the cost of the items (for example, dwelling (Dw), education) verified by UBN. Thus, the pertinent Y for items included in the IPMM-PL is available income (Ya_j).

All partial achievement indicators, including the integrated $IPMM_J$, might vary from 0 to 2 (given the explicit reduction of higher indicator ranges to this one), with the norm at 1, while the deprivation indicators might vary from −1 to +1, with the norm at 0. The poor (positive values in the deprivation scale) have been classified in three poverty (deprivation) strata for all indicators: very intense poverty (VIP), intense poverty (IP), and moderate poverty (MP). The sum of the first two has been labelled as extreme poverty (EP). The population above the norm (0 or negative values in the deprivation scale) has also been classified in three strata: minimal satisfaction stratum (MSS), medium stratum (MS), and upper stratum (US). The values delimiting the strata are given in Table 8.3.

The Integrated Poverty Measurement Method (IPMM)

Table 8.2: IPMM basic procedure

Form of verifying need satisfaction				Income comparable with the PL
UBN	Mixed	PL	Time	
1. Sanitary conditions 2. Domestic energy 3. Housing quality and spaces 4. Communications 5, Education 6. Durable goods	7. Health and SS. If person has access to SS institutions, needs are considered satisfied. Otherwise, their condition is assessed by income capacity.	8. Food 9. Fuel and electricity 10. Hygiene 11. Clothing and shoes. 12, Transportation 13. Recreation and culture 14.Expenditures on housing services 15. Private expenditures on health and education 16. Other required expenditures PL = cost of $\sum 8 \ldots 16$.	Deprivation indicator of free time (FT), calculated on FT norms and norms for reposition of capacities, domestic and extra-domestic work, and study.	Available income (Ya) after expenditures on items considered in UBN or mixed procedures. Ya <=> PL. PL is the cost of the items in the NBES verified by PL.
I(UBN) by HH: weighted average of 1 to 7	I(IPMM) = I(UBN + mixed)(0.33) + I(PL)(0.40) + I(FT)(0.27): weighted average of the three components			

Source: Own elaboration

Table 8.3: Strata used in IPMM

	Deprivation values (DV) that define the stratum
1 Very intense poverty (VIP)	$0.5 < DV \leq 1.0$
2 Intense poverty (IP)	$0.5 \geq DV > 1/3$
3 = 1 + 2 Extreme poverty (EP)	$1/3 \leq DV \leq 1.0$
4 Moderate poverty (MP)	$1/3 \geq DV > 0$
5 = 3 + 4 Sum of poverty (Total poverty) (TP)	$DV > 0$
6 Minimum satisfaction stratum (MSS)	$-0.1 < DV < 0$
7 Medium stratum (MS)	$-0.5 \leq DV \leq -0.1$
8 Upper stratum (US)	$-1.0 \geq DV \leq 0.5$
9 = 6 + 7 + 8 Sum of non-poverty (TNP)	$0 \geq DV \leq -1$

8.3 Detailed description of IPMM poverty indicators, Part 1: UBN

This section describes the methodology used to calculate the indicators used in the IPMM in detail. The incidence of deprived (poor) population in Mexico in 2020 (H = q / n, where q is the number of poor people and n is the pertinent population) is provided after each significant indicator. In some cases, a commentary is added. The first part of this discussion is devoted to the UBN dimension, while the second part addresses the dimensions of Y and time. Finally, the way in which the previous dimensions are combined to generate the IPMM achievement and deprivation indicators is explained. All indicators at the HH level are built without considering resident domestic workers or guests.

As can be seen in Figure 8.1, the UBN dimension comprises eight subdimensions: housing, sanitary services, durable goods, communication services, domestic energy, education, HS, and SS. The first six are verified directly: the information provided by the HH is used to verify whether the HH or its members comply with the thresholds (standards) and to what degree. The last two indicators are verified with a mixed procedure: all HH are verified directly and via their paying capacity, and the best result is selected. Thus, although all the members of a HH might be deprived, they will be considered at the norm or above it if they can pay for market solutions (after considering the amount required to cover their PL). Two sets of alternative market solutions were considered: public and private, both for HS and for SS.

8.3.1 Housing quality and space ($QSDwA_J$)

The housing dimension comprises two subdimensions: the quality of the building materials and adequacy of the space available in the dwelling (Dw) vis-à-vis the number of persons in the HH or Dw. Combining both, we obtain the indicator of achievement/deprivation of quality and housing space.

Housing quality

This subdimension is measured by a composite indicator, which is the result of the weighted average of the indicators of the materials used on the Dw's walls, roofs, and floors. Materials should be easy to clean and provide structural stability, weather protection, and good thermal behaviour. In principle, these indicators are referred to the Dw and not to the HH, but to facilitate the notation I will use the same subscript J for both.

These types of indicators do not have an original numerical variable; therefore, each solution was associated with a level of OWB. As previously explained, this exercise can be seen as providing an extension of the usual dichotomic variables by recognising the existence of intermediate solutions. This implies that solutions can, and are, very different (for example, coated floor compared to cement and soil), and provide very different levels of OWB (the coated floor is better than the cement floor, and the latter is better than the soil floor). Going beyond dichotomisation means recognising that there are solutions that do not comply with the standard but are nevertheless better than the worst solution. The following are scores, standards, and indicators for different solutions, as captured and grouped in ENIGH.

Wall scores (W_J)

Waste material and cardboard sheet = 0
Asbestos or metal sheet, bamboo, reed or palm, and 'embarro' or 'bajareque' = 0.25
Wood or adobe = 0.6
Cement brick, brick, block, stone, quarry, cement, or concrete = 1 (Norm, $W\star$)

As seen in Equation 8.1, the achievement indicator is the quotient between the score of HH_J and the norm ($W\star$), which is 1. All HH with a score < 1 will therefore be deprived.

$$WA_J = W_J / W\star \tag{8.1}$$

WA_J will vary between 0 and 1. This is a truncated indicator where no solutions better than the normative one are possible. The deprivation indicator will be:

$$WD_J = 1 - WA_J \tag{8.1a}$$

All HH with a score > 0 in WD_J are considered deprived. In 2020, using ENIGH databases, 9.05% of the population lived in Dw with walls below the norm; they are thus considered deprived in this indicator (H = 9.05%).

Roof scores (RJ)

Waste material and cardboard sheet = 0
Metal or asbestos sheet, corrugated fibre cement sheet, palm or straw, wood or 'tejamanil' and roof with beams = 0.5
Roof tile, concrete slab, joists with vault = 1 (Norm, $R\star$)

$$RA_J = R_J / R\star \tag{8.2}$$

RA_J will vary between 0 and 1. This is a truncated indicator with no solutions above the norm.
(H = 22.01%)

Floor scores (F_J)

$$\text{Soil} = 0$$
$$\text{Cement or firm} = 0.5$$
$$\text{Wood, mosaic, or other coating} = 1 \text{ (Norm, F\star)}$$

As seen in Equation 8.3, the achievement indicator is the quotient between the score of HH_J and the norm (F★), which is 1. Thus, all HH with a score < 1 will be deprived.

$$FA_J = F_J / F\star \qquad (8.3)$$

FA_J will vary between 0 and 1, with no solutions better than the normative one.

The deprivation indicator is $FD_J = 1 - FA_J$. It varies from 1 (the worst situation) to 0 (the best). All values > 1 mean deprivation. In 2020, 57.64% of Dw had $FD_J > 0$, which was the value of H.

The composite housing quality adequacy indicator (HQA_J) is calculated as a weighted average of the three indicators of material quality specified above. Weights reflect the relative costs of walls, roof, and floors (at the norms) and are indicated with K in the following equation. Weights are taken from COPLAMAR (1982, vol. 3) and from Boltvinik (1999).

Composite indicator of housing quality adequacy (HQA_J)

$$HQA_J = (WA_J\, K_W) + (RA_J\, K_R) + (FA_J\, K_F) \qquad (8.4)$$

Where: $K_W = 0.55$; $K_R = 0.30$; $K_F = 0.15$. HQA_J varies from 0 to 1. The corresponding deprivation indicator is:

$$HQD_J = 1 - HQA_J \qquad (8.4a)$$

and varies from 1 to 0.

The three indicators are truncated, meaning there is no compensation. A Dw with defective walls could have floors and roofs above the norm, so that the combined indicator H could be expected to be either above or below the norms. But with truncated indicators, the only Dw that can have an overall normative quality would be those with achievement scores of 1 for the three indicators. Truncated indicators have serious unplanned consequences, which is why they must be avoided at all costs when designing surveys. The following equation gives a hypothetical example of a given Dw_j:

$$HQD_J = (1 \star 0.55) + (1 \star 0.30) + (0.5 \star 0.15) = 0.925 < 1$$

Ergo, this Dw is deprived. In 2020, 32% of the Mexican population lived in Dw with exactly this profile: solid walls and roofs, and a cement floor. In the same year, 43.1% lived in Dw with adequate conditions in the three indicators. The latter were not deprived, but the remaining 56.9% were deprived in various degrees. This is the value of H for the HQD_J. To illustrate the opposite condition, let us visualise a Dw with $(0 \star 0.55) + (0.5 \star 0.30) + (0 \star 0.15) = 0.15 < 1$. This Dw is also poor, but significantly poorer than the previous one. Only 0.11% of the population lived in Dw as deprived as this one, or more. Dichotomists would classify the Dw in our two examples as poor, and the big differences among them would go unnoticed. But in the IPMM every HH maintains the scores it is given for all indicators, so that when they are combined with others, they will not be poor/not poor indicators but have a specific score, as in our examples: 0.925 and 0.15. When these two scores are combined with one or more non-truncated indicators (like housing space, Y, or education) that have values above the norm (up to a score of 2), one HH could turn out to be poor but not the other.

Adequacy of space availability

Space norms, like quality of materials, are in principle applied to Dw and not to HH. A Dw can be shared by two or more HH (this was the case with 1.5% of Dw in Mexico in 2020). But ENIGH does not identify how the space in those Dw is shared between the two or more HH inhabiting it. With this in mind, what follows below refers to both spaces (rooms) in the Dw, and persons inhabiting the Dw (except domestic workers that sleep in the Dw). To simplify, I refer below to Dw as HH.

For any HH with two or more people, the required space types are: exclusive-use kitchen; bathroom; one bedroom for every two persons; and a multipurpose room (living room, dining room, or study) for every four people. For single-person HH the standards include a bathroom and a multipurpose room that can also be used for cooking and sleeping.

To calculate available spaces in the HH, the following variables of living spaces must be defined:

1. **Number of total rooms (TR):** This variable, contained in the ENIGH, does not count bathrooms or corridors, but it does count the exclusive-use kitchen.
2. **Bedrooms (B):** This variable, contained in the ENIGH, indicates the number of rooms used as bedrooms, regardless of whether they are also used as a kitchen.
3. **Kitchen for exclusive use (KE):** This refers to the existence of a room exclusively used for cooking, that is, not used for sleeping. In this variable, the score 1 indicates that the kitchen is exclusive, while the score 0 indicates the opposite case. This is not required in unipersonal HH.
4. **Multipurpose rooms (MR):** These are rooms with no specialised use, such as the kitchen and bedrooms. It is obtained by subtracting B and KE from TR.

These definitions can be expressed in equation form as follows:

$$MR_j = TR_j - (B_j + KE_j) \qquad (8.5)$$

$$TR_j = KE_j + B_j + MR_j \qquad (8.6)$$

The norms on space requirements in the HH are divided according to the number of HH members. If the HH is unipersonal, the requirement for TR equals 1, which indicates that KE and MR are not required. If the HH possesses either, it will be above the norm:

$$TR\star = 1 \mid \text{unipersonal HH} \qquad (8.7)$$

In HH with more than one member ($M_j > 1$), that is, a multi-person HH, the space requirements are the following:

$$KE\star = 1 \qquad (8.8)$$

$$B\star = M_j / 2 \qquad (8.9)$$

$$MR\star = M_j / 4 \qquad (8.10)$$

From the equations presented above, one can derive a single normative variable on the number of TR required:

$$TR\star_j = KE\star + B\star + MR\star \qquad (8.11)$$

$$TR\star_j = 1 + M_j / 2 + M_j / 4 \qquad (8.12)$$

The Integrated Poverty Measurement Method (IPMM)

$$TR^\star_j = 1 + 0.75 M_j \qquad (8.13)$$

Based on the definition of these standards, partial indicators of achievement (A) can be developed for each type of space in the HH:

$$AKE_j = KE_j / KE^\star \mid \text{for dwellings with 2+ persons} \qquad (8.14)$$

$$AB_j = B_j / B^\star_j \qquad (8.15)$$

$$AMR_j = MR_j / MR^\star_j \qquad (8.16)$$

On the basis of these partial achievement indicators, one can form the housing space achievement indicator (ATR_j), a global variable that equals the sum of the three partials (Equation 8.18) which, once replaced with the previous equations (8.14, 8.15, and 8.16), can be simplified as follows:

$$ATR_j = TR_j / TR^\star_j \qquad (8.17)$$

$$\begin{aligned} ATR_j &= (KE_j + B_j + MR_j) / (KE^\star_j + B^\star_j + MR^\star_j) \\ &= TR^\star_j / (1 + 0.75M) \end{aligned} \qquad (8.18)$$

However, this ATR_j achievement indicator is not the one used, since it assumes that all the spaces of the HH (bedrooms, kitchen, and multipurpose room) are homogeneous and fully interchangeable. But this is not so. The architectural design is different, and the average size of a KE is smaller than that of a B, which in turn is smaller than a MR. Therefore, it becomes necessary to express the different types of spaces according to their size vis-à-vis that of a B. The following equivalences – drawn from housing designs by COPLAMAR (1982b: vol. 3) – are used:

$$KE = 0.5\ B \qquad (8.19)$$

$$MR = 1.5\ B \qquad (8.20)$$

Based on this, it is possible to construct the concept of equivalent bedrooms (EB). This indicator of housing spaces relates the TR – in a comparable way – with the norm in terms of normative equivalent bedrooms (EB*):

Equivalent bedrooms (EB) per household

$$EB = KE\ (0.5) + B + MR\ (1.5) \qquad (8.21)$$

Normative EB per HH (for 2+ members)

$$EB^\star_J = KE^\star_J (0.5) + B^\star_J + MR^\star_J (1.5) \qquad (8.22)$$

which, when substituting with Equation 8.21, is:

$$EB^\star_J = 0.5 + B^\star + MR^\star_J (1.5) \qquad (8.23)$$

The ratio of observed EB_J to normatively required $EB^\star_J$ is the indicator of achievement of housing space (AHS_J), which does consider space equivalencies in the HH and thus replaces Equation 8.18:

$$AHS_J = EB_J / EB^\star_J \qquad (8.24)$$

In the case of single-person HH, the indicator is simpler due to the norm enunciated in Equation 8.7:

$$AHS_J = EB_J / TR^\star = EB_J \qquad (8.25)$$

since $TR^\star = 1$ when the HH is unipersonal.

AHS_J can vary from values very close to 0, for HH with many members and a single room, to values well above 1, where HH_J far exceeds the standard. It is not a truncated indicator. High extremes in the values of the indicators can also occur in the dimensions of education and Y. Since such indicators are subsequently combined, it is necessary to prevent extremely high levels in one of them from distorting HH average scores. This is one of the reasons to rescale the values of these three dimensions so that their variations remain in the same range. The maximum is 2, which has the same distance to the norm (1) as the minimum (0).

For such a rescaling, a maximum must be defined. This can be a *conceptual maximum*, which is the only one consistent with the principle of full normativity, or an *observed* one, which is problematic. The use of a conceptual maximum is also required by the principles of decreasing marginal WB and of the existence of a maximum WB level.

The maximum value for AHS was set at 3, which is three times the threshold or normative value. The maximum observed in 2020 was 23. When rescaled, it was set at 2, since additional spaces above the maximum do not add OWB to HH members. The maximum conceptual value equals three EB for a single-person HH, and three times the number of EB required by the normative standards for HH of two or more individuals. This implies that, for a four-person HH, where the norms require one KE, two BR, and one MR, that is, four EB, the maximum conceptual value of 3 implies 12 EB, which could comprise one KE, four BR, and five MR. The maximum value of 23 observed in 2020 implies a 92 EB HH for four persons, a completely absurd condition. The rescaling is expressed as follows:

$$AHS'_j = 1 + [(AHS_j - 1) / (\max AHS - 1)]$$
$$= 1 + [(AHS_j - 1) / 2] \mid AHS_j > 1 \qquad (8.26)$$

After values of the original distribution above the norm have been rescaled, all HH (if any) that remain above the value of 2 are given a final value of 2 by applying the principle of the existence of a maximum WB. This would be the case of the HH with an AHS value of 23. This is the *truncating operation*:

$$AHS'_j = 2 \mid AHS'_j > 2 \qquad (8.27)$$

The deprivation indicator of housing space (DHS'_j) is:

$$DHS'_j = 1 - AHS'_j \qquad (8.28)$$

whose range is between close to $+1$ to -1, with the norm at 0.

In 2020, space H was 57.64% of the population, who lived in overcrowded HH not complying with the norms that we have just set, particularly EB★. This figure is slightly above the H in HH quality.

Integrated indicator of housing quality and space adequacy ($HQSA_j$)

This integrated indicator aims to express both the quantitative and qualitative adequacy of the Dw. To be adequate, the Dw must comply with the qualitative (material quality of building materials) and the quantitative (spaces or rooms) thresholds discussed above. Since these thresholds are co-realisable (both a gigantic Dw made with throwaway materials and a doll house made of perfect materials would be useless), the appropriate way of combining them is by multiplying their achievement scores. Thus, the Dw qualitative and quantitative achievement indicator is:

$$HQSA_j = (HQA_j)(AHS'_j) \qquad (8.29)$$

Since the range of HQA_j is from 0 to 1 and that of AHS'_j (after rescaling) is from 0 to 2, the range of the $HQSA_j$ indicator will be from 0 to 2, and the norm will be located at 1. If the ENIGH questionnaire allowed for additional housing quality features (for example, painted walls or carpets on floors) plus other questions related to the quality of the dwelling (for example, windows), the range of $HQSA_j$ could reach a maximum of 4, in

Table 8.4: Stratification of population (%) by the value of $HQSD_j$ in their corresponding Dw

1 Very intense poverty (VIP)	26.27
2 Intense poverty (IP)	15.19
3 = 1 + 2 **Extreme poverty (EP)**	**41.45**
4 Moderate poverty (MP)	28.83
5 = 3 + 4 **Sum of poverty (TP)**	**66.28**
6 Minimum satisfaction stratum (MSS)	10.28
7 Medium stratum (MS)	16.08
8 Upper stratum (US)	7.36
9 = 6 + 7 + 8 **Sum of non-poverty (TNP)**	**33.72**

which case a standardisation procedure would be required to reduce it to the usual 0 to 2.

The housing quality and space deprivation indicator is:

$$HQSD_j = 1 - HQSA_j \qquad (8.30)$$

with a range of −1 to 1, and the norm at 0. In 2020, the percentage of the population in Dw with $HQSA_j < 1$ or $HQSD_j > 0$ was 66.28%. Expressed in terms of the population living in the type of Dw thus classified (which has the virtue of weighing HH/Dw by their size), the resulting stratification is presented in Table 8.4.

8.3.2 Durable goods

ENIGH contains information on the HH's reported possession of certain common durable goods (including their quantity, for example, how many TV sets or computers; see Table 8.5). To calculate this indicator, the durable goods value (DGV_j) owned by HH_j is contrasted with the value of a normative minimum value ($DGV\star$), defined for this purpose in the IPMM (this includes the value of the items marked with $\star$ in Table 8.5). The quotient between DGV_j and $DGV\star$ is the achievement indicator of HH_j in this dimension. Table 8.5 shows the prices used in 2020 to calculate the respective values. The achievement indicator of DGV possession is defined as:

$$DGVA_j = \Sigma DGV_j / \Sigma DGV\star \qquad (8.31)$$

where the numerator (ΣDGV_j) is the sum of the goods owned by HH_j and the denominator ($\Sigma DGV\star$) is the sum of the durable goods that a HH

Table 8.5: Updated prices of durable goods, August 2020

Goods	Prices at August 2020, pesos
Car	$164,178.01
Pickup truck	$183,997.81
Pickup (truck with box)	$183,997.70
Motorcycle	$37,031.31
Bicycle*	$1,775.20
Radio/recorder*	$581.10
Stereo*	$1,246.90
TV*	$2,905.10
Video player (DVD)	$532.67
Video game	$4,930.47
Computer*	$10,393.14
Fan*	$373.40
Sewing machine	$3,354.88
Stove*	$3,918.26
Refrigerator*	$6,437.38
Blender*	$427.81
Water pump	$1,116.69
Iron*	$197.19
Washing machine*	$4,358.50
Vacuum cleaner	$546.84
Printer	$1,550.08
Toaster	$519.40
Heater* (only normative in cold areas)	$1,087.46
Gas or solar water heater*	$2,383.30
DGV* (HH in non-cold areas)	$33,701.44
DGVCA* (HH in cold areas)	$34,788.90

* Denotes that the good forms part of the minimum basket of durables all HH should possess.
Source: Own elaboration. Price and market research Evalúa CDMX.

should have – bicycle, radio or recorder, TV or screen, stereo, fan, stove, refrigerator, blender, iron, washing machine, computer, heater (in cold weather areas only), and water heater. The ENIGH allows us to know the number of each good owned by a HH. It is for this reason that the number of possessed goods in the case of some HH can be larger than the 21 items captured by the ENIGH. The DGV of the numerator can far exceed the norm.

A quotient higher than 1 in Equation 8.31 indicates that the HH also possesses non-basic durable goods, which could be sold or pawned without affecting the satisfaction of basic N.

Prices of DG were updated by using information available in INEGI and, where necessary, by surveying well-known national stores. This was done by Evalúa CDMX. The most austere models were selected. Table 8.5 contains the list of DG captured by ENIGH, the ones constituting the DGV★, and the updated prices for August 2020, when field work for ENIGH 2020 started.

Note: Goods marked with ★ are those added to the denominator of Equation 8.31. Total DGV★ and DGVCA★ are the sums of costs for HH in non-cold and cold areas, respectively.

The range of the $DGVA_J$ can go from 0 to several times the norm (which is 1). For this reason, all values higher than 1 must be rescaled, so that the maximum becomes 2. The maximum is defined in the same way as in the rescaling of the adequacy of space indicator: a conceptual maximum is defined considering the decreasing marginal WB and the maximum WB level. In this case, the maximum level is set at 10.

Thus, the rescaling is as follows:

$$DGVA'_J = 1 + [(DGVA_J - 1) / (\max DGVA_J - 1)]$$
$$= 1 + [(DGVA_J - 1) / 9] \mid DGVA_J > 1 \qquad (8.32)$$

After rescaling the values above the norm of the previous distribution, a final modification is required for HH that still maintain a value > 2.

$$DGVA'_J = 2 \mid \text{for } DGVA'_J > 2 \qquad (8.33)$$

Once the range for $DGVA'_J$ has been reduced to 0 to 2, the deprivation of DGV_J is as follows:

$$DGVD_J = 1 - (DGVA'_J) \qquad (8.34)$$

with a range of −1 to +1, and the norm at 0.

In 2020, 38.55% of the population were members of HH with a set of DG whose value (DGV) was below the norm: H = 38.55%.

8.3.3 Sanitary services

The sanitary adequacy dimension measures the degree of (un)satisfaction of the hydric–hygienic cycle. This cycle is captured through three indicators: water provision, drainage, and toilet.

Water provision (WP)

This is a composite indicator integrated by two further indicators: water source (WS) and water frequency (WF).

Water Source (WS). The following WS receive the indicated *initial scores*:
Well, river, stream, lake, other/rainwater collectors/piped water hauled from other Dw = 0
Public tap (or hydrant)/tank truck = 1
Piped water outside the Dw but inside the housing lot = 2
Piped water inside the Dw = 3 (Norm, WS★)

The achievement indicator for WS is:

$$WSA_J = WS_J / WS\star \tag{8.35}$$

This achievement indicator ranges from 0 to 1. It is a truncated indicator.
 In 2020, H = 24.82%, which represents the percentage of the population living in Dw where $WSA_J < 1$.

Water frequency (WF). The initial scores for WF are:
Occasionally = 0.4
Once a week = 0.6
Twice a week = 1.2
Every third day = 2
Daily = 4 (Norm, WF★)

The achievement indicator for WF is:

$$WFA_J = WF_J / WF\star \tag{8.36}$$

WFA ranges between 0 and 1. It is a truncated indicator.
 Calculations with ENIGH data showed that H = 36.18%, which is the percentage of the population that lived in Dw where WF was below the norm of daily flow.
 The combined indicator of water provision (WP_J) is constructed based on the achievement indicators WS_J and WF_J. For solutions of WS scored 0 and 1:

$$WP_J = WS_J, \tag{8.37}$$

as WF_J does not apply.
 For solutions of WS scored 2 and 3:

$$WP_j = (WS_j)(WF_j) \qquad (8.37a)$$

The result for WP (product of WS_j and WF_j where applicable) in 2020 was H = 44.5%.

Drainage service

Drainage (Dr). Scores are given to the following solutions:
Has no drainage; a pipeline which releases served waters to a canyon/rift or to a river, lake, or sea = 0
Public drainage system; septic tank = 1 (Dr★)

The Dr achievement indicator is:

$$DrA_j = Dr_j / Dr\star \qquad (8.38)$$

DrA_j will vary from 0 to 1. It is a truncated and dichotomic indicator. In 2020, H was 5.1%.

Toilet (To). Initial scores for To are given to the following solutions:
No toilet; a toilet into which water cannot be poured = 0
Shared toilet (with another Dw) flushed by pouring water with a bucket = 2
Shared toilet (with another Dw) with direct water discharge = 3
Exclusive-use toilet flushed by pouring water with a bucket = 3
Exclusive-use toilet with direct water discharge = 4 (To★)

The achievement indicator for To is:

$$ToA_j = To_j / To\star \qquad (8.39)$$

ToA_j ranges from 0 to 1. It is a truncated indicator. In 2020, H was 33.57%.

Consolidated indicator of sanitary achievement (SA_j)

This indicator is calculated as the product of WP, Dr, and To indicators, since they are co-realisable:

$$SA_j = (WP_j)(DrA_j)(ToA_j) \qquad (8.40)$$

The indicator of sanitary deprivation (SD_j) is:

$$SD_j = 1 - SA_j \qquad (8.41)$$

SD_j ranges from −1 to 1, with the norm at 0. In 2020, the sanitary deprivation (SD_j) scores were such that H = 52.13%.

8.3.4 Communication services (CS)

The communication services achievement indicator (CSA_j) is calculated by combining two indicators: telephone service (landline or fixed and/or mobile) and internet access.

Telephone (fixed line and/or mobile) (Tl_j)

Scores for Tl_j are given to the options available in the ENIGH questionnaire:

$$\text{No landline/fixed and no mobile phone} = 0$$
$$\text{Has a fixed line or a mobile phone} = 1 \; (Tl\star)$$
$$\text{Has a fixed line and a mobile phone} = 1.5$$

The achievement indicator of Tl_j is:

$$TlA_j = Tl_j / Tl\star \qquad (8.42)$$

which ranges from 0 to 1.5.
The corresponding deprivation indicator is:

$$TlD_j = 1 - TlA_j \qquad (8.43)$$

which ranges from −0.5 to 1. In this case, 4.91% were deprived: H = 4.91%.

Internet access/connection (IA_j)

Scores for IA_j were assigned to the following dichotomic options:

$$\text{No access/connection to internet} = 0$$
$$\text{Access/connection to internet} = 1 \; (IA\star)$$

The internet access achievement (IAA_j) score is:

$$IAA_j = IA_j / IA\star \qquad (8.44)$$

which varies from 0 to 1. In 2020, 56.29% of the population had no internet access at home: H=56.29%.

The combined achievement communication services (CSA_j) indicator is obtained by averaging the indicators of the two partial components, as they are not co-realisable:

$$CSA_j = (TIA_j + IAA_j) / 2 \qquad (8.45)$$

which ranges from 0 to 1.25.

The deprivation indicator is:

$$CSD_j = (1 - CSA_j) \qquad (8.46)$$

and ranges from −0.25 to 1. In 2020, H was 43.97%.

8.3.5 Energy adequacy (EnAJ)

The HH energy adequacy indicator is built by combining two basic S: electricity (El) and home-cooking fuel (CF). An alternative to this very simple indicator was to incorporate heating and cooling in the Dw, as well as heating water for the shower and the sink. Instead, these additional S were incorporated in the PL cost and in the normative package of DG.

Electricity access and quality indicator

This indicator is built by combining the electricity access indicator (El_j) and a proxy indicator of the in-house electricity network quality: lightbulb achievement (LB_jA).

Electricity access receives the following achievement scores:
No electricity = 0
Electricity access via solar panel or another source = 0.5
Electricity access via the public service or a private plant = 1 ($El\star$)

The achievement indicator of El_j is:

$$ElA_j = El_j / El\star \qquad (8.47)$$

ElA_j varies from 0 to 1.

Lightbulb achievement

An achievement indicator of the number of lightbulbs (LB_jA) in the Dw is included as a proxy variable to distinguish precarious in-house electricity networks from adequate ones. The normative threshold defined for the number of LB in a Dw is related to the TR – as defined in Section 1.2 – which includes an exclusive-use kitchen (KE) *plus bathrooms*, which I call modified total rooms (MTR).

$$LB_j^\star = (MTR_j)(1.25) \qquad (8.48)$$

where factor 1.25 is the number of LB normatively required per MTR. The achievement indicator of LB_j is the quotient between observed LB_j and normative $LB_j^\star$:

$$LB_jA = LB_j / LB_j^\star \qquad (8.49)$$

LB_jA can vary from 0 to a number that far exceeds 1. Therefore, as in other indicators, values above 1 must be rescaled, so that the maximum value of the indicator becomes 2. To do this, we must define a conceptual maximum above which an increase in the number of LB does not increase WB. A reasonable number for this maximum is four times $LB_j^\star$: max $LB_jA = 4LB_j^\star$. Hence, rescaling is done with the following equation:

$$\begin{aligned} LB_jA' &= 1 + [(LB_jA - 1) / (\max LB_j^\star - 1)] \\ &= [(LB_jA - 1) / 3\star] \mid LB_jA > 1 \end{aligned} \qquad (8.50)$$

LB_jA' will vary between 0 and 2.

If despite this rescaling LB_jA' values above 2 still remain, all such values will be made equal to 2:

$$LB_jA' = 2 \mid LB_jA' > 2 \qquad (8.51)$$

This indicator was surprisingly low as captured in ENIGH 2020: H = 51.1%. This shows how precarious the installations and use of electricity are in Mexican HH.

Electricity access and quality achievement indicator ($ElLB_jA$)

This indicator equals the product of both components, as they are co-realisable:

$$ElLB_jA = (ElA_j)(LBA'_j) \qquad (8.52)$$

which can vary from 0 to 2, with the norm at 1.

The corresponding deprivation indicator is:

$$ElLB_jD = 1 - EILB_jA \qquad (8.53)$$

which ranges from −1 to 1, with the norm at 0. In 2020, the value of H was 51.2%.

Home-cooking fuel (CF_j)

The achievement indicator of this component is calculated by scoring the options in the ENIGH questionnaire as follows:

$$\text{Firewood, charcoal/coal, or other fuel} = 1$$
$$\text{Gas (liquefied or natural), or electricity} = 3 \ (CF\star)$$

The CF achievement indicator (CFA_j) is:

$$CFA_j = CF_j / CF\star \tag{8.54}$$

which can vary from 0.33 to 1. Since most Dw in Mexico cook with gas, H was low: 15.83%.

Domestic energy achievement indicator (EnA_j)

Finally, the domestic energy achievement indicator (EnA_j) is obtained by combining the indicators $ElLBA_j$ (electricity access and quality achievement) and CFA_j (home-cooking fuel achievement). The variables are weighted in terms of costs at the normative level solutions. The weights adopted here are 0.7 for El and 0.3 for CF:

$$EnA_j = EILBA_j \ (0.70) + CFA_j \ (0.30) \tag{8.55}$$

EnA_j will vary between 0.1 and 1. The domestic energy deprivation indicator (EnD_j) is:

$$EnD_j = 1 - EnA_j \tag{8.56}$$

which ranges from of −1 to 0.9, with the norm at 0. In 2020 we found that 55.76% of HH were deprived.

8.3.6 Educational achievement indicator (EAI)

The educational minimum or normative educational threshold changes between countries according to various factors, one of which is legislation. In the following paragraphs I will resort to the Mexican Constitution and the General Law of Education as examples to show the relations between legal changes and the educational thresholds applied in the IPMM in Mexico.

As of 2022, Article 3 of the Mexican Constitution establishes 15 years of compulsory schooling for the new generations, starting with pre-school education at three years old and finishing with preparatory school (high school in the US), after which the individual might enter university or other higher education. These 15 years are complemented by the constitutional, though not yet regulated, statement that the universal right to education includes initial education – before pre-school – for children under 3 years old. Before 1993 the Constitution only defined a norm for primary school (six years of education starting at age six). The prevailing text of Article 3 states that 'initial education, pre-school, primary, and secondary education form the basic compulsory education'. Since initial education is not a pre-requisite to enter pre-school, its compulsoriness is not operational.

It should be noted that Article 3 of the Mexican Constitution starts with the statement, 'Every person has a right to education'. This right includes everyone, not only children and adolescents, as reflected in the existence of the Instituto Nacional para la Educación de Adultos (National Institute for Adult Education), devoted to educate adults who have not attained the normative minimum. Based on this, we can conclude that: the right to education applies to all the country's population, not only to children aged 15 or under; people who did not attend school 'on time', in childhood or adolescence, do not lose this right; the state is legally obligated to provide educational services from pre-school to preparatory school; and attending to all those adults below the threshold is an obligation of the state. This analysis of educational legislation clearly shows that, strictly speaking, the educational norm established in Mexican law is the right that every inhabitant of the country has to three years of pre-school education, six of primary education, and six of secondary education.

These legislative standards coincide with prevailing perceptions among the population. The survey 'Perceptions of the Urban Population on Minimal Norms of Basic Needs Satisfaction' – carried out by Profeco among 2,470 households of 18 cities in 2000 – has shown that more than 75% of the urban population considers preparatory education as the minimum for everyone. Regarding the question on the minimal educational level that any person should attain these days, only 20.7% answered lower secondary school (nine years); 45.9% answered preparatory school (12 years); and 25.7% (a higher percentage than for lower secondary school) said higher and postgraduate education. Thus, 71.6% of the interviewees answered preparatory school or more: convincing evidence. More recent surveys on population perceptions on basic needs reached similar conclusions. In short, for the young population the norm should be set at preparatory education (12 years plus pre-school), while lower secondary school should be the norm for those aged 39 or above. Given the fact that adult education becomes more difficult for people aged 69 and above, the norm for poverty measurement among this group can be set at primary school (nine years).

The COPLAMAR study carried out in 1982, when the knowledge economy was still incipient, set two alternative thresholds: primary and secondary. Additionally, one should consider that the conception of poverty adopted in the IPMM is relative poverty. In 1970, only 29.5% of the population over 15 years of age had completed primary education, and only 8.5% of those aged 18 and above had completed secondary education (COPLAMAR, 1982c: Graphic 5, 51, and 55). In 2000, 70.9% of people aged 15 years and above had completed primary education, more than twice the figure in 1970. The proportion of the population over 15 that had completed secondary education reached 45.9%, 5.4 times the figure in 1970 (INEGI, National Population Census, 2000). Recent figures are still higher: according to the ENIGH 2005, the proportion of people who completed secondary education was 54.5%, and 75.6% for primary education. In 2020, 63% of the population had attained the educational norms established here, which includes population aged 4 years and older, as will be shown below.

The achievement threshold currently used in the IPMM by Evalúa CDMX and by me is close to the average HH educational achievement level. For persons aged 18 and older, the educational norm is 15 years of schooling (with completion of higher secondary/preparatory education).

The pre-school educational standard in Mexico was modified in 2003, making young children's attendance in pre-school compulsory for three years prior to primary school, starting at three years old. Before this modification, only one year was compulsory.

In contrast to Dw and sanitary indicators, the educational indicator accounts for adequacy or deprivation at the individual level, not the HH. It is a combined indicator that comprises the adequacy of the education level attained according to the age of the individual; attendance to school (if between ages four and 17); and literacy level. The latter acts basically as a control variable. Therefore, the indicator is calculated for people aged three and older, for whom the ENIGH reports whether they attend school, their literacy level, as well as the last completed level and grade of education.

Although preparatory school is already a right for all adults in the country and the state is obligated to provide the necessary means for every adult to complete it, for the purposes of the IPMM I considered that adult education becomes difficult from a certain age onwards. Therefore, to set the standards I also considered the characteristics of historical advances in Mexico's educational levels. The standard of having a complete preparatory education was set only for people aged 19 to 39; the threshold for individuals aged 40 to 69 is lower secondary school (nine years plus pre-school); finally, the primary school threshold is applicable to those aged 70 and older. The thresholds for minors are established according to the grade they should have completed according to their age, allowing for one year off. So, for example, individuals who are 7 years old at the time of the interview are

Table 8.6: School attendance standard/threshold

Age	Normative educational grades (E*)	Normative school attendance (SA*)
3	0	No
4	0	Yes
5	1	Yes
6	2	Yes
7	3	Yes
8	4	Yes
9	5	Yes
10	6	Yes
11	7	Yes
12	8	Yes
13	9	Yes
14	10	Yes
15	11	Yes
16	12	Yes
17	13	Yes
18	14	No
19	15	No
20–39	15	No
40–69	12	No
70+	9	No

Source: Own elaboration based on ENIGH 2020

only required to have completed pre-school and be attending school, that is, the first year of primary school (see Table 8.6).

Indicators of attendance, years of schooling, and literacy

The variable that accounts for school attendance of individuals (SA) takes a value of 1 when the individual attends school, and of 0 otherwise. This indicator, like all the following ones, are only calculated for persons aged three years or older, since the ENIGH does not capture these data for children under three. The indicator of completed years of schooling (E) is taken from the individual report of the last grade and level of schooling approved. The literacy achievement variable (LA) takes the value of 1 for people who report that they can read and write, and of 0 for those who cannot. The normative value of years of schooling (E★) expresses the schooling level that each person should have achieved according to their age (Table 8.6). In addition, the table includes the normative value of school attendance (SA★) for persons between four and 17 years of age.

Individual and HH educational achievement/deprivation indicators

Below is the formula for calculating individual educational achievement (IEA_{IJ}). It includes the following elements: observed years of schooling (E_{IJ}) for each individual of age A; normative years of schooling given the individual's age ($E\star^A$); school attendance (SA_{IJ}) required for all individuals aged four to 19 who have not completed 15 years of total schooling; and literacy achievement as a control variable (LA_{IJ}). SA_{IJ} and normative $SA\star^A$ will be valued 1 when attending or attending required, respectively, and 0 when not attending or attending not required, respectively. For its part, literacy is required from age 10 onwards; LA_{IJ} will be valued 1 if not required, 1 if required and achieved, and 0 if required but not achieved. In all formulas, individuals are denoted with subscript I and HH with subscript J. In all cases an asterisk denotes normative and superscript A denotes age of individual:

$$IEA_{IJ} = [(E_{IJ} + SA_{IJ}) / (E\star^A + SA\star^A)] [LA_{IJ}] \qquad (8.57)$$

In (8.57), IEA_{IJ} has not been transformed into a WB indicator. It is still expressed in terms of years of schooling vis á vis the norm, plus attendance at school. For persons aged 70 and older with a Ph.D., its value can reach 3 (since E_{IJ} can reach 26–27 and $E\star^A$ is 9, values which total almost 3 when applied to Equation 8.57). As already stated, WB achievement indicators should range from 0 to 2 with the norm at 1. In this case, the norm is indeed at 1, but the maximum value can exceed 2. We must therefore rescale the values above 1 so that they range from 1 to 2. This is necessary only for persons aged 40 or older (below this age it is impossible to reach an IEA_{IJ} above 2). As education is a special type of good, where one can assume a constant marginal WB (a later year adds as much WB as an earlier one), a linear adjustment is adequate. This is the general expression for rescaling IEA values above 2:

$$IEA'_{IJ} = 1 + [(IEA_{IJ} - 1) / (\max IEA_{IJ} - 1)] \mid IEA > 1, \text{ and ages 30+} \qquad (8.58)$$

As we have already seen, this type of rescaling formula is employed in other indicators, including Y poverty. The maximum in the formula has two types of interpretation: one is as an empirical maximum (in the case of education, it is the maximum attainable IEA_{IJ}) and the other one is a conceptual maximum – the level at which WB is assumed to reach a maximum. The latter is the interpretation applied to space in the Dw: as one adds rooms to a Dw, WB increases up to a point where marginal WB becomes either null or negative. This would clearly be the case when the number of rooms is such that finding a person requires electronic communication, or when moving within the Dw requires transport systems or long walks. In the case of education, no conceptual maxima seem acceptable, as learning is a non-satiable activity (since knowledge accumulated by humanity can be regarded as infinite in terms of an individual's lifespan). Therefore, in this case only a practical maximum can be identified: the PhD, considered the maximum-level formal diploma available and interpreted as 26 years of formal study (including three pre-school years). The ENIGH surveys do not identify anything beyond the PhD.

The maximum IEA_{IJ} for the age groups 40–69 and 70+ can be above 2. These values are rescaled in (8.58) to obtain IEA', thus attaining the desired range 0 to 2 for the achievement indicator. For people under 40 years of age, IEA' = IEA.

Finally, the individual educational deprivation indicator is:

$$IED_{IJ} = 1 - IEA'_{IJ} \qquad (8.58a)$$

IED_{IJ} ranges from −1 to +1, with the norm at 0.

Using the ENIGH 2020 databases, we found that 37.8% of the population had educational scores that do not comply with the norms presented. Thus, they are educationally deprived (H = 37.8%, 47.9 million persons). Out of this segment, more than 12 million persons aged eight years or above were illiterate. However, the great majority of this deprived population (63%) were classified as moderately poor, which shows that they are not too far away from the norm.

The HH Educational Achievement Indicator (HEA_J) is the simple average of the individual indicators:

$$HEA_J = \Sigma IEA'_{IJ} / m \qquad (8.59)$$

where m is the number of persons aged four or above.

And, finally, the HH Educational Deprivation Indicator (HED_J) is:

$$HED_J = 1 - HEA_J \qquad (8.59a)$$

8.3.7 Health Services (HS) and Social Security (SS)

As already mentioned, unlike the previous dimensions of UBN, the HS and SS indicators are built based on a mixed verification procedure. All HH are scored for affiliation to a health system and their Y is compared with two factors: first, the cost of voluntary (V) subscription to the compulsory regime of IMSS (Mexican Social Security Institute) ($VSS), which covers not only in-kind health services but also all other risks covered by SS in Mexico, except work risks, and second, the private market possibilities for HS and SS.

In HS the concept to be measured is access to (and economic capacity to access) adequate and complete HS for each person. The adequacy standard is access to comprehensive health services – without exclusions of diseases or medical interventions – covering the primary, secondary, and tertiary HS levels, including rehabilitation and dental care.

HS achievement (HSA_{IJ}) and SS achievement (SSA_{IJ})

HSA_{IJ}. People entitled to the services provided by the SS institutions (IMSS, ISSSTE (Institute for Social Security and Services for State Workers), individual states' ISSSTE) are regarded as being in the normative condition in both HS and SS; they are protected (P_R) in both and their score is 1.0. People entitled to the HS and SS provided by PEMEX (the Mexican state-owned oil company), the army, or the navy – which are also SS institutions – are considered above the normative level, both in HS and SS, given that the quality of these institutions' overall services is better than that of IMSS or ISSSTE. They are therefore regarded as over-protected (OP_R) and have a score of 1.2 in both HS and SS.

I will now refer to HS institutions that do not provide SS. People entitled to the services provided by 'Seguro Popular', INSABI (Health Institute for Well-Being), or IMSS-Bienestar – which provide truncated or incomplete HS – are below the normative level, are classified as under-protected 1 (UP_R1), and receive a score of 0.51 in HSA. Individuals registered in 'other medical services' receive an even lower score (0.33) and are classified as UP_R2. Interviewees (only those aged 12 years or above) who declared being affiliated to university services (which provide only primary health services) were also scored 0.33, while those who declared being affiliated to private medical services or having private medical insurance were given a score of 1.5 in HSA. In all these cases, persons are classified as not protected (NP_R) in SS.

All persons who are NP_R by their job, or who do not qualify to receive SS by being relatives (dependants) of an affiliated person, and who declared not being affiliated to SS, are considered NP_R in SS. As in HS, people affiliated to PEMEX, the army, or the navy are given a score of 1.2 in SS. Individuals aged over 65 years who receive the alimentary pension for older adults (APOA) – which was 35% of the minimum wage in 2020 – will receive a score of 0.3 and will be considered UP_R1 in SS.

The institutionally NP_R might still have access to HS via two voluntary paths in IMSS: one is called voluntary affiliation to IMSS in-kind medical services (only) (VHSSS), sometimes referred to as family services, and the

The Integrated Poverty Measurement Method (IPMM)

Table 8.7: Annual $VIMSS$_i$ per person, voluntary IMSS HS insurance, 2020

Age group	Ages	Annual costs
AG1	Children under 19 years old	$4,650
AG2	From 20 to 29 years old	$5,500
AG3	From 30 to 39 years old	$5,850
AG4	From 40 to 49 years old	$8,100
AG5	From 50 to 59 years old	$8,450
AG6	From 60 to 69 years old	$12,250
AG7	From 70 to 79 years old	$12,700
AG8	Over 79 years old	$12,750

Source: Mexican Social Security Institute web page (www.imss.gob.mx)

other is the voluntary affiliation to the compulsory SS regime (VCSSR). These are the publicly produced 'market' forms of access. IMSS sells two kinds of insurance: one that only includes HS and the other that also includes SS. The costs of these options are denoted as $VHS and $VSS. The former has an individual character, and its cost changes according to age, as specified in Table 8.7. The latter includes HS and all the insurances provided by SS (except work risks): invalidity and life; retirement, unemployment in advanced age; old age; and playgroups and social benefits. Private insurance companies also sell medical and retirement insurances, so that the option to obtain a vital capacity to access adequate market VHS or VSS becomes a function of Y.

For the purposes of these two indicators, HH_j is deemed capable of accessing adequate HS and SS when their Y is higher than the sum of the HH_j PL plus $VHS and $VSS. A good option for a HH with several dependants is VSS, as the cost is independent of the number of dependants. A good strategy for a HH with several dependants, but that also has one or more non-dependent persons as defined in the law of IMSS (and who are therefore not entitled to SS via the affiliation of the 'virtual worker', VW) is to pay IMSS for additional individual VHS for said persons. The $VSS covers the affiliated person (considered as a worker without an employer, or a virtual worker) and their dependants as defined in the law of IMSS. The affiliated person's payment includes both the amount paid by ordinary dependent employees to SS, and the amount paid by employers (except payments made for work risks and to INFONAVIT, which is a fund for housing loans for dependent workers). The monthly payment depends on the amount declared by the VW as their monthly Y (payment is around 16% of their monthly Y). When the VW retires, they will receive a life annuity according to the prevailing rules in the national system of pensions. Said annuity will be a function of the VW's monthly savings, the number of months these savings have been maintained, and the real rate of interest earned on them. Due to the great variations of this last variable, and because commissions are charged by the financial institutions managing the savings, the amount of the monthly pension is undetermined, as it depends on the real rate of return for savings, age of retirement, and life expectancy. This is an important shortcoming of present-day SS that applies not only to VW but to dependent employees as well. An important advantage is that the government guarantees a minimal pension equal to the minimum wage when the amount saved by the worker is not enough; in other words, the worker receives a subsidy.

This means that the sum with which available Y in HH J – without subtracting HS and SS observed expenditures – denoted as Ya'$_J$, would be compared is PL$_J$ + \$VSS$_J$ + \$VHS$_J$. If Ya'$_J$ ≥ PL$_J$ + \$VSS$_J$ + \$VHS$_J$, HSA$_J$ and SSA$_J$ will both be ≥ 1.0. Note that the required \$VHS$_J$ will be null in HH where VSS$_J$ covers all its members. The best strategy for any NP$_R$ HH is to cover \$VSS$_J$ first and only then pay VHS to cover young persons without dependants and not covered by SS. However, income-poor HH will not be able to follow this path and will remain deprived in HS and SS. This path is applicable to non-Y-poor HH whose Y is not enough to cover all their NP$_R$ or UPR members. The lessons learnt from poverty survival strategies suggest the following coverage priorities, in decreasing order: breadwinners, starting with the one whose Y is the highest; active women who take care of one or more children aged under 12 years; non-economically active children, starting with the older ones; students; and adults who do not work or study, starting with the youngest. Individuals in HH with one or more NP$_R$ individuals will be ranked from 1 to n, according to these priorities. These decisions are reflected in the table of scores (Table 8.8).

NP$_R$ or UP$_R$ HH/I with a larger Y than the one required for paying \$VSS can opt for private medical insurance (PMI), which is many times more expensive than VSS (Z\$VSS > \$PMI > X\$VSS), where Z is 55.4 and X is 5.7). For ages 20 to 59, \$PMI are much higher for women than men. To simplify the notation, I have calculated the quotient \$PMI / \$VSS for each age/sex group and used them to express \$PMI. The table of scores is presented in Table 8.8. The concept of Y used is available Y (Ya'$_J$) after expenditures on S verified by UBN (education, Dw, basic Dw-related services, durable goods, but not the payment of VSS or VHS, nor observed health expenditures) have been subtracted from CY. To obtain the per capita available Y of each I in HH$_J$, I divided HH$_J$ by the number of HH members (N) in J: Ya$_{IJ}$ = Ya$_J$ / N. Also, to obtain the proxy[1] PL$_{IJ}$, I divided PL$_J$ by N when Ya$_J$ was larger than PL. The table of scores for HSAAj and HSSj (with the norm at 1) is:

---

[1] There is no correct per capita PL concept, since PL must be calculated by HH given the presence of family G&S. Thus, the proxy PL$_J$ is only a helpful quantity to quantify the sufficiency of Ya'$_J$.

The Integrated Poverty Measurement Method (IPMM)

Table 8.8: Scores for $HSAA_{ij}$ and HSS_{ij}

First part: access criterion only

1 P_i and $(Ya'_j \leq PL_j) = 1 = HSA_{ij} *$ normative level $= SSA_{ij} = 1$

2 OP_i (PEMEX, Army, or Navy) & $(Ya'_j \leq PL_j) = 1.2$ in both HSA and SSA

2a OP2: Private medical services or private medical insurance = 1.5 only in HSA

3 NP_i in HS and $(Ya'_j < PL_j) = HSAIJ = HSS_{ij} = 0$

4 $UP2_i$ in HS and $(Ya'_j < PL_j) = 0.33$ in HAS_i and $= 0$ in SSA_{ij}

5 $UP1_i$ in HS and $(Ya'_j < PL_j) = 0.51$ in HAS_i and $= 0$ in SSA_{ij}

In cases 1 to 5, HH_j are Y poor and the access criterion prevails absolutely both in HS and SS

6 NP or UP_i in SS (APOA) and $(Ya'_j < PL_j) = 0.3$ in SS

Second part: economic capacity to access voluntary insurances in IMSS

7 NP_i, $UP1_i$, $UP2_i$, and $(Ya'_j \geq PL_j + \Sigma \$VSS_{ij}) = P_i = HSA_i = SSA_i = 1$

7.1 NP_i, $UP1_i$, $UP2_i$, & $(PL_j + \$VSSIJ < Ya'_j < PL_j + \Sigma \$VSS_{ij}) = 1$ for the affiliated person and the lawfully dependent HH members

7.2 NP_i, $UP1_i$, $UP2_i$, not protected in 7.1 and $(PL_j + \$VHS_{ij}) < Ya'_j < PL_j + \Sigma \$VSS_{ij}) = 1|$ not protected in 7.1; if 7.2 is valid only for one NP person, the remaining persons will maintain their access criterion score

Third part: economic capacity to access PMI and private vital rent (PVR)

8 For the cases in 7 where $Ya'_j \geq PL_j + \Sigma \$VSS_{ij}$, a second test is performed to determine if the HH has the economic capacity to pay for PMI and for a private savings programme that will provide the person with a vital rent or life annuity (a private alternative to a pension in SS)

Note: 8.1 Ya'_j has been contrasted with the cost of PMI ($\$PMI_i$) according to age groups (AG#, where # = 1 to 8) and sex group, identified by the corresponding symbols (♀ and ♂). PMI annual costs are expressed as multiples (M) of $\$VHS$: M$\$VHS$. When a PMI is bought for an individual, the latter's HSA score can be upgraded from the access criterion score to the highest HSA score: 1.5. A triage procedure is applied for allocating Y above PL_{ij} to PMI if Y does not suffice to pay all HH member's $\$PMI$. The order of priority is as follows: 1) the main breadwinner; 2) in HH with children aged under 12, the mother or caretaker of the children; 3) children; 4) the remaining HH members from younger to older. The results are the following (regardless of the score obtained in the access criterion):

8.1.1 $Ya'_j > (PL_{ij} + 5.8\$VSS) = 1$ member of AG1 ♀/♂ = 1.5

8.1.2 $Ya'_j > (PL_{ij} + 6.5\$VSS) = 1$ ♂ member of AG2 = 1.5

8.1.2a $Ya_j > (PL_{ij}^P + 8.5\$VSS) = 1$ ♀ member of AG2 = 1.5

8.1.3 $Ya_j > (PL_{ij}^P + 7.9\$VSS) = 1$ ♂ member of AG3 = 1.5

8.1.3a $Ya_j > (PL_{ij}^P + 10.8\$VSS) = 1$ ♀ member of AG3 = 1.5

8.1.4 $Ya_j > (PL_{ij}^P + 8.3\$VSS) = 1$ ♂ member of AG4 = 1.5

8.1.4a $Ya_j > (PL_{ij}^P + 10.8\$VSS) = 1$ ♀ member of AG4 = 1.5

8.1.5 $Ya_j > (PL_{ij}^P + 13.1\$VSS) = 1$ ♂ member of AG5 = 1.5

8.1.5a $Ya_j > (PL_{ij}^P + 14.9\$VSS) = 1$ ♀member of AG5 = 1.5

8.1.6 $Ya_j > (PL_{ij}^P + 16.5\$VSS) = 1$ ♀/♂ member of AG6 = 1.5

8.1.7 $Ya_j > (PL_{ij}^P + 31.2\$VSS) = 1$ ♀/♂ member of AG7 = 1.5

8.1.8 $Ya_j > (PL_{ij}^P + 55.3\$VSS) = 1$ ♀/♂ member of AG8 = 1.5

(continued)

Table 8.8: Scores for HSAA$_{IJ}$ and HSS$_{IJ}$ (continued)

Note: In case 7, Ya'J is enough for a HHJ to pay $VSS for all NP or UP HH members. This may involve the affiliation to VSS of more than one HH member. All members are considered at the norm in both HS and SS. In 7.1, Ya'J is enough for a HHJ to pay $VSS for all lawfully dependent members that become entitled to SS with one affiliated VW, but not enough for two or more affiliations to VSS; in this case, (7.2) is tested: if Ya'J is enough to pay for 1 or n persons affiliated to VHS (see Table 8.7 for annual costs of $VHS according to age), these 1 to n persons will be considered P in HS, though not in SS, and will maintain their access score.

As both VSS and PIM are not divisible, all monetary residuals below the required quantities for an additional member will not be considered.

Economic capacity to access a private vital rent (PVR). Some private insurance companies have plans that combine life insurance with a form of saving. After paying a monthly prime during a pre-established period, the policyholder obtains a guaranteed life annuity of Y$ per month. For this P measuring exercise, I defined the guaranteed life annuity as equal to the proxy average per capita PL of 2020 – 4,012.9 Mexican pesos – for people retiring at age 65. The monthly prime is a function of the age at which one starts paying. If this happens at age 20 and payments continue for 45 years, the monthly prime would be $1,041 ($12,492 per year); if one starts paying at 30 and pays for 35 years, the monthly payment would be $1,435 ($17,220 yearly); starting at 40, one would pay $2,318 monthly ($27,816 yearly); and lastly, if one starts paying at 50, one would pay $4,379 monthly ($52, 548 yearly). In case of death one would receive $872,794. In all cases, one receives $4,012 from 65 until death. But $4,012 is the PL per capita. Assuming that older persons have few dependants, $PVR will be multiplied by 2. This PVR does not apply for persons over 50. For intermediate years, I apply the closest figure: if a person is 43 years old, the payment is the same as at 40. This is indicated below as PVR^A, and all payments are annual.

Since both PMI and PVR must be bought, I will assume that the third test for PVR is applied only to HH whose Y has passed the second test (PMI). This is reflected in the following equations.

If Ya'$_J$ > (PL$_j$ + 16.5$VSSS + 2$PVR^A) = SSA$_I$ = 1.5, the deprivation indicators will be:

$$HSD_{IJ} = 1 - HSA_{IJ} \qquad (8.60)$$

$$SSD_{IJ} = 1 - SSA_{IJ} \qquad (8.61)$$

whose range will be from −0.5 to +1, with the norm at 0.

As explained above, a complex (but as yet incomplete) research on these two last indicators was carried out for this book. Considering only the population with a complete and acceptable access to these two services (via public institutional providers and with no payments or very low payments by the beneficiaries), the population covered with acceptable and mostly free HS (mainly via IMSS, but also PEMEX, the army, and the navy) was of 79.65 million in 2020 according to ENIGH, that is, 62.83% of the national population (POP), while the corresponding figure for SS was of 78.94 million, 62.28% of POP. The difference is explained by students covered by IMSS only in HS. But the alternative paths to adequate HS and SS explained above – both of which are market solutions offered by both by IMSS and private insurance companies – as evaluated by the HH's paying capacity, meant that 3.0% of the national population could cease to be deprived in HS by paying market health services (either IMSS or private). If everyone who could afford them would pay for these services, deprivation (H) in HS could drop from 40.2% to 37.2%. Surprising is that the number of people who can pay for PMI – which corresponds to the highest score in HS available in Mexico – sky-rocketed from 5.59 million to 14.4 million, 11.4% of POP, who were thus classified in the high stratum of HS. By adding the population now classified in the middle stratum to these figures, one reaches 12.1% of POP, compared with 4.8% without considering these private paths. A substantial proportion of this increase is reflected in a drastic drop in the number of people with only right of access to HS in the SS institutions, which suggests that they were able to pay for private medical services. In everyday life, many Mexican citizens are or know people who are affiliated to IMSS or ISSSTE but who never use these services. Most of these people do not have PMI, but when in need go to private medical services (including quite expensive ones). The prevailing opinion (which is partly correct) is that IMSS and ISSSTE provide low-quality HS, especially at the first level. Some people only use these services when confronted with an illness/treatment that they could not afford in a private hospital. One argument supporting this methodology is that, conceptually, it is equivalent to adding the private cost of medical attention in the PL of HH/persons with no access to SS HS.

As expected, given that the innovations introduced in both HS and SS are related to high levels of satisfaction of the need, the HS new methodology (NM) implied a very small change in the levels of HS deprivation when compared with the previous methodology (PM) (40.2% before the changes and 37.2% after them, but a very impressive change in the composition of the HS's non-P. With the PM most of the non-poor were in the minimum satisfaction stratum (MSS); with the NM the middle and upper strata went up to 15.1 million (12.1% of the whole population) and the MSS diminished to 64.3 million. SS proportion of deprived diminished substantially 37.7% to 47.1 million), while the proportion represented by middle and upper strata moved from zero to 9.1%. This innovation corrected a big mistake of the previous methodology that implied having some very rich people classified as poor in SS.

8.3.8 UBN composite indicator

Based on the results of the eight previous indicators, we obtain a global index of UBN for each HH_J and individual HH_{IJ}. The procedure is a weighted average of the eight dimensions, using the costs obtained in the complete NBES as weights. The latter are shown in Table 8.9.

$$UBNA_J = HQSA_J (Q_1) + DGA_J (Q_2) + WSSA_J (Q_3) + CSA_J (Q_4) + EnA_J (Q_5) + EA_J (Q_6) + HSA_J (Q_7) + SSA_J (Q_8)$$

In 2020 I obtained the stratification of individuals in UBN shown in Table 8.10, using the six strata employed in $IPMM_J$ for all its indicators and components.

8.4 Detailed description of IPMM poverty indicators, Part 2: income and time

8.4.1 Income (Y)

Current HH_J Y is constructed by adding the CY of all HH members (excluding guests and HH workers). It does not include purely financial flows:

$$Y_J = \Sigma Y_{IJ} \mid \text{for I belonging to } HH_J \qquad (8.62)$$

Table 8.9: UBN components and weights

Achievement indicators of specific components	Weight (Q)
$HQSA_J$: Housing quality and space availability	0.328 (Q_1)
DGA_J: Durable goods	0.058 (Q_2)
$WSSA_J$: Water and sanitary services	0.037 (Q_3)
CSA_J: Communication services	0.030 (Q_4)
EnA_J: Domestic energy	0.028 (Q_5)
EA_J: Education	0.236 (Q_6)
HSA_J: Health services	0.1415 (Q_7)
SSA_J: Social security	0.1415 (Q_8)
$UBNA_J$: Consolidated UBN	1.0000

The Integrated Poverty Measurement Method (IPMM)

Table 8.10: UBN integrated strata of individuals

Strata	Individuals (millions)	%
1 Very intense poverty	16.680	13.2
2 Intense poverty	19.978	15.8
3 = 1 + 2 Extreme poverty (EP)	36.659	28.9
4 Moderate poverty (MP)	49.538	39.1
5 = 3 + 4 Sum of poverty (TP)	86.197	68.0
6 Minimum satisfaction stratum (MSS)	14.742	11.6
7 Medium stratum (MS)	24.247	19.1
8 Upper stratum (US)	1.576	1.2
9 = 6 + 7 + 8 Sum of non-poverty (TNP)	40.564	32.0
Total population	126.761	100.0

Y_j includes both monetary Y and Y in kind; the following Y sources are distinguished: wages/salaries (W); imputed rent of own Dw (IRODw); Y from own business (YOBSN) (which equals gross operating surplus); property Y/rent (PR) (which includes interests, rents, and profits/dividends from corporate enterprises); governmental transferences (GVT) (monetary and in kind); and transferences from other sources (OT). The total national HH CY is represented as follows:

$$NHHY = \Sigma Y_j \mid \text{all HH in the country} \qquad (8.62a)$$

In terms of Y sources, it is expressed as:

$$NHHY = \Sigma(W, IRODw, BSN, PR, GVT, OT) \mid \text{over all HH in the country} \qquad (8.63)$$

The NHHY obtained by expanding the sample of HH surveyed in ENIGH is substantially below the one calculated for the institutional HH sector in national accounts (NA). Using ENIGH HH data would lead to overestimating Y P and underestimating Y inequality. For this reason, the HH Y figures derived from ENIGH were adjusted to NA before comparing HHY_j with its respective PL_j. Underestimation in ENIGH varies very much according to Y source. Therefore, a specific adjustment factor (AF) was calculated for each of the Y sources. The AF to NA's HH Y in 2020 are shown in Table 8.11.

Table 8.11: Adjustment factors of Y captured by ENIGH to NA, 2020

Sources of Y	Adjustment factor (AF)
Total HH Y	2.22
Wages/salaries (W) (AF1)	1.0
Imputed rent for own dwelling, IRODw (AF2)	1.20
Own business (gross operating surplus) (AF3)	4.8
Property rent (dividends, rents, interests) (AF4)	43.23
Government transfers (AF5)	1.0*
Non-governmental transfers (AF6)	2.59

* This item was left intentionally unadjusted. Given governmental corruption, it is likely that not all reported governmental transferences reach their beneficiaries. There can be substantial leaks.

As can be inferred from the large differences between the AF of the diverse Y sources, ENIGH not only underestimates HH Y but also misrepresents the structure of Y sources, as can be seen in Table 8.12.

The monthly average value of adjusted Y per HH was $38,328 pesos, while the non-adjusted one was $17,273.

The AF shown in Table 8.12 for Y from own business (gross operating surplus) is an average, but specific AF were calculated according to establishment size, available both in ENIGH and in the Economic Censuses. We found that, in general, the larger the establishment, the larger the underestimation of this Y from capital in ENIGH. In non-agricultural establishments, the AF ranges from 1.0 in establishments with one to five workers, up to 181.4 in establishments with 101 workers and more. The middle ranges include AF of 6.6 in establishments with 16 to 20 workers and 13.1 in those with 21 to 30 workers.

Once adjusted, all expenditures by HH_j in items not included in the PL – because, as specified in the methodology, these items are directly verified by UBN – were subtracted from Y_j to obtain Ya_j to acquire the type of G&S included in the NBES. The subtracted expenditure items were those included in educational services, housing expenses, household goods and articles, acquisition of vehicles, monthly rent, and health expenditures. In 2020 the average of this deducted Y was $3,882.9 per month.

The variable Ya_j is compared with PL to measure Y achievement or deprivation. Non-recurring Y items (like compensations for injuries or work accidents) were also subtracted, since they cannot be properly conceived as part of Y.

Table 8.12: Structure of HH Y sources from ENIGH

Adjusted and not adjusted to national accounts		
	% adjusted	% not adjusted
Total Y	100.00	100.00
Wages/salaries	24.34	56.17
IRODw	6.58	12.61
Transferences (gov and non-gov)	20.67	18.34
Y from own business	27.20	11.78
Rent from property	21.21	1.10

PL definition

The cost of the NBES constitutes the PL, the threshold by which HH_j Y is divided to determine whether it is poor and its poverty level. The N whose satisfaction is verified by PL have been enumerated in Section 8.2.

The cost of the NBES for each specific HH as a function of the number of members and EAs is expressed in the following formula, constructed by Boltvinik (2010a: 199) based on Marin (2003):

$$PL^{P, EA} = a + b(P) + c(EA) \qquad (8.64)$$

where P denotes the number of HH members, EA the male equivalent adults, and a, b, and c are parameters derived from the specific NBES for each age group. Thus, the cost of PL-NBES is determined by the fixed costs of the NBES (a), plus the variable costs per person (b), and the variable costs per EA (c). In 2020, this formula acquired the following values – for rural localities (up to 2,500 inhabitants) and for urban localities (over 2,500 persons):

Urban PL $(NBES)^{P, EA}$ = \$1,597.20 + (\$257.72 $\star$ P) + (\$3,886.34 $\star$ EA)

Rural PL $(NBES)^{P, EA}$ = \$1,590.44 + (\$258.00 $\star$ P) + (\$3,514.76 $\star$ EA)

Although every HH has an individualised PL, the empirical average (national, including rural and urban) monthly PL per HH was \$14,245.07, and \$4,017.46 per person. The average HH size was 3.5458 persons, and the average EA size per HH, 2.9038.

Achievement indicator of HH available Y

HH current available Y (Ya_j) is divided by PL_j to generate the achievement Y indicator: YaA_j. PL is the normative threshold for HH Y.

$$YaA_j = Ya_j / PL_j \qquad (8.65)$$

The value of YaA_j in 2020 was 2.6608, which clearly shows that Ya_j was on average well above average PL_j.

As with achievement indicators in other dimensions, the values of YaA_j above 1 must be rescaled and re-expressed in terms of OWB. As in other cases, a conceptual maximum is defined, considering decreasing marginal WB and the existence of a maximum WB level above which the increase in Y does not generate additional WB. A maximum conceptual level of ten times the PL was defined for Y. This means that between 1PL and 9.99PL there is a less than proportional increase in WB, while at 10PL WB attains its maximum. This rescaling is expressed as follows:

$$YaA_j' = 1 + [(Ya_j - 1) / (\max YaA_j)] = 1 + [(Ya_j - 1) / 9] \\ \mid \text{for } YaAj > 1 \qquad (8.66)$$

A final modification is made for HH that still remain above the value of 2: they are assigned a value equal to 2 by applying the principle of the existence of a maximum WB level:

If $YaA_j' > 2$, then $YaA_j' = 2$

This allows us to preserve the range from 0 to 2 for all variables and avoid undesired (and hidden) additional weights. The rescaled Y deprivation indicator (YaD_j') is stated as follows:

$$YaD_j' = 1 - YaA_j' \qquad (8.67)$$

The statistical descriptors of the rescaled indicator (proxy of WB) are set out in Table 8.13.

The results – total poor, non-poor, and their respective strata – for 2020 are shown in Table 8.14.

New methodology for measuring time poverty

The use of time is expressed in terms of hours (hrs) in an ordinary week. The number of annual working weeks is not captured in ENIGH's surveys, which does not allow for calculation of annual FT. The week has 168 hrs; out of these, we estimate that adults must dedicate around 8 hrs daily to sleep and 2 hrs to eating and personal care, that is, 70 weekly hrs to what could be called

The Integrated Poverty Measurement Method (IPMM)

Table 8.13: Some statistical descriptors of the distributions of YaA$_j$' and YaD$_j$

	Mean	Median	Minimum	Maximum
YaA$_j$'	0.859	0.946	0.000	2.000
YaD$_j$'	0.141	0.054	-1.000	1.000

Table 8.14: Income individual's strata by values of YaD$_{ij}$'

	Individual	
	Millions	%
1 Very intense poverty (VIP) (0.5 < YaD$_{ij}$' ≤ 1.0)	32.286	25.5
2 Intense poverty (IP) (0.5 ≥ YaD$_{ij}$' > 1/3)	16.783	13.2
3 = 1 + 2 Extreme poverty (EP) (1/3 ≤ YaD$_{ij}$' ≤ 1.0)	49.069	38.7
4 Moderate poverty (MP) (1/3 ≥ YaD$_{ij}$' > 0)	26.298	20.8
5 = 3 + 4 Sum of poverty (total poverty, TP) (YaD$_{ij}$' > 0)	75.367	59.5
6 Minimum satisfaction stratum (MSS) (-0.1 < YaD$_{ij}$' < 0)	34.970	27.6
7 Medium stratum (MS) (-0.5 ≤ YaD$_{ij}$' ≤ -0.1)	12.452	9.8
8 Upper stratum (US) (-1.0 ≥ YaD$_{ij}$' ≤ 0.5)	3.972	3.1
9 = 6 + 7 + 8. Sum of non-poverty (TNP) (0 ≥ YaD$_{ij}$' ≤ -1)	51.394	40.5
Total population	126.761	100.00

maintenance or replacement of capacities or individual replenishment time (IRT). The time dedicated by adults to take care of minors, elderly adults, and disabled and sick persons (who can be grouped as people requiring care, PRC), I will call replenishment time for PRC (RT$_{PRC}$). The sum of IRT and RT$_{PRC}$ can be called family replenishment time (FRT).

$$FRT = IRT + RT_{PRC} \qquad (8.68)$$

The IRT standard for people aged 18+ is:

$$IRT\star_{IJ}^{18+} = 10 \text{ hrs per day} \mid \text{people aged 18+} \qquad (8.69)$$

IRT$\star_{IJ}$ increases as the age below 18 decreases, since younger persons require more hours of sleep.

The maximum norm for extra-domestic (or market) working time (EDWT$\star$) for people aged 18 to 69 (EDWT$\star^{18-69}$) was established based on Mexican legislation at 48 hrs per week (hrsW). This threshold was adjusted to the expanded concept of work that also includes domestic work time (DWT). That is, the EDWT$\star$ norm becomes the total working time norm TWT$\star$ = EDWT$\star$ + DWT$\star$ = 48hrsW.

For the analytical purposes pursued here, we include in EDWT the time required for commuting to and from the workplace, which in the 1917 Mexican legislation were not included, perhaps because cities were small and transportation times short.

DWT includes time dedicated to three areas. First, HH chores (DWHCT): cooking, washing and ironing clothes, cleaning, and so on; shopping and managing the HH (SMHHT); carrying water and firewood (CWFWT); and repairing the house and its equipment (RHET). Second, caring for other people (the RT_{PRC} mentioned above), which includes exclusive or active care in the HH – passive care times (being on the lookout within the HH) are excluded because other activities are always carried out simultaneously; travel times to take or accompany a PRC to school, the physician, and other activities outside the HH. Lastly, voluntary (unpaid) or community working time (V/CWT):[2]

$$DWT = DWHCT + SMHHT + RHET + RT_{PRC} + V/CWT \quad (8.70)$$

Therefore, in (8.71) we establish the norm for the total time that a (non-disabled) adult aged 18 to 69 can devote to the sum of EDW and DW thus defined, which Araceli Damián (2014) has aptly called socially necessary working time (SNWT):

$$SNWT\star_{IJ}^{18-69} = TWT_{IJ}^{18-69} = EDWT_{IJ}^{18-69} + DWTIJ^{18-69} \quad (8.71)$$

Until the initial poverty estimates of 2020, we had considered the 15–69 age group, but we now realise that this choice contradicted the minimum educational level – equivalent to high school – which is attained at the very least at 17 years of age, so that the population aged 15, 16, and 17 should dedicate their full time to education. In addition, the Federal Labour Law (Article 22 bis) prohibits people under 18 who have not completed high school from working. For these two reasons we corrected the age range and wrote (8.71) considering the age group 18–69.

To establish each person's FT, as well as the corresponding norm (FT★), we need to distinguish available or discretionary time (DT) from FT. For individuals who do not have to study – those aged 18 and above, given the educational and working norms – DT is defined as the subtraction of what can be called compulsory time (CT) from TT (from the 24 daily hrs, or the 168 weekly hrs), which is the sum of the IRT and the TWT (remember

---

[2] By classifying volunteer/community work as part of DWT, we extend the concept of *domestic* to the community and to non-profit organisations, which together comprise the universe of unpaid or non-market-oriented work.

that, for measurement purposes, we reclassified RT_{PRC} as part of DWT). Equations for the age group 18–69 are the following:

$$CT_{IJ}^{18-69} = [IRT_{IJ} + EDWT_{IJ} + DWT_{IJ}]^{18-69} \qquad (8.72)$$

$$TT_{IJ}^{18-69} = [CT_{IJ} + DT_{IJ}]^{18-69} \qquad (8.73)$$

$$DT_{IJ}^{18-69} = [TT_{IJ} - C_{IJ}]^{18-69} \qquad (8.74)$$

For the age group 3 to 17, study time (ST) should be considered part of CT. That is, the ST of this age group is not DT or FT: since it is established normatively, it is CT:

$$CT_{IJ}^{3-17} = IRT_{IJ}^{3-17} + ST_{IJ}^{3-17} + EDWT_{IJ}^{3-17} + DWT_{IJ}^{3-17} \qquad (8.72a)$$

$$TT_{IJ}^{3-17} = [CT_{IJ} + DT_{IJ}]^{3-17} \qquad (8.73a)$$

$$DT_{IJ}^{3-17} = [TT_{IJ} - CT_{IJ}]^{3-17} = TT_{IJ}^{3-17} - [IRT_{IJ} + TE_{IJ} + EDWT_{IJ} + DWT_{IJ}]^{3-17} \qquad (8.74a)$$

FT and DT are the same for people aged 3–17. However, for those aged 18 and above, FT can be lower than DT, since to obtain FT we must subtract the time dedicated to study from the DT, for in this age group study is not part of CT. It is part of the DT but not of the FT. It is a time of autonomous discretionary allocation where the individual decides to commit T to study (or not). Conceptually, the same can be said of voluntary work, although community work can imply a sort of external coercion. As time-use surveys capture these two types of work together, we had no choice but to group them as part of DWT and, therefore, of CT as well. Although the dividing line is blurred, we consider ST after high school part of DT but not of FT, since it involves a decision made under less coercion than V/CW.

$$FT^{18+} = DT^{18+} - ST^{18+} \qquad (8.75)$$

$$FT^{3-17} = DT^{3-17} \qquad (8.75a)$$

We classify ST^{18+} as DT but not as FT, and therefore denote it as non-free discretionary time (NFDT). For those aged 3–17, ST is part of CT, so it is not included in the DT in Equations (8.74) and (8.74a).

The concepts of FT and DT do not apply to the population aged 0–2, who do not work or have to study.

Applying the above equations, the disaggregated definition of FT will be:

$$FT_{IJ} = TT_{IJ} - (IRT_{IJ} + EDWT_{IJ} + DWT_{IJ} + NFDT_{IJ} \mid \text{population 3+}$$
(8.76)

Equation (8.76) is valid for the population aged 3+, but among those under 18 the last term ($NFDT_{IJ}$) is always 0, as it also is for those aged 18+ who do not study.

Time-use surveys are only applied to people aged 12+, so although the definition of FT is applicable to individuals aged 3+, the free time achievement (FTA) indicator must be restricted to the population over 12:

$$FTA_{IJ}^{12+} = FT_{IJ}^{12+} / FT_{IJ}^{\star AG}$$
(8.77)

where AG is the person's age group. The presence of this superscript indicates that FT norms vary with people's age. As already stated, neither ENUT 2019 nor the time-use module (MUT) of ENIGH 2020 (MUT-ENIGH) captured time-use information for the population under 12 years old. They only did so for the population aged 12+. Thus, for empirical measurement purposes, we had to narrow (8.77) to said population.

In the denominator of Equation 8.77, some norms were set for the maximum time that the population of 12 to 17 and 70+ could dedicate to DW (see Table 8.15); also, a null EDW★ for those aged 12 to 14 and 70+ was established.

The values of FT_{IJ} – the denominator of (8.77) – will vary according to the norms defined by age group. Table 8.15 presents the norms for time-use by age group and student/non-student status. The table includes standards for IRT (sleep, eating, and self-care); the sum of EDWT (includes commuting to and from work) and DWT as defined above; and ST (attending school or courses, doing homework, commuting times). The sum of these three sets is total CT. Subtracting this total from 168 hrsW (TT) yields the FT or DT for each age group. Although norms have also been defined for children under 12, they cannot be used in empirical measurement, as stated.

As can be seen in this table, the IRT is 70 hrs per week (hrsW) only for people aged 18+; for people aged 3–5, the IRT was set at 91 hrsW (13 daily hrs), since the required daily sleep hours for this age group are around 11.5; those aged 6 to 14 have 84 hrsW with 10.5 daily hrs of sleep; and individuals aged 15 to 17 have 80 hrsW with daily sleep norms at 9.5. The normative EDWT and DWT sum for all children under 18 is 0, because the study load is combined with their higher FT and sleep T requirements. We have also set at 0 the normative sum of both types of W for students aged 18+ who are in higher education, where the study load plus commuting equals, according to our estimates, that of EDW and commuting (54 hrsW). For people aged 18 to 69, the EDW standard has been set, with some hesitation, at 54 hrsW, the result of adding the average observed commuting time of 6 hrsW to the legal standard of 48 hrsW of work. The mean observed in ENUT 2019 was 44.4 hrsW, commuting included. But this comprises primary and secondary jobs. According to the MUT-ENIGH 2020, the mean EWT for the main work was 42 hrsW (without factoring in commuting); for the secondary job the mean was 36.5 hrs. Average commuting T to the workplace in ENUT 2019 was 6.4 hrsW. If we add this last datum to the average of 42 hrs for the main job (the average subordinate worker with a single job), as captured in MUT-ENIGH, we would slightly exceed the old norm of 48 hrs (without commuting). Despite these doubts, the adopted standard of 54 hrs/W maintains FT at the same level (44 hrsW) as adolescents. This standard was also set for those who only perform DW, so that they would have the same FT norm of 44 hrsW.

For the group of 12+ – and its subclassification into study and non-study – we defined the following AFT expressions based on the normative data in Table 8.15:

$$AFT_{IJ}^{12-69} = FT_{IJ}^{12-69} / FT_{IJ} \star {}^{12}\!-\!69 = FT_{IJ}^{12-69} / 44 \qquad (8.77a)$$

$$AFT_{IJ}^{70-79} = FT_{IJ}^{70-79} / FT_{IJ} \star {}^{70}\!-\!79 = FT_{IJ}^{70-79} / 81 \qquad (8.77b)$$

$$AFT_{IJ}^{80+} = FT_{IJ}^{80y+} / FT_{IJ} \star {}^{80}\!+ = FT_{IJ}^{80+} / 82 \qquad (8.77c)$$

In all cases, disabled persons must be excluded.

AFT_{IJ} is an achievement indicator that could range from 0 – for people aged 12+ without FT – to 98/44 – for people aged 12 to 69 who have 44 hrs W of FT. The maximum achievable would then be 2.2273. In the norm, AFT will be equal to 1. An individual aged 12–69 with 44 hrs of weekly FT would get an AFT score of 1, as would a 70–79-year-old with 81 hrsW of FT. We must ask ourselves whether FT above the norm is subject to DMWB returns. A 65-year-old retired person who does not study or do DW will have an AFT score of 2.23, and 98 hrsW of FT they will hardly be able to occupy with recreational activities, reading, or social interaction. Will this person be 2.23 times better off than someone their age in the norm with 44 hrsW of FT? It seems to us that the negative reply prevails. It is evident that, except for those involved in creative activities or who enter what Mihalyi Csikszentmihalyi (1990) has called a state of *flow* – tasks that are very difficult to sustain for many hours because they involve a high degree of concentration and take up a lot of energy – most people tend to get bored after a certain amount of FT.

Therefore, AFT must be modified so that it reflects decreasing marginal WB. Unlike the norms set in areas such as Y, housing spaces, and education, where the thresholds set can be considered austere, the thresholds we have established in FT are generous: 44 hrs per week of FT for almost all people aged 12 and above, which is equivalent to 6 daily hrs of FT from Monday to Saturday and 8 hrs on Sundays. For this reason – and because, unlike Y, possible FT has a maximum that is (almost) the same for everyone, 98 hrs per week – a conceptual maximum (maxC, above which the marginal WB of additional FT is null) was established at 1.5 times the norm that, in most cases (with a threshold of 44 hrsW of FT), equals 66 hrsW of FT: 9 daily hrs from Monday to Saturday (54 hrsW) and 12 on Sundays.

Therefore, we cannot follow a rescaling procedure like the one used for other indicators, since in those cases the maxC was greater than twice the norm (larger than 2). Now we must convert the values above the norm (where AFT = 1) from a maximum possible range of 1.0–2.23, to one of 1.0–1.5, and from a total range of 1.23 to one of 0.5. As no conceptual or empirical basis for assuming different FT to WB conversion rates could be distinguished in the previous subsections, we will proceed by proportional rescaling, multiplying the FT > 1 values by 0.4065 to obtain FT', which can now vary from 0 to 1.5. In principle, this will not affect the measurement of poverty, because we have only rescaled the WB of the non-poor:

$$AFT'^{AG}_{IJ} = 1 + [(AFT^{AG}_{IJ} - 1)(0.4065)] \mid AFT_{IJ} > 1 \quad (8.78)$$

$$AFT'^{GE}_{IJ} = AFT^{AG}_{IJ} \mid AFT_{IJ} \leq 1 \quad (8.78a)$$

The FT deprivation indicator, DFT^{AG}_{IJ} will be:

$$DFT^{AG}_{IJ} = 1 - AFT^{AG}_{IJ} \quad (8.79)$$

which may vary from −0.5 to +1, with the norm at 0.

We will calculate two versions of the FT_{IJ} variable observed: one captured as 'the time you had left to perform the activities you like' (and corrected with the imputations made to missing cases) in the MUT-ENIGH 2020, and one obtained with the same formula used in Table 8.15:

$$FT_{IJ} = 168 - [IRT + (DWT_{IJ} + EDWT_{IJ} + 6) + ET]$$
$$\mid \text{people who do EDW} \quad (8.80)$$

$$FT_{IJ} = 168 - [IRT + (DWT_{IJ} + ET)] \mid \text{people who do not do EDW} \quad (8.80a)$$

Both versions should be run and a comparative table should be made with the results.

The Integrated Poverty Measurement Method (IPMM)

Table 8.15: Norms for: IRT, (EDWT + DWT + comm), ET + comm, by AG. HrsW

Age group and condition of study (1)	IRT (2)	EDWT + DWT + commW. (3)	ST + transfers S (4)	DT or FT = (5) = 168 − [(2) + (3) + (4)]
3–5	90	0	20	58
6–11	84	0	26	58
12–14	84	0	40	44
15–17	80	0	44	44
18+ higher education	70	0	54	44
18+ other studies	70	24	30	44
18–69	70	48 + 6 = 54 54 *DWT only*	0	44
70–79 (who do not study)	75	12 DWT only	0	81
80+ (do not study)	80	6 DWT only	0	82

Note: IRT: Individual replenishment time, which includes sleep, feeding, self-care, rest, prayer/meditation, and self-health care; EDWT: extra-domestic work time; DWT: domestic work time, which includes active care of people, housework, voluntary, and community work, repairs of housing and its equipment, and hauling of firewood and water; ST: study time, which includes associated commuting.

The integrated indicator of IPMM

Unlike the previous procedure used for many years in the IPMM – which first combined Y and time to obtain the Y-time indicator, and then combined the latter with UBN to obtain the IPMM – the new procedure turns the dimension of time poverty (TP) into something more than a modifier of HH Y, which was the central role it played in the previous methodology. This forces us to rethink how to combine the FT indicator with those of Y and UBN. Time is the fundamental resource of human beings (HB). We sleep around 8 hrs daily and dedicate another 2 hrs approximately to eating, hygiene, personal care, and self-health care. We have 14 hours a day to do everything else. To survive and have a healthy development, both physically and mentally, HB require a broad set of S that far exceed survival or material N. What Boltvinik has called monetisable resources – which correspond to the N covered by UBN and PL (Y) – are present as S of all HN, but they are only major S of survival or material N, while they are secondary S in other groups of N (cognitive, emotional and esteem, and growth N). In these last groups, the main S are the subject's activities, knowledge and theories, capacities, and primary and secondary relationships. The WBS (or resources) associated with all these S are T and knowledge and skills (see Table 3.2). Table 8.2 lists the N verified in the IPMM by UBN, PL, or mixed procedures. A set of 17 items are listed; 15 of them are monetisable resources – the main WBS (or resources) – with the exceptions being education, recreation, and culture, where the main resources are time and knowledge and skills. The emotional, esteem, and growth N are left out of PL and UBN PMM. On the other hand, FT to perform other activities – such as activities (AV) with friends or with a partner – as well as the subject's capacities – the main S of the N excluded by UBN and PL – are only covered by means of the FT indicator. FT is clearly the main WBS for the N of education, recreation, and culture, where monetisable resources are a secondary source, as we have pointed out.

Therefore, a cost-weighted IPMM would maintain the object-centred character of UBN and PL considered together. But the IPMM, as we have seen, seeks to transcend this object-centred vision (to have) and introduces the person-centred vision (to be). For this reason, we propose a system of weights that, on the one hand, reflects the greater weight of PL with respect to UBN in the monetisable cost dimension and, on the other hand, strongly introduces FT.

$$A(IPMM) = A(UBN)(0.33) + A'(PL)(0.40) + AFT(0.27) \qquad (8.81)$$

As an alternative – and for simulation purposes – that seeks to show that in a multidimensional method the weighting of components is less important than is usually thought, we also calculated but do not show here the results for the following modified version of (8.81), which reduces the weight of T and increases those of UBN and PL:

$$A(IPMM) = A(UBN(0.35) + A'(PL)(0.45) + AFT(0.20) \qquad (8.81a)$$

The central results are presented in Table 8.16. The change in weights shown in Equations (8.81) and (8.81a) render a very small change in the incidence of the decrease in percentual points (pp) is 1.072. The importance of weights (in terms of numerical results) is overrated, as this example shows. Moreover, in Boltvinik (2010a: 240–243) I simulated the results of the IPMM by wildly changing the weights used, even to an absurd point. As would be expected, weights matter more the more the levels of poverty incidence differ between the weighted elements. *Poverty incidence in IPMM is highly robust: its range goes only from a maximum of 83.7% to a minimum of 73.1%, with 20 combinations of weights* (four weighting combinations within UBN and five between UBN and Y). And this happened with 'sets of selected weights for the simulation exercise', which I qualified as 'very radical, extreme, and arbitrary', and which included a random procedure for (internal UBN) weight selection, as well as the same weights for all dimensions. In the weights between UBN and Y, two of the combinations

Table 8.16: A big contrast: IPMM's and Coneval's diagnosis of poverty in Mexico, 2020

	UBN	PL	Time	IPMM%	IPMM-millions
Weights – I	0.33	0.40	0.27	1.00	1.00
Poverty H – I	68.0	59.5	60.5	76.7	97.222

are non-realistic cost weights; 0.75–0.25 and 0.25–0.75. The incidence of what I then called indigence (now very intense poverty) is more sensitive to changes in weights.

9

Aggregate poverty measures (APM)

9.1 Description and critique

In the study of poverty, it is necessary to distinguish between poverty measuring methods (PMM) and aggregate poverty measures (APM). Amartya Sen distinguishes between *identification* (who is poor and who is not) and *aggregation*, which makes it possible to obtain poverty indicators at the social level (how wide and deep social poverty is). To this I add an intermediate level, which can be called the poverty intensity measurement (PIM). PIM takes place at the same level at which identification is performed (individual/HH) and tells us how poor the poor are.

As Nolan and Whelan (1996, p 1) point out, the 'value of sophisticated synthetical (or aggregated) measures is associated with the adoption, first of all, of a satisfactory approach to the identification of the poor, which has been relatively neglected'. Or, in even clearer terms, there is no point in calculating highly sophisticated aggregate measures of poverty if the method to identify the poor is flawed.

We have already addressed PMM in detail. It is now time to introduce the reader to the most widely used APM, including what I call the individual/HH PIM. In this chapter I seek to provide a personal vision of the usual measures, aiming at some degree of originality. At the end I present a new APM that incorporates social inequality in two variants: between poor and non-poor, and through the Gini coefficient (G) of the entire WB distribution.

I will begin by clarifying the problem of the observation unit. Conceptually, this comprises individuals who experience the deprivations related to poverty. Moreover, assuming that the degree of solidarity between the members of a HH and a family is limited, we must accept that there may be poor people in non-poor HH and non-poor people in poor HH. However, observing the distribution and use of resources within HH is almost impossible, so that for all practical purposes the HH – understood as the group of people who live under the same roof and share, at least, food expenses – becomes the usual unit of observation and identification of poverty. In other words, it is usually HH that are tested, and if they meet the poverty criteria, they will be identified as poor. All members of a poor HH are regarded as such.

Aggregate measures must be expressed in more or less homogenous units. Therefore, since HH are not homogeneous (they can have from one

Aggregate poverty measures (APM)

member to more than 20), aggregate measures are expressed in units such as individuals or EA; see Chapter 8).

Let us use sub-index J to denote HH, and sub-index I to denote people. A_J will stand for the indicator synthesising the conditions of achievement of HH J (the higher its value, the better the situation). Z_J will denote the synthetic indicator of the minimum normative conditions for HH J[1] not to be poor (the threshold or PL). Let us denote the universe of persons with n[2] and the universe of HH with N_U, the number of poor people with q and the number of poor HH with Q.

In general terms, although there may be methods that do not express it directly, the basic poverty criterion will be:

HH_J is poor if and only if:

$$A_J < Z_J \qquad (9.1)$$

All members of HH J, which has been classified as poor, are also poor. We call q_j the number of members of HH J classified as poor, and q the population of poor that inhabits the set of HH considered (for example, all national HH). Therefore:

$$q = \Sigma q_j \mid \text{from } J = 1 \text{ to } J = Q \qquad (9.2)$$

The intensity of HH_J poverty (I_J), or poverty gap, expresses the distance that separates this HH's conditions from the minimum standards – this measurement constitutes the intermediate operation (between identification and aggregation) that I indicated at the beginning and identified as PIM – and is normalised by dividing it by the norms themselves (and is therefore expressed in multiples/fractions of the norm(s)):

$$I_J = (Z_J - A_J) / Z_J = 1 - (A_J / Z_J) \qquad (9.3)$$

When taking positive values, Equation (9.3) expresses the intensity of HH_J poverty. When taking negative values, it expresses a situation of non-poverty. Considering the universe of the poor only – the one that complies with the

---

[1] The finer the definition of norms, the more they tend to be specific to each HH. For the option with equal standards for all HH, see below.

[2] The contents discussed in this section have been developed and applied, in most of the literature, only for one-dimensional PMM, whose only variable is Y (or consumption expenditure). This text attempts to generalise the discussion for any number of variables. That is why some well-known formulas use A, which expresses a composite index of achievement, instead of Y, which is the usual Y variable.

stipulations of Equation (9.1) – the values will always be positive and will vary from more than 0 to 1. The closer to 1 a positive I_j is, the poorer is the HH. Therefore, I_j is the indicator that allows us to order HH according to their poverty intensity, from higher to lower. I_j also equals the intensity of poverty of every individual in HH J, since for lack of distributive information we usually attribute to individuals the average conditions of the HH.[3] Therefore, we can offer the following general equation:

$$I_I = I_J \mid \text{for every individual I belonging to HH J} \quad (9.4)$$

To properly compare HH in terms of their poverty, we must consider not only the intensity of their poverty but also the number of HH members. Of two HH with the same I_j, the larger in size (q_j) will have more human deprivation in an absolute sense. Thus, we can then define the number of equivalent poor persons (q_{EJ}) or deprivation mass (DM_j) of HH J as the product of the number of people or HH size (q_j) and their poverty intensity (I_j):

$$q_{EJ} = DM_J = I_j \, q_j = q_j \, [(Z_j - A_j) / Z_j] = q_j \, [1 - (A_j / Z_j)]$$
$$= q_j - q_j \, (A_j / Z_j) \quad (9.5)$$

So far, the measures of I and DM refer to a specific HH_j.

The first aggregate measure of poverty on a social scale larger than the HH (calculated for any set of HH defined by a specific attribute, such as the place of residence) is H, which expresses the proportion of poor people in the social aggregate. Therefore, H is the proportion that the poor (q) represent in the total population (n):

$$H = q / n = (q_\mu \, Q) / n \quad (9.6)$$

Where q_μ is the mean size of poor HH ($q_\mu = \Sigma q_j / Q$, where $\Sigma q_j = q$, so $q_\mu = q/Q$).[4]

---

[3] In multidimensional methods, such as the IPMM, there are indicators of achievement/deprivation that are individual by nature, such as education and access to health services. In these cases, we do know the individual situation.

[4] Many writings, for example those of ECLAC, use the proportion of poor HH (Q / N) as the measure of H. This is evidently incorrect, since as noted above, HH are heterogeneous units, with unequal numbers of members, so that the proportion of poor HH does not coincide with the proportion of poor individuals. The only case where both proportions coincide is when the average size of poor HH is equal to the average size of non-poor HH, in which case n is to N as q is to Q.

Aggregate poverty measures (APM)

In Table 8.16, I presented empirical results for the integrated H (or H_{IPMM}) in Mexico for 2020, according to a set of weights for UBN, PL, and T and for the first set of weights imputing children up to 11 the HH average value of AFT. The results of H for UBN, PL,T were 68.0%, 59.5%, and 60.5% while IPMM was 76.7% and the values of q were 86.177 m★, 75.367 m★, and 76.711m★. IPMM was 97.2m★.

The second aggregate measure of poverty is poverty intensity (I), which expresses an average of how far the poor are below minimum standards. I is equal to the weighted average of HH poverty gaps (using HH size as weights) or, in other words, to the simple average of the poverty intensity among poor individuals:

$$I = (1 / q)(\Sigma I_j q_j) = (1/q) \Sigma q_{EJ} = (q_E / q) \mid \text{from } J = 1 \text{ to } J = Q \tag{9.7}$$

$$I = (1 / q) \Sigma [\{(Z_j - A_j) / (Z_j)\}(q_j)] \mid \text{from } j = 1 \text{ to } j = Q \tag{9.7a}$$

$$I = (1 / q) \Sigma I_I = (1/q) \Sigma [(Z_I - A_I) / (Z_I)] \mid \text{from } I = 1 \text{ to } I = q \tag{9.7b}$$

In cases with a set of equal norms for all HH/individuals, Z_J and Z_I are equal for all HH and individuals, and can be expressed simply as Z.[5] Under these conditions, and obtaining the mean of A_I (denoted A_μ) by dividing its summation by q, we have the following:

$$I = (Z - A_\mu) / Z = 1 - (A_\mu / Z) \tag{9.7c}$$

Since I is the weighted average of I_J or the simple average of I_I, it will also vary from 0 to 1 and indicates, for the poor as a whole, the relative magnitude of the standardised average gap or average intensity of poverty.

The numerator of Equation (9.7) – $\Sigma (I_j q_j)$ or Σq_{EJ} or ΣI_I – is the total deprivation mass. If we divide this datum by the number of poor (q), we obtain the deprivation mass per poor person or deprivation mass per capita among the poor, which is a way of interpreting I. Given that the total deprivation mass is measured in number of poverty thresholds or norms (for we have normalised it by dividing it by the poverty threshold Z), it expresses the *number of equivalent poor*, that is, a homogenised number of poor, whose poverty intensity is equal to 1 and is denoted as q_E. The relationship between

---

[5] In much of the literature, the thresholds/norms are presented as unique for all individuals or HH. However, as seen in other chapters of this book, this cannot always be the case. For example, it is obvious that educational standards cannot be the same for a 10-year-old as for a 25-year-old.

q and this number of equivalent poor (q_E) can be observed if we rewrite the numerator; instead of expressing it as the sum of each poor person's intensities, we will now express it as the average intensity of poverty among individuals, which is our known I, multiplied by the number of poor.

$$q_E = \Sigma I_i = qI \tag{9.8}$$

Since I is a number ranging from 0 to 1, it is evident that q_E will be a fraction of q, as high as the intensity of poverty. If I were equal to 1, q_E would be equal to q. When I approaches zero, q_E becomes a very small fraction of q.

The aggregate poverty index (I) is only possible if we assume that the poverty gaps of the poor are summable without first transforming them into a WB gap using some sort of WB (or ill-being) function, or by assuming that this function is proportional, that is, that the ill-being of the poor grows in direct proportion to their poverty gap. This matter is discussed below.

P.K. Chaubey (1995) calls 'aggregate poverty gap' what I have designated as total deprivation mass: the sum of I_i. Likewise, he presents three 'normalisations' of this gap: when it is divided by the norm, the result is what Chaubey calls the 'normalized poverty gap', which is equal to the numerator of Equation (9.7a); when it is divided by the number of poor, the result is the average absolute gap; and when it is divided by the two (the norm and the number of poor), the result is what Chaubey calls the 'poverty intensity rate', which is our equation Equation (9.7), particularly (9.7b). Chaubey focuses on the limited properties of these indices, which paves the way for the most elaborate indices; however, for this reason he does not analyse their meaning. Most authors omit these simple indexes and directly address the more elaborate ones.

The concept of equivalent poor is very useful to analyse the geographical and strata distribution of poverty, and to design the resource allocation policy to combat poverty. Table 9.1 presents empirical results of H, q, and q_E for integrated poverty measurements in Mexico for 2020, disaggregated by poor strata. It also includes $H_E = q_E / n$, which is explained below.

Amartya Sen (1981/1991/1992), based implicitly on premises that make it impossible to aggregate the gaps of the poor without previously modifying them, has pointed out that the previous measures, H and I, have serious defects. On the one hand:

> The income-gap ratio *I* is completely insensitive to transfers of income among the poor so long as nobody crosses the poverty line by such transfers. It also pays no attention whatever to the number or proportion of poor people below the poverty line, *concentrating only on the aggregate short-fall, no matter how it is distributed or among how many*. These are damaging limitations. (1981/1991/1992, p 33; emphasis added)

Table 9.1: H, q, I, and q_E results for the IPMM by poor strata in Mexico, 2020

Poor strata	H	q (millions)	I	$q_E = qI$ (millions)	$H_E = HI = qI/n$
1 Very intense poverty	0.0992	12.570	0.5921	7.442	0.0587
2 Intense poverty	0.1918	24.311	0.4098	9.964	0.0786
3 = 1 + 2 Extreme poverty	0.2909	36.880	0.4720	17.406	0.1373
4 Moderate poverty	0.4760	60.342	0.1690	10.198	0.0804
5 = 3 + 4 Poverty sum	0.7670	97.222	0.2839	27.604	0.2178

On the other hand:

> The head-count measure H is, of course, not insensitive to the number below the poverty line; indeed, for a given society it is the only thing to which H is sensitive. But H pays no attention whatever to the extent of income short-fall of those who lie below the poverty line. It matters not at all whether someone is just below the line or very far from it, in acute misery and hunger. (p 33)

And then Sen adds:

> Furthermore, a transfer of income from a poor person to one who is richer can never increase the poverty measure H – surely a perverse feature. The poor person from whom the transfer takes place is, in any case, counted in the value of H, and no reduction of his income will make him count any more than he does already. On the other hand, the person who *receives* the income transfer cannot, of course, move below the poverty line as a consequence of this. *Either* he was rich and stays so or was poor and stays so, in both of which cases the H measure remains unaffected; *or* he was below the line but is pulled above it by the transfer, and this makes the measure H fall rather than rise. So a transfer from a poor person to one who is richer can *never* increase poverty as represented by H. (p 33, emphasis in original)

This critique has led to the development of a vast literature on aggregate measures of poverty. Sen's specific critique regarding the income-gap ratio's exclusive focus on the aggregate shortfall (see text in italics in the first paragraph cited) carries with it the idea that gaps cannot be aggregated without a prior transformation.

A first index – our third aggregate measure – that overcomes some of the disadvantages noted above (except insensitivity to transfers among the poor) is the multiplicative combination of H and I, which I call *equivalent incidence*.

Chaubey (apparently wrongly) attributes this index to Watts (1968). It is also often identified as the P_1 poverty index:

$$P_1 = HI = (q/n)(1/q) \Sigma_j [(Z - A_j)/(Z_j)](q_j)$$
$$= (q/n)(1/q) \Sigma_j (I_j q_j) \quad (9.9)$$

q is eliminated on the right side of both expressions, thus leaving the index as follows:

$$P_1 = HI = (1/n) \Sigma_j [(Z - A_j)/(Z_j)](q_j)$$
$$= (1/n) \Sigma (I_j q_j)$$
$$= (\Sigma q_{Ej}/n) \quad (9.9a)$$
$$= (\Sigma I_i/n)$$

Since $\Sigma(I_j q_j)$ or Σq_{Ej} or ΣI_i is the total deprivation mass, its division by n expresses the deprivation mass per capita, which makes it possible to compare different societies/groups. As total deprivation mass has also been called the number of equivalent poor (q_E), this allows us to designate P_1 as the equivalent incidence, that is, the proportion of equivalent poor in the population, which we can denote H_E:

$$P_1 = HI = qI/n = H_E = q_E/n \quad (9.9b)$$

It thus becomes evident that the improvement of H_E on H lies in the fact that the measurement unit 'poor people' has been homogenised by multiplying it by its average degree of I, which results in a 'comparable' incidence between societies and through time.

Amartya Sen has criticised the HI combination as well, noting that:

> If a unit of income is transferred from a person below the poverty line to someone who is richer but who still is (and remains) below the poverty line, then both measures **H** and **I** will remain completely unaffected. Hence any 'combined' measure based only on these two must also show no response whatsoever to such a change, *despite the obvious increase in aggregate poverty* as a consequence of this transfer in terms of relative deprivation. (1981, p 34, emphasis added; bold emphasis in original)

Based on these criticisms, a whole bibliography has emerged of APM that meet the conditions of being sensitive to the type of transfers Sen refers to. When a poor person transfers resources to another person who is also poor, but less poor than them, it is evident that the distribution of Y has worsened. However, Sen (and after him almost every author) goes further and points out that aggregate poverty has also increased in terms of relative deprivation. This means that poverty is conceived as a phenomenon that increases when inequality among the poor increases, which is not obvious. More specifically, it means that the amount of money that the poorest lose entails an increase in their poverty greater than the decrease in the poverty of the recipient (who is less poor), so that aggregate poverty increases. This indicates that marginal 'WB' decreases among the poor: it increases less than proportionally to Y – or rather ill-being decreases less and less as Y increases. This assumption is questioned below.

Amartya Sen (1986/1972) himself spearheaded these developments, giving rise to an index that is known in the literature as the Sen Poverty Index (P_s), which is expressed as:

$$P_S = H\,[I + (1 - I)\,G_p] = H\,I + H\,(1 - I)\,G_p = HI + HG_p - HIG_p \tag{9.10}$$

Where G_p is the Gini coefficient of income distribution among the poor,[6] and H and I are, respectively, poverty incidence and poverty intensity, as defined above.

Sen (1981) explains how this index is derived from the combination of two axioms. The first axiom is the 'Ranked Relative Deprivation', which postulates that the weights of an individual's gaps must be equal to the rank that individual occupies among the poor (classified from the less poor to the poorest), in such a way that the rank and weight for the poorest will be q, while the rank and weight for the least poor will be 1. The second axiom is what Sen calls the 'Normalised Absolute Deprivation', which holds that when no problem of distribution exists among the poor – everyone has the same Y level (or equal rate of achievement, we would add from the perspective of a multidimensional measurement) – the HI output adequately expresses the magnitude of poverty.

Imagine a small community with 1,500 inhabitants, of whom 1,000 are poor. Suppose that the gap of the least poor is 0.1; by applying P_s, we would obtain its rank (and thus also its weight), which would equal 1. Now suppose that the gap of the poorest is 0.9; then its weight would be 1,000. In contrast, by applying the HI, the gap of the least poor, which is nine times greater than the gap of the poorest, weighs just nine times more. In the Sen index, the gap of the poorest will be weighted by a thousand and, therefore, will count as a value of 900, while that of the least poor will be

---

[6] Virtually all discussion on poverty measures concerns the measurement of Y poverty. In this text I have tried to generalise the measures so that they can be applied to any method. In principle, it is possible to calculate the Gini coefficient among the poor for any set of indicators expressed in metric units.

weighted by 1, and will thus count as a value of 0.1. That is, the gap of the least poor will be worth nine thousand times less. If this same calculation is carried out at the level of a country with 100 million poor inhabitants, the gap of the poorest will be multiplied by 100 million, while that of the least poor will be multiplied by 1. The difference between the two will now be almost 90 million! This amounts, in practice, to disregarding the smaller gaps. The rank of relative deprivation axiom would then have two defects: first, the absence of any basis for such a system of weights; second, the fact that the weight of the poorest depends on the absolute number of poor people, and not on the level of the gap, so that the weight of the poorest in Mexico will amount to only a small fraction of the equivalent weighting in India or China, even if the gap is equal in all cases.

When examining the formula of the Sen index, one will notice how when G_p is equal to zero, the situation of the second axiom obtains (the distribution among the poor is totally equitable), and P_s is equal to HI. When G_p is equal to 1 (one poor person accounts for all the achievements of the poor), the index becomes H (as can be seen when replacing G_p by 1 in Equation (9.10)). In general, the higher H, I, and G_p are, the higher the index.

The meaning of the Sen index is greatly clarified if presented in the following way:

$$P_s = H\,[(I - (A^{ee} / Z)] = H\,(Z - A^{ee}) / Z = H\,[I - A_\mu\,(1 - G_p) / Z] \tag{9.10a}$$

Where A_μ is the mean achievement indicator (mean Y in the case of the PL method) of all individuals, Z is the norm that we assume equal for all, and A^{ee} is the product of A_μ and $(1 - G_p)$. Multiplying an indicator by $(1 - G_p)$ generates the concept *egalitarian equivalent*, so that A^{ee} is the egalitarian equivalent achievement. In this way, as Blackorby and Donaldson (1980) note, and as Amartya Sen (1981/1991/1992, p 191) relates, the measure P_s can be 'seen as the product of the head-count ratio *H* and the proportionate gap between the poverty-line income π [in our case replaced by Z] and the Atkinson-Kolm "equally distributed equivalent income"... of the incomes of the poor'. That is, what the Sen index does is recalculate the gap by modifying the concept of the achievement of the poor index: instead of A, the product of A by $(1 - G_p)$. Since the Gini coefficient measures the degree of inequality of the distribution, $(1 - G_p)$ measures the degree of equality: the higher G_p is, the higher the inequality and the closer $(1 - G_p)$ is to zero. In this extreme situation, the output is zero (the equal equivalent Y is zero). In the opposite extreme case, when G_p is equal to 0, $(1 - G_p)$ is equal to 1 and Y is not modified, in which case P_s is equal to HI. The equidistributed or egalitarian equivalent Y is a lower Y that, however, due to its equal distribution, translates into the same level of social WB as the one observed, whose concentration is G_p. Therefore, equidistributed Y would be comparable between societies and over time since it has been standardised by its dimension of equality.

In light of this, the Sen index assumes a double standardisation of H: on the one hand, the standardisation of the intensity of poverty to obtain the H_E shown above; on the other hand, the standardisation of inequality, which would lead to the concept of *poor egalitarian equivalence*. Therefore, we can conceive the Sen index as *egalitarian equivalent incidence* (H_{eE}) and write it as follows:

$$P_s = H_{eE} = H(I_e) = qI_e / n = \{q[I - (A^{ee} / Z)]\} / n \qquad (9.10b)$$

Where I_E is equal to $[I - (A^{ee} / Z)] = (Z - A^{ee}) / Z = 1 - [A_\mu (1 - G_p) / Z]$, that is, an equivalent egalitarian intensity of poverty calculated not from A_μ (the average achievement) but from its egalitarian equivalent by multiplying it by $(1 - G_p)$, that is, A^{ee}.

With the Sen index we conclude a triad of incidence concepts: simple incidence (H), equivalent incidence (H_E), and the equivalent egalitarian incidence (H_{eE}). This is a new way (not available in the literature) of construing the triad of best-known aggregate measures: incidence, P_1, and Sen index. As will be seen later on, H_{eE} can also be obtained with other indices.

Behind Sen's index lies the idea that social poverty increases when a poor person loses Y gained by another (less) poor person, and that the more acute a person's poverty, the more value a unit of Y (or deficit) represents. This is the old idea of diminishing marginal utility, albeit translated to a format where cardinal measurements are not required, only ordinal (although see below).

Before examining other distribution sensitive indices (among the poor) and addressing the critique of them as a whole, it is worth delving into Sen's view of the reasons behind the index and the role played by relativistic considerations before and after identifying the poor. Let us first review a few paragraphs taken from *Poverty and Famines* (Sen, 1981):

> The income short-fall of a person whose income is less than the poverty-line income can be called his 'income gap'. In the aggregate assessment of poverty, these income gaps must be taken into account. But does it make a difference whether or not a person's short-fall is unusually large compared with those of others? *It seems reasonable to argue that any person's poverty cannot really be independent of how poor the others are. Even with exactly the same absolute short-fall, a person may be thought to be 'poorer' if the other poor have short-falls smaller than his, in contrast with the case in which his short-fall is less than that of others.* Quantification of poverty would, thus, seem to need the marrying of considerations of

absolute and relative deprivation *even **after** a set of minimum needs and a poverty line have been fixed*.

The question of relative deprivation can be viewed also in the context of a possible transfer of a unit of income from a poor person – call him 1 – to another – christened 2 – who is richer but still below the poverty line and remains so even after the transfer. Such a transfer will increase the absolute short-fall of the first person by exactly the same amount by which the absolute short-fall of person 2 will be reduced. Can one then argue that the over-all poverty is unaffected by the transfer? One can dispute this, of course, *by bringing in some notion of diminishing marginal utility of income*, so that the utility loss of the first may be argued to be greater than the utility gain of the second. But such cardinal utility comparisons for different persons involves the use of a rather demanding informational structure with well-known difficulties. In the absence of cardinal comparisons of marginal utility gains and losses, is it then impossible to hold that the overall poverty of the community has increased? I would argue that this is not the case.

Person 1 is relatively deprived compared with 2 (and there may be others in between the two who are more deprived than 2 but less so than 1). When a unit of income is transferred from 1 to 2, it increases *the absolute short-fall of a **more** deprived person and reduces that of someone **less** deprived, so that in a straightforward sense the over-all relative deprivation is increased.* (1981/1991/1992, pp 31–32, emphasis added; bold emphasis in original)

The first sentence in italics poses the idea of interdependence between the condition of a poor person and the rest of the poor people but it does not mention the non-poor. In Appendix C of *Poverty and Famines* (1981/1991/1992), Sen notes:

In the light of the perspective of relative deprivation it may be reasonable to think of the weight v_i of the poverty gap of [person] i to be dependent on i's relative position *vis-à-vis others in the same reference group*. If the reference group is the group of the poor, this causes $r(i)$, that is, the rank of the poor person i among the poor, a relevant determinant of v_i. (p 187, emphasis added)

Here Sen takes a more open stance, compatible with his discussion of the concept of relative deprivation in chapter 2 of the same book, where he points out:

A second contrast [concerning the concept of relative deprivation, the first of which refers to the contrast between *feelings of deprivation and conditions of deprivation]* concerns *the choice of 'reference groups' for comparison*. Again, one has to look at the groups *with which the people in question actually compare themselves, and this can be one of the most difficult aspects of the study of poverty based on relative deprivation.* (Sen, 1981/1991/1992, p 16; my emphasis)

If it is so difficult to know with whom the poor compare themselves, then why the total absence of doubt when Sen (1981/1991/1992, p 31) says: 'Any person's poverty cannot really be independent of how poor the others are.' Without discussing it, Sen eliminates the possibility that the reference group includes the non-poor. In the original article in which Sen developed the index that bears his name (Sen, 1976/1982), the Focus Axiom is not included among the axioms to derive or substantiate the index, but it was incorporated in *Poverty and Famines*. The Focus Axiom implies that only the Y of the poor should be considered in the measurement of poverty, thus excluding the Y of the non-poor.

Going back to the long quotation above, the second phrase in italics maintains that absolute and relative considerations must be involved in the measurement of poverty, 'even after having defined a set of minimum needs and having set a poverty line'. This suggests that, according to Sen, relativistic considerations should intervene both in the setting of the PL and in the way in which APM are calculated. Regarding the former (fixing a PL), if we return to *Poverty and Famines*, Sen (1981/1991/1992) makes it clear (although not very explicit) that the level of the PL should be determined by some (or several) of the following elements: existing social prescriptions (conventions or customs); opinions (perceptions) about N in each society; and contemporary standards. He also approvingly cites Townsend, who stresses the importance of defining the lifestyle that is generally shared or approved in each society and then assessing the difficulties of HH in sharing said lifestyle. Therefore, his full position includes considering, somehow, the standard of living (and Y distribution) of the entire population to define the PL,[7] and the distribution among the poor to obtain the APM.

In the last two paragraphs of the long quote above, Sen introduces diminishing marginal utility of Y as a possible line of argument in support of the statement that a transfer from a poor person to another better placed,

---

[7] Although Sen has never defined which procedure is correct to define the PL in a society, Foster and Sen (1997, p 165) point out: 'Indeed, a "relativist" view of income poverty can take us forcefully in the direction of *making the poverty line responsive to the distribution of incomes as well as the mean income* (e.g., the poverty line may be fixed at half the median income level of that community)'. Although they keep some distance from this statement, they do not reject it completely.

but poor as well, increases poverty. Although he does not choose this as his preferred contention, he adopts arguments that can be described as soft, referring to the complex informational structure of the interpersonal comparison of utilities, without rejecting the egalitarian idea behind the concept of decreasing marginal utility of Y. Instead, he chooses to hold that, when such transfers occur, relative deprivation increases in an obvious and direct manner (that is, without the need for measures of utility), because the most deprived person loses and the least deprived one wins, something that takes us back to his statement in the first paragraph of the long quotation: 'any person's poverty cannot really be independent of how poor the others are'. This rejection of cardinal utility is, however, denied in his own index. Sen himself explains that to transform the 'axiom' of the weights of the ordinal ranks (axiom R) into a theorem,[8] his index incorporates the procedure of equidistanced cardinalisation *of an ordering* followed by Borda in 1781. Professor Sen adds: 'Using Borda's procedure combined with appropriate normalization of the origin and unit, we arrive at Axiom R' (Sen, 1976/1982, p 377). Although Sen considers that there is another way to transform this 'axiom' into a theorem, this is, again, a much softer one based on Runciman's relativistic conception (note that here the indicator based on rank is one of the possible ways to express the relative position of the individual):

> The second is to take a 'relativist' view of poverty, viewing deprivation as an essentially relative concept (see Runciman, 1966). *The lower a person is in the welfare scale*, the greater his sense of poverty, and his welfare rank *among others* may be taken to indicate the weight to be placed on his income gap. Axiom R can be derived from this approach as well. (Sen, 1976/1982, p 377, emphasis added)

We must point out that being lower on the social ladder can occur because the rich are getting richer. On the other hand, the rank on the welfare scale should obviously include the non-poor, not just the poor. Sen's argument about the difficulty of determining who the reference groups of the poor are defeats the position assumed in his index, which entails the assumption that the reference group is always the poor group. The poor of an urban neighbourhood (of Mexico City or New York) see how their neighbours (who are not all poor) live, but they seldom see

---

[8] If ordinal range weights are presented as an axiom, one has to accept the axiom. This is Sen's stance. Although in his original article (1976/1982) Sen leaves open the possibility of handling ordinal range weights as a theorem, in *Poverty and Famines* this alternative is closed.

how the rest of the city's poor, who live in places they never visit, live. The Sen index (and the other indices sensitive to distribution within the poor) assume that if a group of poor people in a city improve their situation, the condition of the poor who remain in the same condition (for example, those of other cities or neighbourhoods) worsens (their rank within the poor has become larger, so the weights of their gaps increase). However, Sen argues that the enrichment of the richest, their increasingly extravagant luxury, does not affect the poor (unless it changes the PL, which is linked, at least for Sen and Foster, as we have seen, to the average value of HH income but not to its inequality). Nevertheless, it is very likely that the wealth of the richest (for whom the poor work and whom they see in the streets) is more visible for the poor than the poverty of the poor in other neighbourhoods, and that, in Runciman's terms, the sense of poverty is influenced to a greater degree by the former than by the latter.

Moreover, as Sen's position is that relativist positions must influence both the definition of the PL and of the APM, he should propose the definition of the PL and the choice of the APM as an integrated package.

The fashionable index, developed by Foster, Greer, and Thorbecke (FGT) (1984), is based on a related idea: what the authors call the *degree of extreme poverty aversion*. The greater this degree, the greater the weight given to the largest gaps – those of the poorest. So that, as in the Sen index, the greater the inequality among the poor, the greater the index, given the aversion coefficient. If we adjust the Foster Index or FGT to the notation adopted here, we can express it as follows:

$$P_{FGT} = 1/n \, \Sigma \, [(Z_i - A_i)/(Z_i)]^{\alpha} \mid \text{from } i = 1 \text{ to } i = q; \text{ for non-negative } \alpha \quad (9.11)$$

Where α is the parameter of aversion to extreme poverty. When its value is zero, the FGT index becomes H; when it is equal to 1, it becomes HI; and when it is greater than 1 (the most employed value is equal to 2), a greater value is given to the gaps the larger they are, thus weighting the gap of the poorest to a greater extent. Therefore, the novelty in this index arises when α is greater than 1.

When α is equal to 2, as shown by the authors themselves, the FGT index is similar to Sen's in that it takes into account the incidence, intensity, and inequality among the poor, although in this case measured with the α squared coefficient of variation (C^2) and not with the Gini coefficient. The FGT, when α is equal to 2, which is the most commonly used value, can be written as:

$$P^2_{FGT} = H \, [I^2 + (1-I)^2 \, C^2_p] = H \, [I^2 + A^2_{\mu} \, C^2_p] \quad (9.12)$$

Where, in the last expression on the right, A_μ is our average indicator of achievement among the poor. Along with the difference in the measure of inequality, when comparing Equation (9.12) with (9.10), the fact that both I and A_μ are squared stands out in FGT, while in the Sen index they are elevated to power one. That is, the FGT (when α equals 2) depends on the incidence of poverty (H), the square of poverty intensity (I^2), and the product of multiplying the squared coefficient of variation and the squared average indicator of achievement [$A_\mu^2 \, C_p^2$].

The Khare index (1986, cited by Chaubey, 1995), which uses the Champernowne inequality index, is very similar to the Sen index as well. According to Chaubey, the Champernowne inequality index among the poor (K_p) is equal to 1 minus the quotient of the geometric mean and the arithmetic mean of the income of the poor. Hence, the Khare Poverty Index is expressed by Chaubey as follows:

$$I_K = H_p \, [I_p + (1 - I_p) \, K_p] \qquad (9.13)$$

The expression, as can be seen, is similar to the Sen index, except that the Gini coefficient has been replaced by the Champernowne inequality index. A surprising feature of this index is that it is obtained simply by multiplying H by its geometric mean, which we can denote as A_G, through a modification where A_G substitutes the arithmetic mean of the indicator of achievement (A_μ) in Equation (9.7c) – this implies that H is not multiplied by I, which would lead us to our equivalent incidence (HI) or P_1. By making this substitution we would get a new I that we can denote as I_G. That is, the Khare index can also be expressed as:

$$I_K = HI_G \qquad (9.13a)$$

Finally, Chaubey (1995) shows that the Watts Index (1968) is also sensitive to incidence, intensity, and inequality among the poor. It is a very simple index, symmetrical to Khare's, which consists in multiplying the incidence (H) by the logarithm of the quotient between the PL and the geometric mean of the Y of the poor.

9.2 Critique of aggregate measures sensitive to distribution among the poor

Two objections can be made to the central idea behind the indices developed by Sen, FGT, and others that were discussed in the preceding section. First, it is not clear why the distributive dimension of poverty, which Sen presents as relative deprivation, should be expressed through a measure of inequality among the poor only. Indeed, from the standpoint of the conceptualisation of relative poverty, it is the inequality between the poor and the non-poor which is significant, all the more since it is the non-poor that express the dominant social lifestyles to which Townsend, for example, refers. Whether it is someone's neighbour's improvement that triggers the suffering caused by deprivation remains unclear. Instead, it seems more plausible that what defines relative deprivation is the improvement of general standards of living in society. A person suffering from third-degree malnourishment does not compare their situation to someone suffering second-degree malnourishment but to well-nourished people.[9]

The second objection touches upon the level of appearance of decreasing marginal WB. Implicit in the Sen index (as well as the FGT and other indices sensitive to inequality among the poor) is the immediacy of this decreasing character. We could say that it starts, so to speak, from the second tablespoon of soup. The issue is whether we should assume that decreasing marginal WB starts at such starving levels. Desai (1991/1998) responds: 'we may question the relevance or realism of assuming as one does in the neoclassical approach that the marginal utility of consumption is positive but declines immediately no matter how low the level of consumption'. And he goes on to propose: 'the perfectly plausible and realistic assumption that we should be able to define the individual as having "well-being" or even deriving "utility" until his/her consumption level has reached Z(C) [the normative level or poverty line]. *As consumption goes from zero to C, the individual is merely surviving, not enjoying himself/herself* (Desai, 1991/1998, p 86, emphasis added).

---

[9] Moreover, a good part of the inequality observed among the poor is more apparent than real. In some pieces of my empirical research, I have broken down the Y differences between HH belonging to different strata of the poor (such as extremely poor, moderately poor) into two components: the average Y per occupied person (which reflects their occupational status and can be called the economic factor of poverty) and the ratio of occupied persons to total persons in the HH (which reflects the rates of occupation, LF participation, and proportion of the population of working age, which I have called the demographic factor). Whenever I have carried out this exercise at the national level, the economic factor has invariably explained most of the difference (around 80% in Mexico in 1989; see Boltvinik, 1999). On the contrary, whenever the exercise has been carried out in a low class neighbourhood (the immediate population for the 'relative deprivation among the poor'), the decomposition of the Y differences between strata of the poor, and between the non-poor and the poor, has been explained in greater measure by the demographic factor (56% of the difference in four low class neighbournhoods in the Metropolitan Area of Mexico City; see Boltvinik, 1997). This evidence shows that Y differences among the poor, at least in some cases, are mainly due to the stages of the HH lifecycle and are therefore temporary. These differences do not seem to be a solid basis for the conception of relative deprivation.

Desai's argument sounds compelling, but its consequences in terms of the effect of transfers between the poor seem controversial. If we accept his stance, then support for each group of poor people must be proportional to their average I. Such neutral position on inequality among the poor poses a stark contrast to the strong emphasis on equity between the non-poor and the poor that his equation of decreasing marginal WB above the PL entails (see below). All the more since, in the hands of the non-poor, resources mean less additional WB the richer the possessor. The SPI Opportunity Set, which I developed (Boltvinik, 1992b), holds a stance similar to Sen's. Indeed, the Gini coefficient used in said index is sensitive to changes in the distribution in any of its segments, so much so that a transfer from a poor to someone less poor, or in fact from anyone to someone who is in a better situation, will increase the Gini coefficient. However, the SPI is insensitive to distributive changes between the poor and the non-poor (except when these changes imply a decrease in the absolute Y of the poor).

Desai argues that marginal utility is constant for the whole group of the poor as consumption grows. He also points out that it is above the PL that marginal utility starts to decrease, and it does so faster the further we move away from it. The specific welfare function he uses is:[10]

$$W_i = (C_i - C\star) + 2(C_i - C\star)^{1/2} + 3(C_i - C\star)^{1/3} + \ldots n(C_i - C\star)^{1/n} \quad (9.14)$$

In (9.14) each section of individual consumption (C_i) is dealt with in a separate member of the equation. The first term applies to consumption up to less than $C\star$, which is the PL level. The second term applies to the section between one and less than two times the PL, and so on. Naturally, if an individual's C_i is less than $C\star$, only the first term will apply. In this case, their WB will be negative (it will be ill-being) and equal to their poverty gap (I_1). The first and second terms will apply to those who have a consumption between one and two times the PL, etc. It is evident that from the second term onwards, WB grows more slowly than consumption. What follows is a specific application of a welfare function that Atkinson (1970; 1983) has used to construct his inequality index and which Desai expresses as:

$$W_i = [1/(1-e)][C - C\star]^{1-e} \quad (9.14a)$$

---

[10] This welfare function, as proposed by Desai, served to manage GDP per capita in the first eight or nine years of the UNDP's Human Development Report, but was later replaced by a logarithmic function.

However, one can go further and think of extreme situations in which marginal WB (the marginal decrease in deprivation) increases. Indeed, if 100 grams of bread a day do not prevent a person from starving, but 500 grams do, it becomes evident that the marginal WB of the last 100 grams of bread is higher than that of each of the first four. If we apply this argument to a family of five, we would find that the rational course of action for a family that only has 500 grams of bread a day (without any hope that this will change) would be for one person to ingest the 500 grams – the result would be one survivor, whereas any other form of distribution would yield none.[11] These circumstances are usually described as requiring a 'triage' solution.

In such extreme cases, equality would not be defensible. Arguments like the former suggest that we need a different solution between zero and a physical subsistence consumption line (C_s), probably a function of increasing marginal WB (see the curve from the origin to Cs in Figure 9.1). Above C_S there would be two possibilities: either to apply a Sen-type solution for the rest of the poor (the curve from Cs to PL), or to introduce an intermediate segment in which deprivation decreases (and WB increases) proportionally to the level of resources, that is, the Desai-type solution (the straight line).

A report by experts jointly convened by FAO/WHO/UNU (1985) presents the standard energy N of a variety of people: a male clerk with a light workload; a subsistence farmer with a moderate workload; a man with an intense workload; a healthy retiree; a housewife in a developed country; and a rural woman in a developing country. In each case, the daily activities are broken down according to the number of hours they take and the energy requirements for each one. First, in all cases, rest (sleep) is considered to take eight hours, consuming energy at the basal metabolic rate (BMR), which is different for each type of person depending on their age, weight, height, and body mass index (BMI). Second, energy expenditure per hour varies in occupational activities according to their intensity, from 1.7 times the BMR in the case of the clerk worker, to 3.8 times the BMR when intense work is performed. Third, so-called discretionary activities, which include a subgroup called 'socially desirable activities' and housework require 3.0 times the BMR and, for the sedentary population, 20 minutes of aerobic exercise require 6.0 times the BMR. Finally, the experts add a surplus called 'remaining time', in which energy is supposed to be spent at 1.4 times the BMR, with only minimal activities performed.

For a 'dependent and totally inactive' person, the aforementioned report calculates an energy requirement equal to 1.27 times the BMR, which

---

[11] The WB to which I refer is OWB, measured in nutritional condition, and not the utility (pleasure or happiness) that the consumer feels when consuming a S.

Figure 9.1: Well-being as a function of access to resources

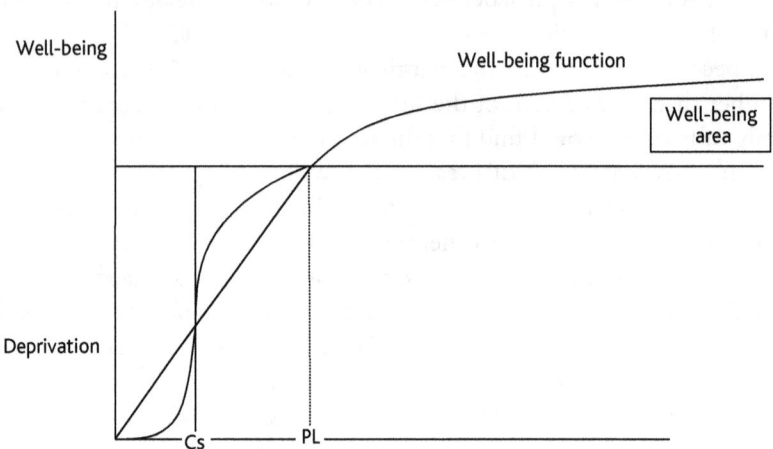

results from eight hours of sleep at 1 BMR and 16 hours awake at 1.4 BMR (1.27 = 2 / 3 * 1.4 + 1 / 3 * 1). The report calls this requirement *survival forecast*. However, the authors warn that this level of energy 'allows only minimal movements; it is not compatible with long-term health, nor does it take into account the energy needed to earn a living or prepare food' (FAO/WHO/UNU, 1985, p 80). Based on three of these six tables, Partha Dasgupta (1993) notes that this survival forecast, which he calls *maintenance requirement (r)*, represents between 65% and 75% of the total energy requirements in the three cases he analyses. Therefore, he notes, there is a very high fixed cost in living, and this has substantial implications for the economy of living. Although his conclusion stands, his calculations are based on 1.4 BMR, while the FAO/WHO/UNU report suggests the survival forecast to be 1.27 BMR. In Table 9.2 I have calculated the proportion that the fixed cost *r* represents in the six tables of the FAO/WHO/UNU report, based on both 1.27 BMR and 1.4 BMR as a survival forecast. My calculation is consistent with the report itself, which clarifies in a footnote (1985, p 86) that the maintenance requirement can rise up to 1.4 BMR if a person stands for two hours a day or walks 1.5 hours. As the table shows, the survival forecast represents an amount of total energy requirements that ranges from 59.4% (in persons with an intense workload) to 84% (in the case of a healthy retiree) when using 1.27 BMR as *r*, and from 65.5% to 92.6% when using 1.4 BMR as *r*. This categorically confirms Dasgupta's thesis on the very high fixed cost of staying alive even when performing no activity whatsoever. Therefore, there is a totally indivisible minimum in the survival requirements. In the examples cited, it ranges from 1,615 to just over 2,100 kilocalories per day using 1.27 BMR and from 1,781 and 2,352 kilocalories using 1.4 BMR. These are the survival minimums for a dependent and totally inactive adult. The most important conclusion from the argument developed here is that below these caloric intakes, food amounts are irrelevant since they do not allow the individual to survive.

Therefore, even if the total addition of Y (at a very low level) were to be destined for food, its marginal value in terms of WB would be zero until reaching the survival requirements. Above the level of survival (and up to the levels of nutritional requirements of the individual), marginal WB will increase. If we introduce, as we should, other N, the decreasing character of marginal WB (increasing marginal ill-being) will extend beyond the satisfaction of nutritional requirements. This confirms the hypothesis held in Figure 9.1, published in 1993 without having read Dasgupta's book (also published in 1993).

Partha Dasgupta (1993) presents his conclusions on the connection between health and BMI – the indicator considered most appropriate to express the nutritional condition of a person – in a graph imitated here as Figure 9.2. The BMI is calculated by dividing body weight (in kilograms) by squared height (in metres). When the BMI has a value ranging from 18.5 to 25, the person is well nourished. A value below 18.5 indicates some degree of malnutrition; above 25, some degree of obesity. Dasgupta explains that his graph is simplified ('stylized'), 'but only to a small extent' (p 415). The graph expresses the curve associating the BMI (on the x axis) with the probability of not getting sick (on the y axis). When the BMI is between 0 and 12, this probability is zero, so the curve is a horizontal straight line at value zero. The probability 'rises slowly until [BMI] reaches 15 or so', and 'then rises rapidly until [BMI] $\approx$ 18.5'. It then becomes horizontal between 18.5 and 25. Above 25 it descends again. Dasgupta concludes: 'the analytical point of interest in nutritional economics' is that the probability of not getting sick in the range of BMI values between 12 and 18.5 is 'non-concave', that is, the second derivative of the probability with respect to BMI is positive. And he clarifies: '*This is the (probabilistic) generalization of the fact that there is a large maintenance (that is, fixed) cost involved in the process of living*' (pp 415–416; my emphasis). Dasgupta's graph is, in its initial portion, very similar to that of Figure 9.1.

The preceding arguments and evidence call seriously into question the basis for supporting not only the SPI but the entire family of indices sensitive to inequality among the poor, which give an increasing weight to the highest gaps. All of them are based, directly or indirectly, on the idea that the WB function is concave in all its extension, meaning that decreasing marginal WB prevails throughout it.

Table 9.2: Energy survival requirements (r) and % of total requirements for two estimates of survival (1.27 and 1.4 BMR), various occupations

Concept/occupation	Male clerk	Subsistence farmer	Intense work	Healthy retiree	Housewife*	Rural woman
(1) BMR (kcal per day)	1,680	1,560	1,632	1,296	1,308	1,272
(2) Total requirements (TR) (daily kcal intake)	2,580	2,780	3,490	1,960	1,990	2,235
(3) TR in # of BMR	1.54	1.78	2.14	1.51	1.52	1.76
(4) Low survival estimate = (1) * (1.27 BMR)	2,134	1,981	2,073	1,646	1,661	1,615
(5) = (4) / (2) * 100. % of r in TR	82.7	71.3	59.4	84	83.5	72.3
(6) High survival estimate = (1) * (1.4 BMR)	2,352	2,184	2,285	1,814	1,831	1,781
(7) = (6) / (2) * 100. % of r in TR	91.2	78.6	65.5	92.6	92.0	79.7

* In a developed country
Source: Own elaboration based on Tables 9 to 14 in FAO/WHO/UNU (1985)

Figure 9.2: Probability (π) of not having a health breakdown as a function of BMI

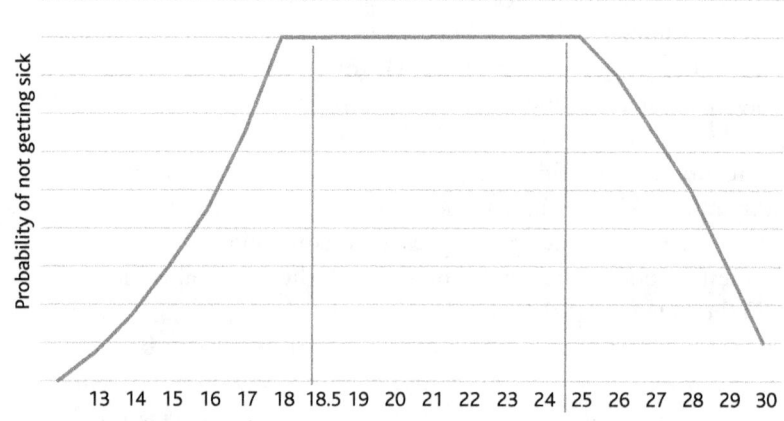

Source: Inspired by P. Dasgupta (1993, figure 14.3, p 416)

9.3 A new aggregate measure of poverty sensitive to social inequality

The arguments presented in the preceding section are very strong, both for their logical truth and their empirical basis. In my opinion, they shatter the bases of poverty indices sensitive to distribution among the poor. The remaining question is whether those arguments also provide the basis for building alternative indices. First, we must pose some queries about the scope of such arguments. If we were to accept that the fixed cost of survival is set at a very low level, so that no PL and very few or no HH fall in said level, the arguments would be empirically irrelevant. I concluded above that the energy requirements to survive doing any kind of activity represent between 59% and 84% of the total energy requirements in five different types of persons. Let us agree that the average is 71%. The additional 29% of caloric requirements, when available, allow people to perform their basic biological and social reproduction activities, and nothing more. The difference between surviving biologically lying in a bed and being a person who can work at home and outside is not insignificant. The WB gain consists in moving from a socially dysfunctional biological entity to a human being that can be socially functional. Therefore, the difference in WB between a 1,600–2,100 caloric intake and a 1,960–2,580 one is quite substantial. There cannot be any DMWB in this stretch. The Dasgupta curve reproduced in Figure 9.2 shows that the probability of not getting sick increases very quickly when the individual approaches a BMI ranging from 15 to 18.5, when they are no longer malnourished. The last soup tablespoons that allow a person to reach the nutritional minimum are objectively the most valuable. In most countries and international organisations, the usual PL – and not only those called EPL – are thresholds of non-malnutrition. I am not going to repeat the proof (presented in Chapter 6) that most PL are lines of non-malnutrition (meaning any person whose conditions reach the usual PL has a BMI of around 18.5 and, in the best-case scenarios, their other needs are met with minimum biological conditions). Those who fall below that PL, therefore, can be classified into two groups: persons whose BMI score is between 12 and 15 (severely malnourished) and persons whose BMI is between 15 and 18.5 (moderately malnourished). No one can be alive with a BMI under 12. A transfer of resources from a severely malnourished person – one that allows them to remain in that same category but causes a drop from a BMI of, say, 15 to 14 – to another person with moderate malnutrition – that pushes their BMI from, say, 16 to 17 – would mean a drop in the probability of not getting sick of the first person, compensated by a large rise in this probability for the person receiving the transfer (given that the slope of the curve is steeper in this section than in the previous one, as can be seen in Figure 9.2). The poor's average probability of not getting sick would increase. If we consider this probability as an inverse indicator of poverty, aggregate poverty would have decreased – exactly the opposite of what Sen, FGT, and similar indices measure. To properly describe this result, in the Sen index (equation 9.10 above) we would have to replace G_p, which measures inequality among the poor, with $(1 - G_p)$, which measures equality among the poor. Indeed, since all the poor (as they are usually identified) were to fall in the two tranches I have just described – whatever their distribution between both tranches – we could increase inequality by making transfers such as the one exemplified, always producing an increase in the average probability of not getting sick, that is, decreasing poverty.

The complex ethical issues raised by any proposal that would systematically follow this line would make its defence very difficult. This ethical stance, together with the arguments expressed above that the inequality that matters is not the one between the poor, but the one between the poor and the non-poor, leads me to propose an APM that modifies HI with an indicator of inequality between the poor and the non-poor. The individual indices remain unchanged, while the aggregate I is the simple average of the all the poor's I, which means equal weights for all rather than gigantic weights for the poorest and insignificant weights for the less poor – as the Sen index and the FGT do – and instead of higher weights for the less poor and smaller for the poorest, as the evidence suggests – with complex ethical implications.

A simple indicator of the relative condition of all the poor is the relative gap (G_{PR}) in the average achievement index of the poor ($A_{\mu P}$) with respect to the average achievement index of the non-poor/rich ($A_{\mu R}$):

$$G_{PR} = (A_{\mu R} - A_{\mu P}) / A_{\mu R} = 1 - (A_{\mu P} / A_{\mu R}) \qquad (9.15)$$

To incorporate this measure of inequality, one may do so in the same way that Sen incorporated the Gini coefficient of the poor. The resulting poverty index, which we can call the *relative poverty index*, and denote as P_R, would be:

$$\begin{aligned} P_R &= H\,[I + (1 - I)\,G_{PR}] = HI + H\,(1 - I)\,G_{PR} \\ &= HI + [HG_{PR} - HIG_{PR}] \end{aligned} \qquad (9.16)$$

When inequality between the poor and the non-poor increases, the poor will feel more deprived, even if their absolute situation remains unchanged, so the P_R index will increase appropriately. That is, the index is sensitive to distribution, but not among the poor, since this leads to inconsistencies, as we have seen. As the objective WB function has DMWB above the PL, as in Equations (9.14) and (9.14a) above, the measure of poverty accurately reflects WB variations when there are changes in the distribution between the poor and non-poor. The position of distributive indifference among the poor is most consistent with the evidence on marginal WB decreasing above the PL.

An alternative way of incorporating the inequality dimension in the APM is to calculate the Sen index with the G for the whole population instead of the G for the poor only. We can call this the Sen-Boltvinik APM and denote it as P_{SB}. Table 9.3 presents empirical results for HI, the Sen index

Table 9.3: Values of HI, P_S, P^2_{FGT}, G_{PR}, P_R, P_{SB} by poor IPMM strata, Mexico, 2020

Poor strata	HI	Ps	P^2_{FGT}	G_{PR}	P_R	P_{SB}
1 Very intense P	0.0587	0.0627	0.0353	0.3013	0.0177	0.0656
2 Intense P	0.0786	0.0838	0.0326	0.4715	0.0371	0.0980
3 = 1 + 2 Extreme P	0.1373	0.1540	0.0680	0.3753	0.0515	0.1637
4 Moderate P	0.0804	0.1066	0.0179	0.6685	0.0538	0.1483
5 = 3 + 4 P sum	0.2839	0.2950	0.0859	0.4891	0.1065	0.3119

(P_S), the FGT index (P^2_{FGT}), as well as G_{PR} and my new proposed indices P_R and P_{SB} for the IPMM and the strata of the poor, applied in Mexico in 2020. As we move in any line horizontally through the columns, we will note two things. First, the value of the Sen index for all strata and for the sum of the poor is larger than HI, as the G inequality coefficient among the poor is > 0. Second, the values of the FGT index with α = 2, P^2_{FGT}, are always smaller than HI, as the square of x < 1 are always smaller than x and both A_μ and I are smaller than 1 and are squared in P^2_{FGT}. The three indices are not comparable as they are expressed in different scales. G_{PR} is expressed in larger numbers than the previous ones, as it expresses the proportion of the A(IPMM) indicator of the poor vis à vis the non-poor. Its logic can be seen contrasting the poverty strata: moderate poverty's G_{PR} is twice as large as VIP's G_{PR}. The Sen and Sen-Boltvinik indices have very similar numbers, although one would expect the Sen-Boltvinik index to be substantially higher, whereas the obtained one is only 12% larger. This is explained by the fact that all the indices were calculated on the basis of WB values obtained as achievement scores that are already expressed as WB values. Thus, the G of Y of the non-poor have been truncated and rescaled, as indicated in the next section.

9.4 A final note

The discussion on APM thus far presented in this chapter has been detached from PMM, but the reader should bear in mind that, as explained in Chapters 5 and 8, in the IPMM the APM are applied to databases of achievement/deprivation scores of HH/individuals which have gone through various processes of standardisation, and the scores above the thresholds have been rescaled to ensure that all complete achievement indicators (that is, not truncated; not derived from questionnaires that did not provide response options above thresholds) range from 0 (or near 0) to 2, and that deprivation indicators range from −1 to +1 (or near +1). The first step, in all cases, is to divide the original variables (for example, income per capita) by the threshold or normative value so that variables are re-expressed in multiples (or fractions) of the threshold level. Thus, considering a threshold of $3,000, a HH with a per capita score of $1,000 per month will have an achievement score of $0.333 = \$1{,}000 / \$3{,}000$. These processes imply the application of various principles discussed in Chapter 5. The scores thus obtained are meant, in all cases, to express the position of the HH/individual in the specific WB scale of each indicator at various levels of aggregation. This means that, although the discussion of APM presented above is valid for any variable, in the IPMM they are applied to WB integrated indicators obtained from an elevated number of specific indicators which are meant as WB indicators.

Epilogue

One can add plenty, or just a few words at the end of a complex book. I am happy to have got to the point of writing this Epilogue. I am also happy with the book's structure, which has at its centre the distinction between poverty conceptualisation (Part I) and measurement (Part II), and the view that measurement ought to be based on conceptualisation. All too often, this *ought to* is not observed in poverty studies. For instance, the World Bank (WB) identifies the lowest PLs used in the world and averages them to obtain what it calls the IPL (International Poverty Line), which it then uses to measure poverty in peripheral countries. According to Reddy and Pogge (2020, p 43), the 'bank's estimates of the level, distribution, and trend of global poverty are marred by three serious problems', the first of which is the one that interests me now: 'The bank uses an *arbitrary* IPL that is *not adequately anchored in any specification of the real requirements of human beings*' (emphasis added). One could say that the WB does not comply with the abovementioned *ought to* because it excludes any kind of conceptualisation. Another very different example of a text that does not fulfil the normative statement that measurement should be based on conceptualisation is Altimir (1979): after thoroughly analysing the concept of poverty, and the relations between poverty and basic needs, in chapters 2 and 3, with arguments that clearly point to a multidimensional PMM and multiple human needs, the author adopts a one-dimensional PMM that reduces the WBS to income and recognises only one need, food. Chapter 6 discusses ECLAC's procedure in more detail. Moreover, this procedure is the core object of a very detailed empirical and simulation-oriented research in Boltvinik and Damián (2020).

This distinction also involved breaking the narrative on principles (P) and good practices (GP) into two chapters, each of them in a different part of the book. This felt slightly forced at times, since the dividing line between what constitutes conceptualisation and what constitutes measurement can become blurry on occasion. However, I think that all in all it benefitted the book.

I think devoting two chapters of Part I (1 and 4) to the conceptualisation of poverty and another two chapters to what I have called CPEP was a good decision. The conceptualisation is incomplete without the critique. Complementing them clarifies the difference between the conceptualisation I adopted here and those prevailing in the literature. The CPEP is an external critique (done from the vantage point of the NP, which will be fully developed in Volume 2 of this work and is here synthesised in Section 2.5), complemented by the internal critique of both the PMM (Chapters 6 – especially Section 6.3 – and 7) and the APM (Section 9.2). This paragraph has evinced the importance attributed in this book to critique (understood as the rational appraisal of other authors' approaches, rejecting what is found to be flawed and assimilating what is considered correct). I use the word 'critique' in the original sense it had for Marx, although not in the spirit of dogmatic Marxism, which rejects almost everything (without any previous rational appraisal) coming from non-orthodox Marxists or non-Marxists.

Critique (both external and internal), together with the P and GP (both on conceptualisation and measurement), conform the complementary foundations of my approach to *economic poverty* in a broad sense, which can be seen as the object of this volume; Volume 2, for its part, will address *human poverty*. To my knowledge there is no other approach to economic poverty based on critique-built P and GP. This is the first global original contribution of the book. The second comprises primarily the IPMM and complementarily the new distribution-sensitive APM.

Although what I have called the improved variant of the IPMM (IV-IPMM) was developed in 1992 and has been empirically applied since 1994, the method presented and applied in Chapter 8 – while part of a 30-year tradition – incorporates so many changes that it should be called the New Improved Variant of the IPMM: NIV-IPMM. Some of these changes were implemented some years ago, especially since 2010, but many other improvements resulted from the preparation of this volume. Although these improvements were detailed in Chapter 8, I will herein offer a global consideration of them and their significance.

First, although most indicators are calculated at the dwelling (Dw) or HH level, surveys and censuses capture inequalities between members of the same HH regarding HS, SS, education, and time. Averaging these individual scores (both achievement and deprivation scores) – as I used to do up to 2010 and even after – conceals internal inequality. This is why Evalúa CDMX made some changes in 2019: now all indicators are expressed as individual scores, even those that were calculated at the Dw or HH level, attributing the aggregated scores to every member of the Dw/HH.

Second, although adjusting income data captured in the ENIGH to NA is an old practice carried out by ECLAC (since 1979), by COPLAMAR (1983), and by Boltvinik and Hernández Laos (1999), I only applied it when the NA data for HH were available on time, which was rare. Since 2019, the period where the NA by institutional sectors are regularly published, Evalúa CDMX has consistently applied this adjustment, turning it into an institutionalised procedure.

Third, although the family budget approach to income poverty was adopted by COPLAMAR (1983) through the NBES (CNSE in Spanish), it only included the required quantities of each satisfier and their costs for the average national HH, made up of 4.9 members in 1977. There were urban and rural distinctions, but of no consequence (the cost of the rural NBES was only 4% below the urban one). This is a big contrast with the huge differences between rural and urban PLs in CONEVAL's and ECLAC's PMM, where the differences are of 71% and 62.5%, respectively. This was not a casual result but the consequence of a decision applied throughout COPLAMAR's research programme: 'Although austere, minimal satisfiers [the thresholds] should have the same quality for all the population. For this reason, the differences between rural and urban areas do not result from differences in quality, but rather from customs, objective needs, and short- or medium-term viability' (Coplamar 1982 [Necesidades esenciales y estructura productiva]: 118). Thus, for example, daily transport costs and requirements were considered objectively smaller in rural areas than in urban areas; meanwhile, hats and shawls (*rebozo* in Spanish) were included in the NBES in rural areas but not in urban ones.

This lack of flexibility forced the use of the same PL per capita for all HH. This practice was maintained until Marín (2003) calculated the quantities and costs for 1- to 10-member HH and for all possible member compositions according to age and gender. This allowed consideration of the differences between individuals (adult equivalents), as well as the economies of scale derived as the number of HH members grows while some family goods are constant and others change at a slower rate than the number of members. This is described and compared with other procedures used to consider equivalence requirements and economies of scale in Boltvinik and Marín (2003). Since this procedure is applied to a normative basket of S covering all market-related N, it became completely normative. This allowed analysts to overcome the practice of an equal PL per capita for all HH, and therefore to have different PL for each HH according to their size and structure. The latter practice shows a great difference from the homogeneous per capita PL, which underestimates the cost of the NBES for small HH and overestimates it for large HH. It also overestimates the costs of HH with several small children. In Boltvinik (2010b), I developed the equation which made calculating the PL for each HH a very quick procedure. I have applied this in my practice ever since, and Evalúa CDMX has applied it since 2019.

Fourth, many adjustments have been made to UBN indicators. A very unfortunate one was eliminating the waste disposal indicator, as the ENIGH (starting in 2010) omitted the question on the frequency of waste collection and rendered the corresponding indicator useless. In other UBN indicators, thresholds were modified according to the law and social trends. In education, for instance, the Mexican Constitution extended compulsory education to 15 years, including three pre-school years and 12 years for primary and secondary education. The thresholds were adapted in consequence. Computers and internet modems were added to the durable goods possessed by the HH, as well as water-heating devices, heaters in cold weather, and fans. These changes led to modifying some of the normative figures that HH must spend (like the costs of gas, electricity, and internet connection service, which in Mexico is usually associated with the landline phone service). Mobile phones had been added some years before as an alternative/complement to landline home phones, but now the telephone indicator was turned into a communications indicator that includes internet connection.

Fifth, HS and SS were radically modified for this book by the introduction of a law which gives unprotected workers the possibility of having access to both HS and SS. This possibility is the voluntary affiliation to every insurance provided by SS in Mexico: sickness and maternity services, disability and old age, and retirement and old-age unemployment. Voluntarily paying a monthly premium to become affiliated to both services and insurances is quite an affordable solution for those HH that are not protected by SS and HS in their jobs. Additionally, workers with higher incomes, many of whom consider (based on much evidence) that HS provided by IMSS are inadequate, can opt for a PMI and a life insurance that provides them with a lifetime rent after a certain age. Private medical services and private insurance instead of public HS, as well as SS for those who can afford it, is a practicable solution.

With all these changes, the NIV-IPMM is now a PMM that achieves the following. First, it identifies observable inequalities within a HH, such as the very highly gendered inequalities in education and FT. The NIV-IPMM can identify poor individuals within non-poor HH and vice versa, although these cases might be rare. More frequently it will identify individuals deprived in education, HS, and SS in HH that are not generally deprived in these services. Second, it does not overestimate income poverty due to the underestimation of income in the ENIGH; rather, it corrects this bias as far as the available information allows. Third, it does not overestimate income poverty in large HH and HH with many children, nor underestimate income poverty in small HH. Fourth, the NIV-IPMM is completely and consistently normative. Fifth, it does not dismiss the need of the human organism to regulate body temperature and consequently considers S as water heaters, heaters, and fans. Sixth, it takes the transformation of modern societies into knowledge societies on board and extends the compulsory education period accordingly, besides giving technological advances their due importance by incorporating S such as mobile phones, computers, and internet connection. Lastly, it takes the fact that it is not only a PMM but also a stratification method seriously (it is a PSMM). In this regard, it incorporates better market solutions for those who can afford them, particularly to cover HS and SS needs. The more non-truncated indicators we include, the better the quality of the IPSMM.

There is a topic I did not analyse in Chapter 8 but that is worth mentioning here for the reader to be aware of, namely the fact that although the NIV-IPMM presented in this Epilogue is the culmination, up to now, of the main line of the IPMM's development, there are other variations on which I have worked in the past and that might be developed further in the coming years. The first variation I will mention appears in Boltvinik (1994a), where I used databases from the 1990 census, which asked all women over 12 years old how many live-born children they had had and how many of them were alive at that moment. The results were interpreted as an indicator on the probability of survival. Moreover, for large population groups they can be construed as the survival rate, which can be added to the other indicators used in the IPMM (which denote the quality of life), where the survival rate would be interpreted as quantity of life. This combination was called *life-time quality of life*.

The second variation is included in Boltvinik (2010b), where I introduced various innovations. The variation enriched the domestic energy achievement indicator by incorporating water heaters and heaters for cold areas as indicators, which were then combined with electricity and cooking fuel achievement. In the solution I adopted in this book, the need for heating both water and the dwelling was introduced as part of the durable goods indicator and included in the cost of the NBES. The need to cool the dwelling in warm/hot areas was also added according to the same procedure, introducing fans in the durable goods indicator and adding the cost of electricity in the NBES. The variation also combined SS (including only its income maintenance function and excluding HS) with income and labour-related indicators (such as belonging to a trade union and having job tenure) to create an income stability indicator, which in turn was combined with the corresponding income level to obtain a stable income equivalent to be used as the income indicator.

Finally, I would like to talk about a more ambitious path to a better informational base for poverty measurement which has nevertheless up to now been a semi-failed experience, namely the surveys conducted by Evalúa CDMX during the period 2008–2012 in Mexico City, and a later survey conducted in 2019. The first group of surveys include the 2009 Survey of Perceptions and Access to Basic Satisfiers (EPASB by its name in Spanish), an innovative time-use survey conducted in 2010, and the 2011 Survey of Access to Basic Satisfiers (ENCASB). The survey carried out in 2019 was called the Survey of Objective and Subjective Well-Being (ENCUBOS). The EPASB was an improved, extended, and adapted-to-Mexico version of Mack and Lansley's (1985) survey on perceptions and access to necessities that led to their PMM (which I call ELSPN; see Chapter 6). The survey was successful and served as a basis for some works: Miguel Calderón and I performed various analyses of the results, published plenty of tabulations on the Evalúa CDMX web page, and held a large press conference revolving around the results; Miguel Calderón (2016) and Paloma Villagómez (2016) published separate articles related to the topic, and the former used the EPASB's databases in his Sociology PhD thesis (El Colegio de México). However, so far no one has fully used the enormous possibilities that these four surveys (EPASB, ENCASB, the innovative time-use survey, and ENCUBOS) offer to enrich the IPMM. These surveys provided, moreover, important foundations to define which satisfiers should constitute a normative family budget. Besides, their questionnaires were designed to avoid – as far as possible – truncated indicators, by adding alternatives for responses above the thresholds, and included many questions on topics not explored by the ENIGH on S that are not (explicitly) included in IPMM's thresholds (windows and their materials in the Dw, for instance) or in the NBES. The ENCASB was designed mainly to update the information captured by the EPASB on access to necessities previously confirmed as such in the EPASB, and to evaluate the observed changes. Evalúa CDMX did not have enough time to explore this survey, since the team was dismantled at the beginning of 2012. ENCUBOS – of which I was the main designer – included many questions on subjective WB, something that had not been applied in Mexico together with objective indicators, as this survey did. To cover the objective dimension of WB, I included a slightly modified version of the ENCASB. As for the subjective perspective, WBS, the survey included three modules: first, the first six questions of BIARE (the self-reported survey on WBS applied in Mexico by INEGI as part of the OECD's efforts to measure people's subjective WB internationally); second, the questionnaire on basic psychological needs by Ryan and Deci, part of their Self-Determination Theory (https://selfdeterminationtheory.org./theory); and third, an online questionnaire that respondents have to answer three or four times a day (at random hours) during one week. It is designed to capture how respondents feel when they do something specific, in a given place, and with certain persons. This last module had a low completion rate. In any case, ENCUBOS has not been analysed yet, although there are some tables available on the Evalúa CDMX website (https://www.evalua.cdmx.gob.mx).

Most applications of the IPMM have been made with the databases of the ENIGH, a highly comprehensive survey that, as was shown in Chapter 8, significantly contributed to the richness of the NIV-IPMM. However, as I argue in this Epilogue, the IPMM could become an even deeper and more holistic method, with fewer truncated indicators and fewer omitted conditions-of-life indicators, if the questionnaire were designed in the same broad spirit as the EPASB and ENCUBOS.

References

Abel-Smith, Brian and Peter Townsend (1965) The Poor and the Poorest, Occasional Papers on Social Administration, 17, London: Bell & Sons; New York: Addison-Wesley Longman (1st edn 1954, 2nd edn 1970).

Alarcón, Diana (1993) 'Changes in the Distribution of Income in Mexico during the Period of Trade Liberalization', PhD Thesis, University of California, Riverside.

Alkire, Sabina (2002) Valuing Freedoms: Sen's Capability Approach and Poverty Reduction, Oxford: Oxford University Press.

Alkire, Sabina and James Foster (2009) 'Counting and Multidimensional Poverty Measurement', OPHI Working Paper 32, University of Oxford.

Alkire, Sabina and Maria Emma Santos (2010) 'Acute Multidimensional Poverty: A New Index for Developing Countries', OPHI Working Paper 38, University of Oxford.

Altimir, Óscar (1979) La dimensión de la pobreza en América Latina, Santiago de Chile: Cuadernos de la CEPAL, 27.

Atkinson, Anthony B. (1970) 'On the Measurement of Inequality', Journal of Economic Theory, 2(3): 244–263.

Atkinson, Anthony B. (1983) The Economics of Inequality, (2nd edn), Oxford: Clarendon Press.

Barreiros, Lidia (1992) 'La pobreza y los patrones de consumo de los hogares en Ecuador', Comercio Exterior, 42(4): 366–379.

Beccaria, Luis and Alberto Minujin (1987) Sobre la medición de la pobreza: Enseñanzas a partir de la experiencia Argentina, Buenos Aires: UNICEF, Documento de Trabajo 8.

Beccaria, Luis, Julio Boltvinik, Oscar Fresneda, Arturo León and Amartya Sen (1992) América Latina: El reto de la pobreza, Bogotá: PNUD Proyecto Regional para la Superación de la Pobreza.

Becker, Gary (1965) 'A Theory of the Allocation of Time', Economic Journal, 75(299): 493–517.

Blackorby, Charles and David Donaldson (1980) 'Ethical Indices for the Measurement of Poverty', Econometrica, 48(4): 1053–1060.

Boltvinik, Julio (1986) 'Modo de producción estatal y satisfacción de necesidades esenciales: El caso de México', Investigación Económica, 45(177): 195–244.

Boltvinik, Julio (1990a) 'Pobreza y necesidades básicas: Conceptos y métodos de medición', Caracas: PNUD, Proyecto Regional para la Superación de la Pobreza, RLA/86/004.

Boltvinik, Julio (1990b) 'Hacia una estrategia para la superación de la pobreza', in ILPES (Instituto Latinoamericano de Planificación Económica y Social), La Paz, Bolivia: ISS (Instituto de Estudios Sociales de la Haya) and ILDIS (Instituto latinoamericano de Investigaciones Sociales), pp 25–50.

Boltvinik, Julio (1992a) 'El método de medición integrada de la pobreza: Una propuesta para su Desarrollo', Comercio Exterior, 42(4): 354–365.

Boltvinik, Julio (1992b) 'Towards an Alternative Indicator of Development' in Meghnad Desai, Amartya Sen and Julio Boltvinik (eds) *Social Progress Index: A Proposal*, Bogotá: UNDP.

Boltvinik, Julio (1993) 'Indicadores alternativos de desarrollo y mediciones de pobreza', Estudios Sociológicos, XI(33): 605–640.

Boltvinik, Julio (1994a) Pobreza y estratificación social en México, INEGI, IISUNAM, El Colegio de México, Colección MOCEMEX.

Boltvinik, Julio (1994b) 'Poverty Measurement and Alternative Indicators of Development', in Rolph van der Hoeven and Richard Anker (eds) Poverty Monitoring: An International Concern, London: Palgrave Macmillan, pp 57–83.

Boltvinik, Julio (1995) 'La pobreza en México II. Magnitud', Salud Pública de México, 37(4): 298–309.

Boltvinik, Julio (1997) 'Perfil sociodemográfico de los pobres', in Martha Schteingart (ed) Pobreza, Condiciones de Vida y salud en la Ciudad de México, Mexico City: El Colegio de México, pp 493–505.

Boltvinik, Julio (1998) 'Poverty Measurement Methods: An Overview', Poverty Reduction Series, Working Paper 3, New York: UNDP.

Boltvinik, Julio (1999) 'Métodos de medición de la pobreza: Conceptos y tipología', (First part) Socialis. Revista Latinoamericana de Política Social, Universidad de Buenos Aires, Universidad Nacional de Rosario, FLACSO (Argentinian office), 1: 35–74.

Boltvinik, Julio (2001) 'Métodos de medición de la pobreza: Conceptos y tipología', in Rigoberto Gallardo, Joaquín Osorio and Mónica Gendreau (eds) Los Rostros de la pobreza, III, Mexico City: Universidad Iberoamericana, Iteso, Limusa Noriega Editores.

Boltvinik, Julio (2003a) 'Evolución y características de la pobreza en México', Comercio Exterior, 53(6): 519–531.

Boltvinik, Julio (2003b) 'Welfare, Inequality, and Poverty in México, 1970–2000', in Kevin J. Middlebrook and Eduardo Zepeda (eds) Confronting Development: Asessing Mexico's Economic and Social Policy Challenges, Redwood City: Stanford University Press, pp 385–446.

Boltvinik, Julio (2005) 'Ampliar la mirada: Un nuevo enfoque de la pobreza y el florecimiento humano', unpublished PhD tesis (two volumes), Centro de Investigaciones y Estudios Superiores en Antropología Social (CIESAS)-Occidente, Guadalajara, México (it is referred to throughout the book as Ampliar la mirada or, in English, *Broadening the Look*).

Boltvinik, Julio (2005–2006) 'El rechazo al concepto de necesidades humanas', Mundo Siglo XXI, 1(3): 37–57.

Boltvinik, Julio (2007a) 'Elementos para la crítica de la economía política de la pobreza', *Desacatos: Revista de Antropología Social*, 23: 53–86.

Boltvinik, Julio (2007b) 'Presentación – De la pobreza al florecimiento humano: ¿Teoría crítica o utopía?', *Desacatos*, 23: 13–52.

Boltvinik, Julio (2010a) 'Coordinar el Número 23 de *Desacatos*: Una Experiencia de Florecimiento Humano' in *Desacatos X Aniversario* 1999–2009, Ciesas, Mexico City.

Boltvinik, Julio (2010b) 'Principios de la medición multidimensional de la pobreza', in Julio Boltvinik, Satya Chakravarty, James E. Foster, David Gordon and Rubén Hernández Cid (eds) Medición multidimensional de la pobreza en México, México City: El Colegio de México-Coneval, pp 43–279.

Boltvinik, Julio (2011) 'Medidas agregadas de pobreza. Heurística de las medidas tradicionales. Crítica de las sensibles a la distribución entre pobres, y propuesta de una medida sensible a la distribución entre pobres y no pobres', Mundo Siglo XXI, CIECAS-IPN, 25(VII): 15–30.

Boltvinik, Julio (2020) Pobreza y florecimiento humano: Una perspectiva radical, México City: Universidad Autónoma de Zacatecas/Editorial Ítaca.

Boltvinik, Julio and F. Cortés (2000) 'La identificación de los pobres en el Progresa', in Enrique Valencia Lomelí, Mónica Gendreau and Ana María Tepichín Valle (eds) Los dilemas de la política social, México: Universidad de Guadalajara.

Boltvinik, Julio and Araceli Damián (2016) 'Pobreza creciente y estructuras sociales cada vez más desiguales en México: Una visión integrada y crítica', Acta Sociológica, 70: 271–296.

Boltvinik, Julio and Araceli Damián (2020) Medición de la pobreza de México: Análisis crítico comparativo de los diferentes métodos aplicados, recomendaciones de buenas prácticas para la medición de la pobreza en México y América Latina, México: Cepal-México, Estudios y Perspectivas 183.

Boltvinik, Julio and Enrique Hernández Laos (1999) Pobreza y distribución del ingreso en México, México City: Siglo XXI editores.

Boltvinik, Julio and Alejandro Marín (2003) 'La canasta normativa de satisfactores esenciales de Coplamar: Génesis y desarrollos recientes', Comercio Exterior, 53(5):473–484.

Bradshaw, Jonathan and Autumn C.S. Yu (1993) Budget Standards for the United Kingdom, Avebury: Ashgate.

Bryant, Keith W. (1990) The Economic Organization of the Household, Cambridge: Cambridge University Press.

Calderón Ch., Miguel (2016) 'Normas sociales y umbrales de pobreza', Acta Sociológica, 70(May–Aug): 73–98.

CEPAL-PNUD (1992) 'Procedimientos para medir la pobreza en América Latina con el método de línea de pobreza', Comercio Exterior, 42(4): 340–353.

Chaubey, Pramod Kumar (1995) Poverty Measurement: Issues, Approaches and Indices, New Delhi: New Age International.

Citro, Constance F. and Robert T. Michael (eds) (1995) Measuring Poverty: A New Approach, Washington, DC: National Research Council, National Academies Press.

Cohen, Gerald A. (1993) 'Equality of What? On Welfare, Goods and Capabilities', in Martha Nussbaum and Amartya Sen (eds) The Quality of Life, Oxford: Clarendon Press, pp 9–29. (Versión del libro en español publicada por Fondo de Cultura Económica con el nombre de Calidad de la Vida. Una traducción independiente de extractos del capítulo de Cohen fue publicada en Comercio Exterior [(2003) 53(5): 427–433]).

Comité Técnico para la Medición de la Pobreza (2002) 'Medición de la pobreza', Variantes metodológicas y estimación preliminar, México: Secretaría de Desarrollo Social.

COPLAMAR (1982a) Necesidades Esenciales y Estructura Productiva en México, México: Presidencia de la República.

COPLAMAR (1982b) Vivienda, Serie Necesidades Esenciales en México, vol. 1 México City: Coplamar-Siglo XXI editores.

COPLAMAR (1983) Macroeconomía de las necesidades esenciales en México, México City: Coplamar-Siglo XXI editores.

Crocker, David (1995) 'Functioning and Capability: The Foundations of Sen's and Nussbaum's Development Ethic, Part 2', in Martha Nussbaum and Jonathan Glover (eds) Women, Culture and Development: A Study of Human Capabilities, Oxford: Clarendon Press, pp 153–198.

Csikszentmihalyi, Myhaly (1990) Flow: The Psychology of Optimal Experience, New York: Harper Perennial.

Damián, Araceli (2003) 'La pobreza de tiempo: Una revisión metodológica', Estudios Demográficos y Urbanos, 18(1): 127–162.

Damián, Araceli (2005) 'Pobreza de tiempo en México: Conceptos, métodos situación actual', in Mónica Gendreau (ed) Los rostros de la pobreza IV, Mexico City: Universidad Iberoamericana, pp 225–288.

Damián, Araceli (2014) El tiempo, la dimensión olvidada en los estudios de pobreza y bienestar, México: El Colegio de México.

Damián, Araceli and Julio Boltvinik (2003) 'Evolución y características de la pobreza en México', Comercio Exterior, 53(6): 519–531

Dasgupta, Partha (1993) An Inquiry into Well-Being and Destitution, Oxford: Clarendon Press.

Deaton, Angus and John Muellbauer (1980/1991) Economics and Consumer Behavior, Cambridge: Cambridge University Press.

Desai, Meghnad (1991/1998) 'Well-Being and Lifetime Deprivation: A Proposal for an Index of Social Progress', in Meghnad Desai, Amartya Sen and Julio Boltvinik (eds) Social Progress Index: A Proposal, Bogotá: UNDP Regional Project to Overcome Poverty (RLA/86/004), pp 67–95.

Desai, Meghnad (1994) 'Poverty and Capability: Toward an Empirically Implementable Measure', Frontera Norte, Número especial: La pobreza, 6: 11–30.

Desai, Meghnad (1995) Poverty, Famine and Economic Development: The Selected Essays of Meghnad Desai, Vol. 2, Aldershot: Edward Elgar Publishing Ltd.

Desai, Meghnad and Anup Shah (1988) 'An Econometric Approach to the Measurement of Poverty', Oxford Economic Papers, 49.

Douthitt, Robin (1992) 'The Inclusion of Time Availability in Canadian Poverty Measures' in Time Use Methodology: Toward Consensus (Symposium in Rome, 15–18 June). Sistema Statistico Nazionale, Instituto Nazionale de Statistica, Note e Relazione, edizione, 3: 83–91.

Doyal, Len and Ian Gough (1991/1994) A Theory of Human Need, London: Macmillan.

EAPN (European Anti-Poverty Network) (no date) www.eapn.eu/what-is-poverty/how-is-poverty-measured/

Escotto, Teresita (2003) 'Situaciones de pobreza en México: La relación entre el nivel e vida y el nivel de recursos de los hogares', PhD Dissertation, El Colegio de México.

Evalúa CDMX (2022) www.evalua.cdmx.gob.mx/principales-atribuciones/medicion-de-la-pobreza-y-desigualdad

FAO/WHO/UNU (1985) 'Energy and Protein Need: Report of a Joint Consultative Meeting FAO/WHO/UNU', Series of Technical Reports, 724, Geneva: WHO.

Fitzgerald, Ross (1977) Human Needs and Politics, Rush Cutters Bay: Pergamon.

Foster, James (2010) 'Informe sobre la medición multidimensional de la pobreza' in El Colegio de México and Consejo de Evaluación de la Política de Desarrollo Social (Coneval), Mexico City: Medición multidimensional de la pobreza en México, pp 323–399.

Foster, James, Joel Greer and Eric Thorbecke (1984) 'A Class of Decomposable Poverty Measures', Econometrica, 52(3): 761–766.

Foster, James and Amartya K. Sen (1997) 'On Economic Inequality after a Quarter Century', Annexe to Amartya Sen (1997) On Economic Inequality, Oxford: Clarendon Press, pp 107–219.

Fromm, Erich (1955/1990) The Sane Society, New York: Henry Holt and Company.

Garfinkel, Irwin and Robert Haveman (1977) 'Earnings Capacity, Economic Status and Poverty', The Journal of Human Resources XII: 49–70.

Gasper, Des (2004) The Ethics of Development, Edinburgh: Edinburgh University Press.

Goedhart, Theo, Victor Halberstadt, Arie Kapteyn and Bernard van Praag (1977) 'The Poverty Line: Concept and Measurement', Journal of Human Resources, 12(4): 503–520.

Gómez de León, José (1998) 'Dimensiones correlativas de la pobreza en México: Elementos para la Focalización de Programas sociales', paper presented at the first meeting of the Lacea/IDB/World Bank Net on Inequality and Poverty, Buenos Aires, 21 October.

Gordon, David and Paul Spicker (eds) (1999) The International Glossary on Poverty, London: CRP-Zed Books.

Gordon, David, Laura Adelman, Karl Ashworth, Jonathan Bradshaw, Ruth Levitas, Sue Middleton, et al. (2000) Poverty and Social Exclusion in Britain, York: Joseph Rowntree Foundation.

Guillén Fernández and Yedith Betzabé (2017) 'Multidimensional Poverty Measurement from a Relative Deprivation Approach: A Comparative Study between the United Kingdom and Mexico', PhD Dissertation, University of Bristol.

Hagenaars, Aldi (1986) The Perception of Poverty, Amsterdam: North Holland.

Halleröd, B. (1995) 'The Truly Poor: Direct and Indirect Measurement of Consensual Poverty in Sweden', European Journal of Social Policy, 5(2): 112–119.

Heller, Agnes (1985) The Power of Shame: A Rational Perspective, London: Routledge and Kegan Paul.

Hernández Laos, Enrique (1992) Crecimiento Económico y Pobreza en México, México: Universidad Nacional Autónoma de México.

INDEC (Instituto Nacional de Estadística y Censos) (1985) La Pobreza en Argentina, Buenos Aires.

Kaztman, Rubén (1989) 'La heterogeneidad de la pobreza: El caso de Montevideo', Revista de la CEPAL, 37: 141–152.

Khare, D. (1986) 'Measuring Poverty', Journal of Income and Wealth, 9.

Lederer, Katrin (1980) 'Introduction' in Katrin Lederer, Johan Galtung and David Antal (eds) Human Needs: A Contribution to the Current Debate, Oelgeschlager: Gun and Hain.

Levy, Santiago (1991) 'Poverty Alleviation in Mexico', World Bank Working Papers, Washington, DC (Reproduced in Spanish in Félix Vélez [ed], La Pobreza en México: Causas y Políticas para Combatirla, México City: Fondo de Cultura Económica, Colección Lecturas, 78).

Linder, Staffan B. (1970) The Harried Leisure Class, New York: Columbia University Press.

Lustig, Nora (1990) The Incidence of Poverty in Mexico, 1984: An Empirical Analysis, The Brookings Institution.

Maccoby, Michael (1988) Why Work? Motivating and Leading the New Generation, New York: Simon and Schuster.

Mack, Joanna and Stewart Lansley (1985) Poor Britain, London: George Allen & Unwin.

Márkus, György (1973/1985) Marxismo y 'antropología', Barcelona/México City: Grijalbo. (There are two editions in English, with the same title and translation: Marxism and Anthropology: Marx´s Concept of Human Essence, Assen: Van Gorcum [1978] and New South Wales, Australia: Mode-Verlag [1988]. The latter adds an introduction by Axel Honnneth and Hans Joas.)

Marx, Karl (1867/1976/1990) Capital: A Critique of Political Economy, London: Penguin Classics.

Maslow, Abraham (1943) 'A Theory of Human Motivation', Psychological Review, 50: 370–396.

Maslow, Abraham (1954/1987) Motivation and Personality, 3rd edn, New York: Longman.

Max-Neef, Manfred, Antonio Elizalde and Martin Hopenhayn (1986) Desarrollo a escala humana. Development Dialogue, special number, Santiago de Chile and Uppsala, Sweden: Dag Hammarskjöld Foundation. (An English edition of this book with two additional chapters by Max-Neef was published in 1991 as: Human Scale Development: Conception, Application and Further Reflections, New York and London: The Apex Press).

Nolan, Brian and Christopher T. Whelan, (1996) Resources, Deprivation and Poverty, Oxford: Clarendon Press.

ODEPLAN, Oficina de Planificación Nacional and Instituto de Economía of the University of Chile (1975) Mapa de la Extrema Pobreza, Santiago de Chile.

OECD (2013) 'The OECD approach to measure and monitor income poverty across countries', Working paper 17, 25 November, Paris.

Orshansky, Mollie (1965) 'Counting the Poor: Another Look at the Poverty Profile', Social Security Bulletin, 28(1), Washington, DC: Department of Health, Education and Welfare.

Penz, G. Peter (1986) Consumer Sovereignty and Human Interests, Cambridge: Cambridge University Press.

Piachaud, D. (1981) 'Peter Townsend and the Holy Grail', New Society, 57: 419–421, extracts reproduced in Townsend (1993), pp 113–120.

Pogge, Thomas and Scott Wisor (no date) 'Measuring Poverty: A Proposal' (multicopied).

Putnam, Hilary (2002) The Collapse of the Fact/Value Dichotomy and Other Essays, Cambridge, MA: University of Harvard.

Rainwater, Lee (1974) What Money Buys: Inequality and the Social Meaning of Income, New York: Basic Books.

Ravallion, Martin (1998) 'Poverty Lines in Theory and Practice', Living Standards Measurement Study, World Bank, Working Paper, 133.

Reddy, Sanjay G. and Thomas Pogge (2020) 'How not to count the poor', in Sudhir Anand, Paul Segal and Joseph E. Stiglitz (eds) Debates on The Measurement of Global Poverty, Oxford: Oxford University Press, pp 42–85.

Ringen, Stein (1995) 'Well-Being, Measurement, and Preferences', Acta Sociologica, Nordic Sociological Association, 38: 3–15.

Robbins, Lionel (1932) An Essay on the Nature and Significance of Economic Science, London: Macmillan.

Rothenberg, Jerome (1974) 'Soberanía del consumidor', in Enciclopedia Internacional de las Ciencias Sociales, Vol. 3, Madrid: Aguilar.

Rowntree, Seebhom (1901/1902) A Study of Town Life, London: Macmillan.

Rowntree, Seebohm (1937) The Human Needs of Labour, revised edn, London: Longmann Greens.

Rowntree, Seebohm (1941) Poverty and Progress, London: Longmann Greens

Rowntree, Seebohm and G.R. Lavers (1951) Poverty and the Welfare State, London: Longmann Greens.

Runciman, W.G. (1966) Relative Deprivation and Social Justice, London: Routledge.

US Department of Health, Education and Welfare (1965) 'Security Bulletin, Washington', 28(1).

Sen, Amartya (1976/1982) 'Poverty: An Ordinal Approach to Measurement', Econometrica, (44): 219–231. (Reproduced in Amartya Sen, Choice, Welfare and Measurement [1982] Oxford: Basil Blackwell, pp 373–387.)

Sen, Amartya (1980) 'Equality of What?', in Sterling M. McMurrin (ed) The Tanner Lectures on Human Values, Vol. 1, Cambridge: Cambridge University Press, pp 195–220. (Reproduced in Amartya Sen [1982] Choice, Welfare and Measurement, Oxford: Basil Blackwell, pp 353–369.)

Sen, Amartya (1981/1991/1992) Poverty and Famines: An Essay on Entitlement and Deprivation, Oxford: Clarendon Press. (Chapters 1, 2 and 3 of this book were translated into Spanish by Julio Boltvinik and Francisco Vásquez and published in Beccaria.)

Sen, Amartya (1983/1984) 'Poor Relatively Speaking', in Resources, Values and Development, Oxford: Basil Blackwell, pp 325–345.

Sen, Amartya (1985) Commodities and Capabilities, Amsterdam: North Holland.

Sen, Amartya (1987) The Standard of Living, Cambridge: Cambridge University Press.

Sen, Amartya (1992) Inequality Reexamined, Cambridge, MA: Harvard University Press.

Shari, Ishak (1979) 'Estimation of Poverty Lines and the Incidence of Poverty in Peninsular Malaysia, 1973', Philippine Economic Journal, XVIII(42): 418–449.

Springborg, Patricia (1981) The Problem of Needs and the Critique of Civilisation, London: George Allen & Unwin.

Sraffa, Piero (1960) Production of Commodities by Means of Commodities: Prelude to a Critique of Economic Theory, Cambridge: Cambridge University Press.

Stewart, Frances (1996) 'Basic Needs, Capabilities, and Human Development', in Avner Offer (ed) In Pursuit of the Quality of Life, Oxford: Clarendon Press, pp 46–65.

Terrail, J.P., Edmond Preteceilleille, Jean-Louis Moynot, Susana Magri, Patrice Grevet, Paul-Henry Chombart de Lauwe, et al. (1977) Necesidades y consumo en la sociedad capitalista actual, México: Grijalbo. (Translation from the French, 'Besoins et Consommation', La Pensée, 180 [1975]).

Thomson, Garret (1987) Needs, London and New York: Routledge and Kegan Paul.

Townsend, Peter (1954) 'Measuring Poverty', British Journal of Sociology, 5(2):130–137.

Townsend, Peter (1962) 'The Meaning of Poverty', British Journal of Sociology, 13(3): 210–227.

Townsend, Peter (1979) Poverty in the United Kingdom, Harmondsworth: Penguin.

Townsend, Peter (1993) The International Analysis of Poverty, London: Routledge.

Townsend, Peter and David Gordon (1993) 'What Is Enough? The Definition of a Poverty Line' in Peter Townsend (ed) The International Analysis of Poverty, London: Routledge, pp 40–78.

UDAPSO (Unidad de Análisis de Políticas Sociales) (1994) Gobierno de Bolivia, La Paz: Mapa de Pobreza de Bolivia.

UNDP (since 1990 annually) Human Development Reports, New York and Oxford: Oxford University Press.

UNDP (1990) RLA/86/004, Bogotá: Desarrollo sin Pobreza.

UNDP, Development without Poverty, Bogotá (1992) PNUD, RLA/86/004, 'Magnitud y evolución de la pobreza en América Latina', Comercio Exterior, 42(4), Mexico, April, pp 380–392.

Vickery, Clair (1977) 'The Time-Poor: A New Look at Poverty', The Journal of Human Resources, XII(1): 27–48.

Villagómez, Paloma (2016) 'Entre lo que se debe y lo que se puede: percepción y satisfacción de necesidades alimentarias en la Ciudad de México', Acta Sociológica, 70(May-Aug): 99–128.

Warr, P. (1987) Unemployment and Mental Health, Oxford: Clarendon Press.

Watts, Harold (1968) 'An Economic Definition of Poverty', in Daniel P. Moynihan (ed) On Understanding Poverty: Perspectives from the Social Sciences, New York: Basic Books.

Wiggins, David (1987/2002) Needs, Values, Truth: Essays in the Philosophy of Value, Oxford: Clarendon Press.

Williams, Bernard (1987/2003) 'Professor Sen on the Capability Approach', in Amartya Sen (ed) (1987) Una traducción de extractos del texto de Williams fue publicada en Comercio Exterior, 53: 424–426(5).

Williams, Bernard (1990) 'The Standard of Living: Interests and Capabilities' in Amartya Sen (ed) (1985) The Standard of Living, The Tanner Lectures, pp 94–102. Extracts in Spanish (2003): 'El nivel de vida. Intereses y capacidades', Comercio Exterior, 53.

Wisor, Scott, Sharon Bessell, Fatima Castillo, Joanne Crawford, Kieran Donaghue, Janet Hunt, et al. (nd) 'The Individual Deprivation Measure: A Gender-Sensitive Approach to Poverty Measurement', International Women's Development Agency, Australian National University, Oxfam.

World Bank (1990) World Development Report, 1990: Poverty, Washington, DC.

World Bank (1993) Poverty and Income Distribution in Latin America: The Story of the 1980s, Washington, DC.

Index

A

Abel-Smith, Brian and Peter Townsend 65, 112–115
ability to achieve 52
achievement (A) 102, 103–104, 123, 151
achievement indicator of individual I (Ai) 102
achievement of expectations 67
achievement of housing space (AHS) 152–153
activities (AV) 186
Acute Multidimensional Poverty Index (AMPI) 125–126
adjustment factor (AF) 175–176
AFT 183
age group (AG) 182, 184, 185
aggregate poverty gap 192
aggregate poverty index or poverty intensity (I) 191
aggregate poverty measures (APM) 103, 124, 142, 188–212
  description and critique 188–202
  distribution among the poor 202–208
  homogenous units 188–189
  literature on 193
  observation unit 188
  poverty intensity 191–192
  social inequality, new aggregate measure 208–211
A(IPMM) indicator 186, 211
alienation 54, 56, 57
alimentary pension for older adults (APOA) 168
Alkire, Sabina 52, 53
Alkire, Sabina and James Foster 125–126
Alkire, Sabina and Maria Emma Santos 126
Altimir, Óscar 59, 60–61, 62, 213
amortisation 22, 23
Aristotle 91, 92
asymmetry 105
Atkinson, A.B. 99, 118n9, 204
authentic threshold 102, 103
available income deprivation indicator (YaD_j) 179
average achievement index of the non-poor/rich $(A_{\mu R})$ 210
average achievement index of the poor $(A_{\mu R})$ 210
axioms of choice 46, 48–50

B

Barreiros, Lidia 115, 116
basal metabolic rate (BMR) 205–207
basic assets (BA) 27, 28, 32
basic capabilities 54
basic lifestyle deprivation 136
Basic Needs Approach to Development (BNAD) 44
Beccaria, Luis and Alberto Minujin 129, 134, 141
Becker, Gary 16, 24, 110
bedrooms (B) 150
Blackorby, Charles and David Donaldson 196
body mass index (BMI) 205, 209
  health and 207, 208
Boltvinik, Julio 59, 61, 62, 129
Boltvinik, Julio and Alejandro Marin 215
Boltvinik, Julio and Araceli Damián 117
Borda, Jean-Charles de 200
Bradshaw, Jonathan and Autumn C.S. Yu 117
Broadening Our Look (Boltvinik) 3, 42, 44, 47, 48, 50, 51, 52, 54, 55, 59, 61, 68
Bryant, Keith W. 32, 33, 45, 48
budget approach 117–118
budget standards 111, 117, 143

C

Calderón, Miguel 217
capabilities approach (CA) 44, 51–55, 93
capacities 51, 57
capacities PL (CPL) 106
capital assets 31
Capital (Marx) 19, 89
capitalism, ideal model of 13–14
capitalist commodity circulation 17
capitalist commodity production 18
capitalist cycle 19–20
cardinal utility 198, 200
cardinalisation 83, 100–105, 122n13, 200
carrying water and firewood time (CWFWT) 179
categorical/absolute needs 34, 35, 41
Champernowne inequality index 202
Chaubey, P.K. 192, 194, 202
choice axioms 46, 48–50
CIESAS (Centro de Investigaciones y Estudios Superiores en Antropología Social) 3
circular evaluation 45
circulation and production schemes 19, 20–21
Citro, Constance F. and Robert T. Michael 63, 66–67, 79n19
cognitive N 71, 72, 75, 78
Cohen, Gerald A. 43, 51–52

Collins English Dictionary 91, 92
combined capabilities 54
combined households (CHH) 23
combined methods of PMM 109
  criteria 134
  description and critique 129–133
  prevailing disagreement on poverty criterion 133–140
combined multidimensional SN and N_o 110
commodities for consumption (CMc) 16, 17
commodities for production (CM_p) 19, 22
commodities for sale (CM_s) 18
commodity fetishism 47
communication services (CS) 159–160
  internet access/connection (IA_j) 159–160
  telephone (fixed line and/or mobile) (Tl_j) 159
completeness axiom 46, 49–50
composite indicator of housing quality adequacy (HQA_j) 148–149, 153–154
compulsory time (CT) 179–180, 181, 182
conceptual maximums 152–153, 178
Concise Oxford Dictionary 37–38
Coneval 86n1, 132, 187, 215
consensual/social indicators (Gordon et al.) 111
consensual truly poor 132
consolidated indicator of sanitary achievement (SaA_j) 158–159
consolidated UBN ($UBNA_j$) 174
consumer durables (CD) 16, 17, 18, 22
  CD_0 16, 17, 22, 24, 25
  CD_1 16, 17, 18, 22, 24
consumer sovereignty 44
consumption (C) 16, 23, 24, 26, 98, 203, 204, 205
  expenditure 22, 24
  G&S 25
  household 24
consumption Time (CT) 98
continuity axiom 46
conventional economic resources 72, 74, 75
convexity axiom 46
cooking fuel *see* home-cooking fuel (CF)
COPLAMAR 1, 7, 117n4, 141, 143, 151, 214, 215
  survey (1982) 164
cost of the normative food basket (CNFB) 106–107
cost of the normative generalised basket (CNGB) 106
cost of the normative non-food basket (CNnFB) 106–107
cost of the normative other needs basket (CNONeB) 106–107
cost of the normative six-N basket (CN6NeB) 106–107
cost of voluntary affiliation to health services (IMSS)($VHS) 169–171
cost of voluntary affiliation to social security (IMSS)($VSS) 169–172
critical thesis 77
Critique of the Political Economy of Poverty (CPEP) 2, 78, 213
Crocker, David 52
CROP (Comparative Research on Poverty) 1n1
cross-dimensional cut-off 132
current income (CY) 27–28, 30, 32, 60, 74, 110, 111, 118

D

Damián, Araceli 119, 120, 143
Damián, Araceli and Julio Boltvinik 117
Dasgupta, Partha 206, 207, 209
Deaton, Angus and John Muellbauer 45, 46–48, 48–49, 67
decreasing marginal WB 203, 204
deficiency N 56
depreciation of the purchased consumer durables ($\omega CD1$) 24
deprivation 124, 125, 128, 136–137
deprivation index 119, 124
deprivation mass (DM_j) 189, 191
Desacatos 3, 4–5, 5–6
Desai, Meghnad 52, 85, 99n1, 130–131, 203–204
Desai, Meghnad and Anup Shah 121n10, 124
desire 34, 37, 38
development and application of capacities (C) 68
dichotomisation 101
dignity 90–91, 91–92
diminishing marginal utility 197, 198, 199
diminishing marginal WB (DMWB) 99, 102, 209
direct deprivation indicators 137n7
direct deprivation scores 128
direct method of PMM 109, 113
direct multidimensional normative 110
direct non-poor 134
direct poor 134
discretionary activities 205
discretionary time (DT) 180, 181
domain-specific poverty cut-off 132
domestic mode of production (DMP) 14, 15, 17
domestic-natural HH 14, 15
domestic production (DP) 15, 16–17, 18, 32, 33
domestic production for self-consumption (DPSC) 14, 33
domestic work time (DWT) 179, 181
dominant economicist approach 60, 66–67, 77

Index

double cut counting methodology 125–126
Douthitt, Robin 119
Doyal, Len and Ian Gough 33, 34, 39–40, 40–41, 44–45, 55
DRAE (*Diccionario de la Real Academia Española*) 36–37, 59, 91
drainage (Dr) 158
drainage service 158
dual cut-off counting method 132, 133
durable goods value (DGV$_j$) 154–156
DGVA$_j$ 154, 156
dwelling (Dw) 146, 149
  quantitative and qualitative adequacy of 153

E

earning capacity 29
ECLAC (UN Economic Commission for Latin America and the Caribbean) 7, 8, 78, 84, 105, 108, 117, 134, 190n4, 214, 215
economic capabilities 66
economic growth 99
economic poverty 5, 6, 56–57
  dominant definitions, critique and comparison 62–68
economic poverty of circumstantial being (CBEP) 68
economic poverty of structural being (SBEP) 68
economic theory 97
economic wealth/poverty 55–56, 56–57, 57
Ecuador 116, 126
education 75, 78
educational achievement indicator (EAI) 162–167
  individual and HH educational achievement/deprivation indicators 166–167
  school attendance standard/threshold 165
egalitarian equivalent achievement (A^{ee}) 196
egalitarian welfarist 43
electricity access and quality achievement indicator (ElLB$_j$A) 161
electricity access and quality deprivation indicator (ElLB$_j$D) 161
electricity (El) 160
elementary social skills 65, 66
emotional N 71, 72, 75
energy 32, 33
energy adequacy (EnA$_j$) 160–162
  electricity access and quality achievement indicator (ElLB$_j$A) 161
  electricity access and quality indicator 160
  home-cooking fuel (CF$_j$) 162
  lightbulb achievement 160–161

energy expenditure 205
energy survival requirements 208, 209
enforced lack, concept of 125, 131, 136
enforced lack of socially perceived necessities (ELSPN) 111, 118, 125, 136
Engel coefficient (E) 105, 108, 116
Engel curves 47
Engel Law 46n7
enterprise decentralisation 14
enterprises 13–14, 19
ENUT (2019) 182, 183
equidistant cardinalisation 102
  of an ordering 200
equilibrium point method 115
equipment (E) 18
equivalence scales 47–48
equivalent adults (EAs) 8
equivalent bedrooms (EB) per household 151
equivalent egalitarian incidence (H$_{eE}$) 197
equivalent incidence (H$_E$) 193–194, 197
equivalent poor 190, 191–192
ethical issues 97
EU (European Union) 108, 115
Evalúa CDMX 7, 156, 164, 214
  surveys 217, 218
excess work (EW) 120
excess working time (EWT) 143
exchange values 81, 82
expensive tastes 43
external critique 6
external objects 69, 70
extra-domestic working time (EDWT) 16, 179, 182
extreme PL (EPL) 128
extreme poverty (EP) 144, 145

F

failed searches for a new approach (FSNA) 60, 80
family budget approach 8
family replenishment time (FRT) 179
FAO/WHO/UNU report (1985) 205–206
FGT index 200–202, 203, 210
Fitzgerald, Ross 35–36
floor score (F$_j$) 148
Focus Axiom 199
food PL (FPL) 106
Foster, James 86, 100, 101
Foster, James and Amartya Sen 59, 60, 62, 63, 65–66, 89, 92–93
free time achievement (FTA) 182
free time (FT) 16, 23–26, 27, 29, 30, 32, 179–184, 186
Fromm, Erich 34
functionings 51–52, 53, 54
fundamental consumer goods 24

G

Garfinkel, Irwin and Robert Haveman (G&H) 29, 32, 33
Gasper, Des 33, 52, 53
generalised dichotomisation (GD) 101–102, 104
  procedure for 103
Generalised Normative Basket (GNB) 111, 117–118
geometric mean of H (incidence of poverty (A_G) 202
Gini coefficient (G) 195, 196–197, 201, 202, 204
Gómez de León, José 127–128
good, definition of 55
good practices of poverty (GPP) 83
  conceptualisation (GPPC) 81, 83
  GPPC1 (holistic) 83, 84
  GPPC2 (sensitive to change) 83, 84
  GPPC3 (based on an objective definition of poverty) 83, 87
  GPPC4 (based on informed value judgements) 83, 88
  GPPC5 (promotes human rights and optimal public policies) 83, 92
  GPPC6 (includes all dimensions of the SLA) 83, 94
  measurement (GPPM) 6, 83
  GPPM1 (Applies PPM1 and PPM2 to measure P and to stratify the whole population) 83, 100
  GPPM2 (minimises errors) 83, 100
  GPPM3 (uses information fully (cardinalisation) and is unbiased) 83, 105
  GPPM4 (full consistency of concepts and measurement procedures) 83, 107
  GPPM5 (full normativity) 83, 107
goods and services (G&S) 7, 8
  consumption of 54, 63, 66
  free access to 32, 73–74, 75
  immaterial N 79
  objects 70, 74, 76, 77, 78
  public sector, free access to 27, 32
Gordon, David and Paul Spicker 38
Gordon et al. 89, 109, 131, 137n7, 139, 140
  methodological approaches for the measurement of P 111
government 21
governmental transferences (GVT) 175
gross ethical concepts 35
growth N 71, 72, 75
Guillén Fernández, Y.B. 130

H

Hagenaars, Aldi 29, 63, 67, 116, 118, 136
Halleröd, B. 132, 136, 139

Haq, Mahbub ul 126
health, BMI and 207, 208
Health Institute for Well-Being (INSABI) 168
health services achievement indicator (HSA_j) 167–174
  scores 171–172
  access criterion 171
  PMI and PVR 171
  voluntary insurances in IMSS 171
health services (HS) 167–174, 216
  new methodology (NM) 173
  previous methodology (PM) 173
Heller, Agnes 91
HH Educational Achievement Indicator (HEA_j) 167
HH Educational Deprivation Indicator (HED_j) 167
home-cooking fuel achievement (CFA_j) 162
home-cooking fuel (CF) 160, 162
household consumption 24
household educational achievement (HEA_j) 167
household income (HHY) 65
household survival strategies 143
households (HH) 3, 8, 73–74
  consumption units 13–14
  heating and water 8–9
  production and circulation schemes 15
  production units 13–14
  reproduction schemes 13–26
  social functions of 13–14
  types of 14
    domestic natural 15
    producers with domestic production 15
    pure producers 15
    pure salaried 15
    salaried with domestic production 15
housing deprivation 136
housing quality and space deprivation indicator ($HQSD_j$) 154
housing quality and space ($QSDwA_j$) 146–154
  adequacy of space availability 149–152
  communication services (CS) 159–160
  composite indicator of housing quality adequacy (HQA_j) 148–149, 153–154
  educational achievement indicator (EAI) 162–167
  energy adequacy (EnA_j) 160–162
  equivalent bedrooms (EB) per household 151
  floor score (F_j) 148
  health services (HS) and social security (SS) 167–174
  housing quality 146–147
  integrated indicator of ($HQSA_j$) 153–154
  normative EB per HH 152–153

Index

roof score (R_j) 147–148
sanitary services 156–159
UBN composite indicator 174
wall score (W_j) 147
housing space achievement indicator (ATR_j) 151
HSS_{ij} 171–172
human beings (HB)
  concept of 69
  consciousness 69–70
  external objects 69
  multiple N 84–85
  social creatures 69
  time 185
  work 69
Human Development Report, no. 20 (2010) 126
human diversity 43
human flourishing 5, 55, 56, 68
human flourishing axis (HFA) 6, 56, 57, 59, 76–77
human need or needs (HN) 4
  in philosophy, concept of 33–36
human rights 83, 92, 108
human wealth/poverty 55–56, 57

I

improved variant of IPMM (IV-IPMM) 7–9, 122, 130, 135, 137–138, 142
  indicators and thresholds 142–143
impulses 39–40
imputed in-kind income 25
imputed rent of own dwelling (IRODw) 175
IMSS-Bienestar 168
IMSS (Mexican Institute of Social Security) 168, 169, 173
incidence concepts 197
income from home business (YOBSN) 175
income gaps 197
income thresholds (Gordon et al.) 111
income-time poverty 119–121
income (Y) 23, 32, 85, 174–187
  achievement indicator of HH 178
  adjustment factors 176
  construction of 174–175
  new methodology for measuring time poverty 178–185
  PL definition 177
  YaA_j and YaD_j 179
inconsistency syndrome 48–49
indirect methods of PMM 109, 113
indirect multidimensional normative 110
indirect non-poor (PL or PLT) 134
indirect one-dimensional NN 110
indirect one-dimensional N_o 110
indirect one-dimensional SN 110
indirect poor (PL or PLT) 134

Individual Deprivation Measure (IDM) 126–127
individual educational achievement (IEA_{Ij}) 166–167
individual educational deprivation indicator (IED_{Ij}) 167
individual replenishment time (IRT) 179, 182
individual unilaterality 56
inertial deprivation 139
INFONAVIT 169
initial capital/money (M) 19, 22
inputs (In) 18
Institute for Social Security and Services for State Workers (ISSSTE) 168, 173
instrumental needs 35, 41
integrated indicator of housing quality and space availability ($HQSA_J$) 153–154
Integrated Poverty and Stratification Measurement Method (IPSMM) 100, 216
Integrated Poverty Measurement Method (IPMM) 7, 30, 60, 120, 123, 128, 140, 145
  basic procedure 145
  cardinalisation 101
  complementarity 137–138
  components and integration procedure 144
  cost-weighted 186–187
  general description of 143–145
  genesis of 141–143
  improved *see* improved variant of IPMM (IV-IPMM)
  income (Y) 174–187
  integrated indicator of 185–187
  object-centred vision 186
  original variant (OV-IPMM) 129
  person-centred vision 186
  strata used in 145
  UBN indicators *see* unsatisfied basic needs (UBN)
intense poverty (IP) 144, 145, 154
intensity of household J poverty or poverty gap (I_j) 189–190
internal capabilities 54
internal critique 6
International Poverty Line (IPL) 82, 213
internet access/connection (IA_j) 159–160
IV-UBN 143, 144

K

Kaztman, Rubén 129, 134, 139, 141
Khare Poverty Index 202
kitchen for exclusive use (KE) 150, 151
knowledge and skills 26, 27, 30, 32, 185

L

labour benefits in kind 31

labour force (LF) 13, 14, 16, 25–26
Latin America 133
Law of Diminishing Marginal Utility (LDMU) 97, 98, 99
Levitas, Ruth 5
life-time quality of life 217
lightbulb achievement (LB$_j$A) 160–161
Linder, Staffan B. 98, 99
literacy achievement variable (LA) 165, 166

M

Maccoby, Michael 90–91, 92
Mack, Joanna and Stewart Lansley 125, 131, 132, 140, 217
maintenance requirement (r) 206
malnutrition 209
marginal utility 204
marginal WB 205, 207
markets 28, 81, 82, 85
Márkus, György 4–5, 33
Marx, Karl 17, 19, 26, 57, 69–70, 89
  needs 34
Marxism 5, 214
Maslow, Abraham 34, 39, 40, 58, 70, 75, 76, 81, 92
material N *see* survival N
Max-Neef et al. 34, 35, 70, 77, 81
mean achievement indicator (A$_\mu$) 191, 196, 202
medium stratum (MS) 144, 145, 154
Mexican Constitution 215
  Article 3 163
Mexican Government (2003–2008) 105
Mexico 1–2, 8–9, 30n3, 88, 117, 126, 132, 138n8, 215–216
  compulsory schooling 163
  education legislation 163
  indicators of attendance, years of schooling, and literacy 165–166
  pre-school educational standard 164
  preparatory education 163, 164
  right to education 163
  school attendance standard/threshold 165
  secondary education 164
minimal capabilities 65–66
minimal error 83, 100
minimum income question 118
minimum satisfaction stratum (MSS) 144, 145, 154, 173
moderate poverty (MP) 144, 145, 154
modified truly poor 132–133
monetary income 25, 28, 31
monetary solution 85
monetary transfers (MT) 22
mortality rates 29
Motivation and Personality (Maslow) 40
multidimensional methods of PMM 109, 113–114
multidimensional poverty 81
  indicators 81
multipurpose rooms (MR) 150, 151
MUT-ENIGH (2020) 182, 183, 184

N

national accounts (NA) 175
National Institute of Statistics and Geography (INEGI) 7, 156
National Survey of Household Income and Expenditure (ENIGH) 7, 102, 164, 165, 167, 173, 175–176, 215, 218
  durable goods 154, 155, 156
  housing quality and space 147, 149, 150, 153
necessity 38
need/needs (N) 34
  biological dimension 89
  capacities 57
  conceptions of 39, 69–71
  conventional approaches 78–80
  definitions 34–35, 36–39, 69
  development of 57–58
  nature of 39–41
  social dimension 89
  types of 70–71, 72, 74–76
  universalisable 39–40
  wants/desires 34
  see also human need or needs (HN)
needs satisfaction 19, 30, 72
Neoclassic Consumer Theory (NCT) 33, 44–50, 67, 107
neoclassical economic theory 97
New Approach to Poverty and Human Flourishing (NAPHF) 4, 6
  conceptual map 74–78
New Improved Variant of the IPMM (NIV-IPMM) 214, 216
New Paradigm (NP) 4, 6, 62–63, 69–80
New Paradigm of Poverty and Human Flourishing (NPPHF) 55–58
NFB PMM 108
Nolan, Brian and Christopher T. Whelan 115, 131, 136–137, 139, 140, 188
non-basic assets (NBA) 27, 28, 30, 32
non-free discretionary time (NFDT) 180, 181
non-monetary current income 28
non-normative method (NN) 109, 112–116
non-protected (NP$_R$) 168
non-satiation axiom 46, 49, 50
norm assumed equal for all (Z) 127, 196
  non-poor (Z$_{np}$) 127, 128
  poor (Z$_p$) 127, 128
  separating poor from non-poor (Z$_{PL}$) 128
Normalised Absolute Deprivation axiom 195

Index

normalized poverty gap 192
normative basket of essential satisfiers (NBES) 8, 117, 144, 177, 214
normative EB per HH 152–153
normative food basket (NFB) 60n3, 78, 105, 116–117
normative generalised basket (NGB) 106, 143
normative method (N_o) 109, 113
normativity 83, 107, 108
norms 108
number of equivalent poor persons (q_{ej}) 189, 191–192, 194
number of poor people (q) 191–192
number of total rooms (TR) 150
Nussbaum, Martha 54–55

O

O-capabilities 53
objective needs 34
objective PL 119, 128, 133, 134–135
objective well-being (OWB) 83, 87, 97–99, 122, 146–147
observed maximums 152–153
OECD (Organization for Economic Co-operation and Development) 108, 115
offensive tastes 43
one-dimensional methods of PMM 109, 113–114
optimisation model 50
optimum objective 49
opulence approach (OA) 43–44
Original Variant of the Integrated Poverty Measurement Method (OV-IPMM) 114, 129, 134, 135
  flaws 142, 143
  limitations 129
  poverty of publicly provided goods 129
original variant (OV) 122
Orshansky, Mollie 88, 116, 119
orthodox procedure 117

P

Pareto optimal 98
partial achievement indicators 144
partial economic capacity 106, 107
partial methods of poverty measurement 30, 61, 82–83, 134, 142
patrimonial poverty line (PPL) 105–106
PEMEX 168, 173
Penz, G. Peter 43, 44, 45, 54
'Perceptions of the Urban Population on Minimal Norms of Basic Needs Satisfaction' survey (2000) 163
petty commodity circulation 17, 18, 19
Piachaud, D. 119
Pigou, Arthur Cecil 97, 99
PL-NFB method 129
Plato 91, 92
pleasures 99
Political Economy of Poverty (PEP) 42, 53
  conceptual map 59, 78–80
  dominant definitions of poverty 59–68
poor egalitarian equivalents 197
poor, the 37–38, 88, 134–135
  consensual truly poor 132
  contingency matrix 142
  dual cut-off counting method 132
  Koran 39
  modified truly poor 132–133
  truly poor 131–132, 138, 139, 140
Poverty and Famines (Sen) 197–198, 198–200
Poverty and Social Exclusion in Britain (Gordon et al.) 111
Poverty in the United Kingdom (Townsend) 64
poverty index (P_1) 194
poverty intensity measurement (PIM) 188, 189
poverty intensity rate (I) 192
poverty line (PL) 7–8, 30, 77–78
  complementarity with UBN 142
  Generalised Normative Basket (GNB) 117–118
  normative food basket (NFB) 116–117
  objective PL 119
  PL_2 105
  PL_3 105
  poor and non-poor by 142
  subjective PL 118
  UBN and 141–142
Poverty Map of Bolivia (UDAPSO, 1994) 123
poverty measurement *see* principles of poverty measurement (PPM)
poverty measurement methods (PMM) 3, 7, 65, 84, 109, 112–116
  combined methods 109, 114
  direct method 109, 113
  indirect method 109, 113
  multidimensional method 109, 113–114
  non-normative method *see* non-normative method (NN)
  normative method *see* normative method (N_o)
  one-dimensional method 109, 113–114
  semi-normative method *see* semi-normative method (SN)
  typology of 109–110, 113–114
  US (United States) 108
poverty (P) 83
  adequate measurement of 28, 30
  change-sensitive 84
  context-sensitive 84
  conventional needs approach 59, 77
  definitions 31, 36–39
  dominant 59–68

dominant economicist approach 60, 66–67, 77
failed searches for a new approach (FSNA) 60, 77
Islamic perspective 38–39
partial view of 30
policy definition of 88
pre-IPMM 134, 134–135
preferences 37, 38, 46, 47, 53
primary goods approach 44
principles of poverty (PP) 83
  conceptualisation (PPC) 81, 83
    PPC1 (principle of totality) 73, 74, 79, 82, 82–83, 85, 107
    PPC2 (principle of sensitivity) 83, 84
    PPC3 (principle of comparability of objective wellbeing [OWB]) 83, 84–85
    PPC4 (entangled nature of the concept of poverty) 83, 87
    PPC5 (dignity: central criterion for defining thresholds) 83, 88–92
    PPC6 (poverty as part of the SLA) 83, 92–94
  measurement (PPM) 6, 77, 83
    indirect and direct forms 77
    multidimensional *see* multidimensional poverty
    PPM1 (decreasing marginal OWB above thresholds) 83, 97–99
    PPM2 (existence of an OWB maximum) 83, 97–99
    PPM3 (minimum error) 83, 100
    PPM4 (full and replicable cardinalisation) 83, 100–105, 122n13
    PPM5 (symmetry) 83, 105–107
    PPM6 (full normativity) 83, 108
principles (Pr)
  of poverty conceptualisation 81–96
  of poverty measurement 97–108
private capitalist enterprises 20–21
private economic resources 27, 72
private income in kind 31
private medical insurance (PMI) 171, 172, 173
private vital rent (PVR) 171, 172
producer households (PHH) 16, 18
producer households with domestic production (PHHDP) 18, 22
producers of commodities (CM_s) 19
productive use-values (UV_P) 14, 15
Profeco 163
Progresa 127, 128, 135
public economic resources 27, 72
public goods 13
public policy 55, 83, 92
public social services 31
pure producing households ($P_U PHHs$) 18
pure salaried HH ($P_U SHH$) 14, 15, 16, 17
Putnam, Hilary 87, 97–98

Q

quantity of life 131

R

Ranked Relative Deprivation axiom 195, 196
Ravallion, Martin 63, 67
Rawls, John 43, 44, 52
ready-to-consume use values (UV_{RC}) 14, 15, 16, 17, 19, 24, 25–26
received transfers 32–33
recently poor 139
Reddy, S.G. and T. Pogge 213
reductionism 64–65, 66, 79–80, 137
  of conventional approaches to P 85
referential level of utility (U_z) 64, 67
reflexivity axiom 46
relative deprivation 195–196, 197–198
relative gap (G_{PR}) 210
relative poverty index (P_R) 210
repairing the house and its equipment (RHET) 179
replicable cardinalisation 102–104
reproduction schemes 13–26
rescaling procedures 122–123
resource typologies 32
resources 31, 71–74
  see also well-being sources (WBS)
revealed or objective UBN thresholds 127–128
Ringen, Stein 109, 110–111
  expenditure approach 111, 112
  measurement of well-being indirect-direct 110–111, 111–112, 115
  narrow-broad 110, 111, 115
  typology of approaches 115
  Y approach 111
Robbins, Lionel 97–98
roof score (R_j) 147–148
Rowntree, Seebohm 8, 117, 137
Runciman, W.G. 200

S

S-capabilities 53
salaried households (SHH) 16
salaried households with domestic production (SHHDP) 16, 22–23
sanitary services 156–159
  consolidated indicator of sanitary achievement (SA_c) 158–159
  drainage service 158
  water provision (WP) 157
satisfiers (S) 34–35, 41, 69–71, 185
  types of 72, 74–76
  typology of 70
saving and borrowing 24
school attendance (SA_{IJ}) 166
schooling € 165

Index

secondary lifestyle deprivation 136
Sedesol (Secretaria de Desarrollo Social) 105–106
self-actualisation 35, 36, 68, 70, 72, 75
self-actualising jobs 57
self-consumption 23
self-esteem 52, 71, 72, 75
semi-normative method (SN) 109, 113, 116–117
Sen, Amartya 35, 61, 86, 88, 89, 197–201
  aggregate measures of poverty 192–193
  aggregate poverty 194–195
  capabilities approach 51–55
  definition of poverty 59, 60, 61, 62, 63, 65–66, 67
  direct methods 112
  expenditure method 112
  HI combination 194
  identification and aggregation 188
  indirect methods 112
  policy definition of P 87
  Poverty and Famines 197–198, 198–200
  utilitarianism 42–44, 53
Sen-Boltvinik APM 210, 211
Sen Poverty Index 195–201, 202, 203, 209, 210–211
shame 90, 91
shopping and managing the household time (SMHHT) 179
simple incidence (H) 197
sleep 205
Smith, Adam 89, 91, 92
social division of labour 56
social multilateralism 56
social norms 89–90
Social Progress Index - Lifetime Deprivation (SPI-LTD) 130–131, 134, 135, 139
social security achievement indicator (SSA_j) 167–174
social security (SS) 9, 167–174, 216
social use values (SUV) 19, 21, 22, 26, 29
socially desirable activities 205
socially necessary working time (SNWT) 179
socio-biology 40
SPI Opportunity Set 204
squared coefficient of variation (C^2) 201, 202
Sraffa, Piero 14, 21
standard dichotomisation 104
standard food basket (SFB) 78
standard of living axis (SLA) 6, 56, 57, 59, 76–77, 92–94
state mode of production (SMP)
  commodity variety 21
  non-commodity variety 21, 22
Stewart, Frances 52
study time (ST) 181

Suarez McAuliffe, Antonio 141, 143
subjective conception of interests 44
subjective desires 34
subjective measures (Gordon et al.) 111
subjective PL 111, 118
surplus value 19
Survey of Access to Basic Satisfiers (ENCASB, 2011) 217, 218
Survey of Objective and Subjective Well-Being (ENCUBOS, 2019) 217, 218
Survey of Perceptions and Access to Basic Satisfiers (EPASB, 2009) 217, 218
survival 206–207, 208, 209, 217
survival constraint 46–47
survival forecast 206
survival jobs 57
survival N 71, 72, 74, 75, 78, 79, 80, 85
symmetry 83, 105–107

T

taxes (T_x) 20, 22, 23
Technical Committee for the Measurement of Poverty (TCMP) 105–106
telephone (fixed and/or mobile) (Tl_j) 159
thick ethical concepts 87
Thompson, Garret 39
thresholds of poverty 83, 88–92
time of domestic work dedicated to household chores (DWHCT) 179
time poverty (TP) 143, 185
  new methodology for measuring 178–185
time (T) 98–99, 185
toilet (To) 158
total current income 23
total deprivation mass 191, 192, 194
total national household current income (NHHY) 175
totality *see* principles of poverty (PP): PPC1 (principle of totality)
Townsend, Peter 112, 116, 121n10, 199
  definition of poverty 31, 60, 61, 63, 64, 66, 67, 89
  deprivation index 119, 124
  reductionism 64–65
  resources 31, 32–33, 65
Townsend, Peter and David Gordon 119, 128
transferences from other sources (OT) 175
transitivity/consistency axiom 46, 50
triage solution 205
truly poor 131–132, 138, 139, 140
truncated PL 105, 106, 107

U

UBN *see* unsatisfied basic needs (UBN)
UBN composite indicator 174
UBN improved variant (UBN-IV) 130
UBN-OV method 124, 125, 129, 132

United Nations Development Programme (UNDP) 113–114, 126
  Regional Project to Overcome Poverty in Latin America (RLA) 129, 141
unmet needs 34
unsatisfied basic needs (UBN) 8, 9, 30, 131, 132, 135, 138, 139
  complementarity with PL 142
  components and weights 174
  direct indicators 86
  durable goods 154–156
  housing quality and space (QSDwA$_j$) 146–154
  improved variant (UBN-IV) 122–124
  indicators 215
  integrated strata of individuals 175
  Latin American applications 141, 142
  norms 133, 134, 135
  PL and 141–142
  poor and non-poor by 142
  restricted original variant 30, 121–122, 125, 141
  thresholds 127–128, 132
unsatisfied needs 1
upper stratum (US) 144, 145, 154
use-value (UV) 14
  domestic production 16–17
  for self-consumption (UV$_C$) 15, 18, 23, 24
utilitarianism 42–44, 53, 67–68

V

vector of consumer goods and services (M$_C$) 17
vector of production commodities including equipment and facilities (CM$_E$) 19
vector of production commodities including inputs (CM$_{In}$) 19
vector of production commodities including labour force (CM$_{LF}$) 19
very intense poverty (VIP) 144, 145, 154
Vickery, Clair 119, 120–121
virtual workers (VWs) 169–170
vitamin model 49
voluntary affiliation to IMSS in-kind medical services (VHSSS) 168
voluntary affiliation to the compulsory SS regime (VCSSR) 169
voluntary or community working time (VCWT) 179

W

wall score (W$_j$) 147
want-satisfaction principle 45
want(s) 34, 38, 45, 69
water frequency (WF) 157–158
water provision (WP) 157
water source (WS) 157
Watts, Harold 115–116, 194
  Watts Index 202
Webster's New World Dictionary 38
welfare economics 44–45, 97, 98
welfarism 43
well-being sources (WBS) 26–33, 71–74, 78–80, 85, 185–186
  concepts in reproduction schemes 27
  principal/secondary 72, 74–76
  specificity of 27, 28
  substitutability of 27, 28
  trends 30
well-being (WB) 28, 73, 85, 122–123
  absolute or practical minimum 86
  conceptual maximum 86
  direct sources 71
  multidimensional index of 86
  normative standard 86
  social trends 29
Wiggins, David 34, 34–35, 41, 55, 69
Williams, Bernard 33, 51
Wolf Point 113, 114, 115, 116
work 69, 75
World Bank (WB) 67, 78, 88, 213

www.ingramcontent.com/pod-product-compliance
Lightning Source LLC
Chambersburg PA
CBHW051534020426
42333CB00016B/1929